MW00353121

The Criminal Investigative Function

A Guide for New Investigators

SECOND EDITION

JOSEPH L. GIACALONE

Looseleaf
Law Publications, Inc.

43-08 162nd Street
Flushing, NY 11358
www.LooseleafLaw.com
800-647-5547

NOTE: All characters, stories and examples are fictional. The thoughts, feelings, stories, notes and opinions are solely that of the author and not the NYPD, John Jay College or the City of New York. This work should not be taken as legal advice and all investigators are strongly encouraged to follow their department's legal and investigative guidelines.

Library of Congress – Cataloging-in-Publication Data

978-1-60885-023-5

Cover by *Sans Serif*, Saline, Michigan

ACKNOWLEDGMENTS

I would like to give thanks to the following:
Dr. Monica Smiddy, MD

A special thanks to Artist Anne Clinton for
allowing me to include her expert forensic drawings
in the Second Edition of this text.
http://www.anneclinton.com

*"The Journey of Criminal Investigation starts with one
giant step backwards and then forward from there."*
— Joseph L. Giacalone

TABLE OF CONTENTS

ABOUT THE AUTHOR

Joseph L. Giacalone is a retired Detective Sergeant from the New York City Police Department. He has an extensive background in criminal investigations. During his more than 20-year career, he held many prestigious positions, but his favorite was the Commanding Officer of the Bronx Cold Case Homicide Squad. Joe has personally worked on hundreds of murders, suicides and missing persons cases throughout his career and is always willing to share his knowledge and experiences with others. More importantly, he is willing to share his mistakes so that future investigators can avoid them. For three years during his tenure, Joe was the Director of the world renowned NYPD Homicide Course. He was a highly decorated member of the Department, including the recipient of the Medal of Valor.

He obtained a Master of Arts Degree in Criminal Justice with a Specialty in Crime and Deviance from John College of Criminal Justice in 2005 and has been an Adjunct Professor at John Jay since January 2006.

In his spare time, Joe writes his own criminal investigation Blog, http://www.ColdCaseSquad.com. Joe is a dynamic speaker and is available for training, insight, lectures, interviews and speaking engagements. He can be reached via e-mail at joe@joegwrites.com, his author's website http://www.joegwrites.com or at 516-557-9591.

You can follow Joe and the Cold Case Squad Blog on Twitter:
@ColdCaseSquad @JoeGiacalone

ABOUT THE SECOND EDITION

What's new in this edition? The second edition of *The Criminal Investigative Function: a Guide for New Investigators* represents a major revision of the text. There have been substantial changes in the law, forensic evidence techniques and the use of social media as an investigative tool. I also included Internet Resources for investigators to make their job easier.

When available, contact numbers and e-mail addresses were made available saving the investigator countless hours researching so that they can spend more time investigating. I have included as much of this material as possible in this revision. This text can be viewed as a mode of information transfer and to be effective it must be updated regularly and comprehensively. I hope I have achieved this goal. Specifically, the following changes appear in this edition:

- Learning objectives and key terms added to the beginning of each chapter
- Photographs and illustrations have been added for emphasis and training purposes
- Additional Criminal Investigation "CI Tip" boxes added
- Criminal Investigation "Stop Sign" Alerts added
- Law updates and changes
- New sample forms added
- Internet Resources for Investigators added at the end of each chapter
- "At the Crime Scene" sections added with current media cases and lessons for investigators
- New investigative techniques added and / or updated
- New topics including: Familial DNA, Touch DNA, Social Media Canvasses, Crime Stoppers, Obtaining DNA Exemplars, Releasing Information to the Media, Statement Analysis, Preparing for CompStat, Forensic Entomology, ViCAP, Making Death Notifications, Identity Theft Investigations
- New Chapters on Report Writing, Missing Persons
- Additional questions added to the end of each chapter

INTRODUCTION

Why did I write this book? With all the criminal investigation textbooks out there, you are probably wondering, "Isn't one text just as good as or better than the next?" The answer to that question is "No." Over the past few years I have used and adopted a variety of textbooks from different companies and authors and I was never happy with any of them in particular. In addition, most academic textbooks are still patrol officer-centric and not in tune with the criminal investigative function. For instance, pick up a textbook on criminal investigation and turn to the 8 Major Felonies (Murder, Rape, Robbery, Felony Assault, Burglary, Grand Larceny, Grand Larceny Auto and Arson). They are more concerned with responding to the scene than with the actual criminal investigation. The investigator's role is a reactionary one and does not respond to in-progress crimes.

My biggest concern was that many of the texts used today in police academies, colleges and universities across the country were written by authors who were never police officers, let alone ever been to a crime scene. This is not an academic textbook; it was written by a practitioner.

This book was written almost entirely from my experiences, my mistakes, what I learned and what I know. I've held the position of Investigator, Executive Officer of the 110th Precinct in Queens, New York and the Commanding Officer of the Bronx Cold Case Homicide Squad. In addition to my field assignments, for three years I was the Director of the NYPD's Homicide School. I hold a Master of Arts Degree in Criminal Justice with a Specialty in Crime and Deviance and I have been an adjunct professor for the past five years.

I'm glad you have interest in the field of law enforcement and more specifically criminal investigation. Even though all law enforcement agents conduct some aspect of criminal investigation, most are involved only in a limited role known as the preliminary investigation. This text was written for the Criminal Justice Student and for the training of new investigators. Today's investigators have to be computer savvy, great communicators, have a strong understanding of physical evidence and be undaunted by politics from inside as well as outside of their department. This text will prepare the groundwork for your new career. It will teach you the necessary investigative techniques, but only through practical experience will you ever master them.

I also gave this text a different kind of look. The book is broken down as if it were a real investigation. You are the investigator sitting at your desk typing a report when the phone rings. From the time the case comes across your desk to the time you'd testify in the courtroom and everything in between is covered. Anytime throughout the text that you see the word "you" I mean "investigator." I wanted you to learn about criminal investigation, not just by learning concepts, but with a little infusion of humor and a number of acronyms that allow the student the opportunity to memorize and never forget. I wanted the reader to feel the investigative experience as best as they could through words by inspiring their imagination. It's easy reading because it's in plain English: no legal mumbo jumbo or scientist "speak."

After each chapter there are a number of "Questions for Discussion and Review" that are designed not only to be thought provoking, but to drill the concepts into your head. Give them a try, its definitely not going to hurt you. I am not going to waste your time with information that you don't need to know, or fill the pages with fluff that prolong the issue. This book was written to give the student investigator what they need to know and go out and do the job.

Good luck with your chosen path. It is most rewarding!

— Joseph L. Giacalone

CHAPTER 1 — THE CRIMINAL INVESTIGATIVE PROCESS

"The difference between a successful person and others is not the lack of strength or a lack of knowledge, but rather in a lack of will."
— Vince Lombardi

KEY TERMS

Criminal Investigation	Reasonable Suspicion	Corpus Delicti
Misdemeanor	Probable Cause	Circumstantial Evidence
Felony	Direct Evidence	Associate Evidence
Arrest Warrant	Real Evidence	Behavioral Evidence
Accusatory Instrument	Exculpatory	Modus Operandi
Inculpatory		

CHAPTER OBJECTIVES

At the end of this chapter, the student should be able to:

- Discuss how a police officer can become an investigator.
- List the qualities of a good investigator.
- Define the term, *criminal investigation.*
- Recall the goal of criminal investigation.
- Recall the police Standards of Proof.
- Discuss the functions of evidence in criminal investigations.

How does one become an investigator? Is probably the most asked question in Criminal Justice classrooms all around the world. I know it is asked in my classes quite often. The investigator position is probably the most sought after position in any police department and is usually bestowed on those that are most worthy. Television has done even more to glorify the investigative position with the myriad of shows surrounding the topic.

It all starts with taking a civil service examination to become a sworn uniformed patrol officer. No one walks out of the academy and into a "suit." During years of patrol service, some officers develop the potential for becoming a good investigator by their quality of work, street smarts, experiences and apprehension record. Eventually, all of these activities get noticed by the higher-ups within the department. A careful selection process is not only based on merit, but officer behavior is also considered. Because the investigator position has a certain level of autonomy coupled with the fact that they wear "regular" or "soft" clothes, officers must have an exceptional background.

Schedules for investigators can be unpredictable at times. Investigators may be required to work odd hours depending on current crime patterns/ trends and sometimes work all day and night when heavy cases (murder, rape, shooting, terrorism) cross their desk. The investigator position is not as neat, clean and "sexy" as it is portrayed on today's television cop shows and could make family life difficult at times. All police work is tough on family life, period, but the life of an investigator is even more unpredictable.

Some large departments such as Los Angeles, Philadelphia and Houston offer a civil service examination to become an investigator. Exams offer one advantage over the "investigative track" program: it eliminates the "hook." However, most police departments dole out their investigator positions as an "investigative track" and not through an exam. Because most police departments have fewer than twenty (20) sworn officers, an individual must perform at an exceptional level to be considered for the investigator position. An investigative track exists to ensure that the very best street cops are chosen to eventually become investigators. A track may consist of the following steps: Patrol Officer ➤ Plain Clothes Officer ➤ Investigator. The patrol assignment develops the officer's skills at conducting preliminary investigations and the plain clothes assignment develops their apprehension abilities as well as developing their skills in analyzing crime trends and criminal behavior.

The sought after "gold shield" is not presented to the officer after a plain clothes assignment, but after they continue the investigative track in the Investigations Bureau of the department for an additional eighteen (18) months. From the time you enter the police academy to the end of the 18-month track within the Investigations Bureau, it could take an individual as long as ten (10) years! Students who want to do this for their future law enforcement career must be mentally prepared for the long road ahead of them.

The investigator, like other police tasks, does more than just investigate cases. The victim/family advocate is a role that is often left off the list of investigator job functions. Investigators represent the victim when he/she is no longer capable of doing it themselves and most importantly they provide closure to families that allow the healing processes to begin. Out of the many roles that I maintained in the police force, it was the most satisfying and rewarding.

Qualities of an Investigator

The qualities of an effective investigator run the gamut. But the most important qualities are to be a **PD COP**:

Persistent	**C**ommunicator
Determined	**O**riented toward details
	Prepared

PERSISTENT

The investigator will have to overcome many obstacles during the course of an entire case. For example, there can be a lack of evidence, frustration with eyewitnesses, missed apprehension opportunities, a series of crimes committed by one perpetrator with no leads in sight, inquisitive media representatives, demanding district attorneys and most frustrating, answering questions about the case to "Downtown." How persistent do you have to be? Like a pit bull, you clamp down on something and don't let go until the facts and evidence prove otherwise.

DETERMINED

After dealing with the frustration and disappointment that often occurs in cases, the investigator has to press on and keep digging for new clues, information and leads that can help solve the case. It may require re-interviewing people, reviewing evidence logs and crime scene photos, conducting follow-up conferrals with the police laboratory, other enforcement agencies and the district attorney. The investigator must remain focused and objective throughout the investigation and subsequent trial.

COMMUNICATOR

The majority of the time an investigator spends on the case will be talking to people: victims, witnesses or anyone who can help. The investigator must have the skill to extract information from people, especially those unwilling to provide information to the police, especially when he is wearing a t-shirt that says, "Stitches 4 Snitches." Say the wrong word, or show bad non-verbal body language and the information can be gone forever. Can you imagine knocking on someone's door at 3 o'clock in the morning and asking him or her to help you?

ORIENTED TOWARD DETAILS

It's the little things that solve crimes, like great observation skills. Examples: Were the lights on or off? Was anything obliviously moved? Is there something present at the scene that shouldn't be? The trace evidence recovered after a careful search of a crime scene, or asking the right question to the right person can mean the difference in solving or not solving the case. If the investigator takes shortcuts, gets lazy or does not prioritize investigative leads then the case will end up cold. The details of the investigation must also be documented carefully. A failure to document could allow a guilty person to walk free. If it was not documented on a report, it is considered never done.

Street Scene © 2012 Joseph L. Giacalone

South

Set a stop watch or alarm clock and take one (1) minute to examine the street scene. Unlike the real world where you may only have seconds to see things and remember them, take the full minute. Following are fourteen (14) questions that will test your observation skills.

OBSERVATION QUESTIONS

1. What is the name of the southbound street you are looking down?
2. What color is the traffic light?
3. What direction is the construction arrow pointing?
4. What University is mentioned in this picture?
5. How many double parked cars are there on the East side of the street?
6. What direction is the West Side Highway?
7. What are the first two (2) numbers or letters of the cab?
8. What is the name of the street that is directly in front of you?
9. What direction is that street going in?
10. In what City was this picture taken?
11. How many taxi cabs are in this photo?
12. If I were looking for a parking garage, what side of the street would you tell me to go?
13. How many traffic control devices are hanging directly in front of you, one or two?
14. Is the cab in front of you stopped or is it moving?
15. What season of the year does it look like? Why?

PREPARED

The investigator has to be "up" on the case because he/she never knows when they are going to get the break they need. As you will learn in a Chapter 7, an interrogation will not take place until all information that is available is obtained. The investigative reports must be typed, submitted in a timely fashion, signed off on by a supervisor and kept neat in the case folder. Proper indexing (Figure 1.1) of reports makes it easier to read and retrieve information, especially in the courtroom years later. An investigator never knows when or if the case will garner media attention and, therefore, Downtown's attention.

Figure 1.1. Indexing of Reports

Case # _____   Complaint # _____

Report #	Date	Description	Observations		
			Day	From	To
1	1/1/2009	Notification of Incident			
2	1/1/2009	Response to the Scene			
3	1/1/2009	Canvass of 123 ABC Street			
4	1/1/2009	Receipt of Victim's Property			
5	1/1/2009	Canvass for Surveillance Video			
	1/1/2009	Suspect Still Created from Surveillance Video			
7	1/1/2009	Subpoena for Cell Phone Information			
8	1/3/2009	Crime Stoppers Tip regarding Surveillance Still			
9	1/3/2009	Computer Checks on Johnny Jones			
10	1/3/2009	DMV request for Photograph			
11	1/7/2009	Photo Array Shown to Witness			
12	1/8/2009	Observation at the home of Johnny Jones	Friday	1600	2000
13	1/9/2009	Receipt of Photos from Surveillance			
14	1/10/2009	Arrest of Suspect Johnny Jones			

The index is short, but you should understand how important it is. It provides an investigative framework for what has been done and what should be done. An index can also allow the investigator to find a specific report. Can you imagine looking through a case folder of 150 to 200 reports without an index? The defense lawyer will label you and your investigation sloppy and disorganized.

What Is Criminal Investigation?

What is criminal investigation? Criminal investigation contains the **CORE** elements to determine what happened, why it happened and who did it. Criminal investigation is the process by which an investigator:

> **C**ollects
> **O**rganizes
> **R**ecords
> **E**valuates evidence and information

An investigator completes these tasks with the thought in mind of someday testifying at trial. An investigation does not end with the arrest, but with the successful prosecution of the case. An investigator must follow a case through until the perpetrator that was responsible is apprehended, tried, convicted and shipped off to corrections.

Goals of Investigation

The goals of investigation are to make sure the case does not go **DOA**:

> **D**etermine whether a crime was committed
> **O**btain information and evidence to identify perpetrators
> **A**rrest suspects and present the case to the prosecutor

DETERMINE WHETHER A CRIME WAS COMMITTED

There are only two (2) categories of crimes: (1) Misdemeanors and (2) Felonies. The definition of a crime does not include violations and traffic infractions. The student must be aware that each public enterprise, whether it is the local, state or federal government, has different names, definitions and penalties for crimes. However, the following information generally applies to all jurisdictions: misdemeanors are considered minor crimes and felonies are more serious. Therefore, penalties are handed down accordingly. If convicted of a misdemeanor, an individual can be punished by a fine and/or imprisoned for a term not to exceed one year. The individual will serve their time in a local jail. If convicted of a felony, an individual can be sentenced to over one (1) year in jail—a year and a day or more in a state penitentiary. The student now knows that the next time they read the newspaper and see, "Johnny Jones was arrested for a crime," that he committed a felony or a misdemeanor. Allegedly of course!

> **CI Tip Sheet**
> Misdemeanor = small crime, small time, small jail
> Felony = big crime, big time, "the big house"

Violations, traffic infractions and civil matters would not rise to the level of a crime (misdemeanor or felony) in most instances; therefore they would not be treated in the same manner.

OBTAIN INFORMATION AND EVIDENCE TO IDENTIFY PERPETRATORS

The investigator searches for trace evidence, body fluids, fingerprints, ballistics and other physical evidence so that these unknown samples can be matched up against known databases: Combined DNA Index System (CODIS), the Integrated Automatic Fingerprint Identification System (IAFIS), Integrated Ballistic Identification System (IBIS), etc.

In addition, victim and witness statements and identification procedures such as a show up, arrays and lineups play a pivotal role in identifying perpetrators (Chapter 5). Investigators spend a tremendous amount of time communicating with people to develop information. Sometimes, statements given by suspects provide crucial evidence in cases. Also, both public and private computer databases provide information regarding people (victim, witness and perpetrator), places (location of occurrence) and things (vehicles, firearms, etc.).

ARREST SUSPECTS AND PRESENT THE CASE TO THE PROSECUTOR

The ultimate goal is to tie a suspect to a crime based on evidence and witness/victim statements. Criminal investigation is not a solo "sport," but requires a team of highly trained and experienced investigators. There is no "I" in Team, but there is an M and an E. An investigator must be careful and not let their ego spoil an investigation.

In order for the police to make an arrest, they must follow specific guidelines. Remember, arresting someone is a "seizure" and the law enforcement community must be mindful of the U.S. Constitution and the rights protected under the Fourth Amendment. In essence, court decisions and legislation have carved out three (3) exceptions to obtaining an arrest warrant. In order for a police officer to seize an individual and place them under arrest, they must remember their **CAPS** before leaving the stationhouse.

Committed in the officer's presence
Arrest Warrant
Probable Cause
Statutory

COMMITTED IN THE OFFICER'S PRESENCE

If a crime or a violation occurs in the officer's presence, he/she can make an arrest without obtaining a warrant. This is also known as a "pick-up arrest." For example, the police officer is driving by in his car and sees a teenager grab a woman's pocketbook and run. He can chase him down and arrest him without a warrant because he witnessed the event. Can you imagine telling the perpetrator, "You wait here while I get an arrest warrant. I'll be back in a few hours to arrest you."

ARREST WARRANT

If you read the Fourth Amendment in the strictest possible sense, no one would ever be arrested unless a warrant was issued (see example in Committed in the Officer's Presence). An arrest warrant is signed by a judge after the officer presents a written affidavit showing satisfactory Probable Cause (see below). The warrant will state the name of the individual to be seized and a demand to bring him/her to court to answer to the charge. Arrest warrants are executable any time of the day and any day of the week. They include weekends and holidays!

An investigator has to be aware of one caveat concerning obtaining an arrest warrant: it is an Accusatory Instrument that means it comes with an absolute right to counsel (Lawyer). The accusatory instrument is the document filed by the prosecutor accusing a person of committing a crime. Another type of accusatory instrument is an Indictment, or "True Bill."

In cases where an accusatory instrument has been filed and the perpetrator is apprehended, the police cannot interrogate him unless his/her lawyer is present. There is zero chance of ever obtaining a confession or admission from the perpetrator (Chapter 7). But sometimes you have no choice. For example, if your perpetrator is located in another state, they can detain him as "For Other Authorities (FOA)," but you have to obtain an arrest warrant to extradite him back to your jurisdiction.

CI BOLO Alert

An Accusatory Instrument comes with
an Absolute Right to Counsel!

Police Standards of Proof (Levels of Suspicion)

There are only four (4) levels of suspicion that dictate police and citizen encounters. At each level the police have different powers granted to them. The student must understand that a police stop could amount to a seizure, which would be protected under the Fourth Amendment. It all hinges on the level of freedom that is taken away.

> ### CI Tip Sheet
>
> A police officer needs Probable Cause for three (3) things:
> (1) To make an arrest
> (2) To obtain an arrest warrant
> (3) To obtain a search warrant.

Here are the four (4) Levels of Suspicion, also known as Standards of Proof, in order from least to most:

- Standard 1—Request for Information

A Request for Information is the lowest level of suspicion. If the police have any suspicion, they can approach anyone for an articulable reason, to inquire and to ask them what they are doing or other general questions. The individual does not have to answer, which is protected under the Fifth Amendment. At this level of suspicion the police cannot forcibly stop the individual or detain them in anyway (*People v. DeBour* 40 NY 2d. 210 (1976)).

- Standard 2—Mere Suspicion

Mere Suspicion is defined as a hunch or gut feeling the officer has that criminal activity may or did take place. At this level of suspicion the police cannot make a forcible stop, but can keep the individual under surveillance or they can walk up to the individual and ask him pointed questions under the common law writ of inquiry (*People v. DeBour* 40 NY 2d. 210 (1976)). Based on the person's answers and actions, the police may develop enough information to rise to the next standard, Reasonable Suspicion.

- Standard 3—Reasonable Suspicion

Observations made by a police officer that would come to the reasonable conclusion that a person is committing, has committed or is about to commit a felony or penal law misdemeanor. At this level of suspicion the police can stop, question and (possibly) frisk. More on reasonable suspicion and the "Terry Stop" can be found in Chapter 3, "Exceptions to a Search Warrant (*Terry v. Ohio* 392 U.S. 1 (1968))."

- Standard 4—Probable Cause

The term Probable Cause comes directly from the Fourth Amendment. It is the standard of proof that is required to make an arrest and obtain both an arrest warrant and a search warrant. "Probable cause exists when evidence or information which appears reliable discloses facts or circumstances which are collectively of such weight and persuasiveness as to convince a person of ordinary intelligence, judgment and experience that it is reasonably likely that such offense was committed and that such person committed it" (New York State Criminal Procedural Law Section 70.10). In simpler terms, the evidence points to the fact that a crime was committed and the person arrested committed it. Probable cause is less than "Beyond Reasonable Doubt," which is the standard used by courts to convict someone.

Statutory

An officer cannot make an arrest for violations not in their presence. For example, a slap to the face leaving no injuries is a violation known as Harassment in most jurisdictions. If this "slap" is not witnessed by the officer, no arrest can be made. Now you may ask yourself, "What's the big deal, there are no injuries." But, what if the case involves a domestic violence (DV) incident? Over the past decade or so, legislators have drafted statutes to provide the police with more discretion regarding making an arrest for violations in DV cases.

A police officer has the final say if an arrest is made even if the injured party does not want an arrest. Once the police feel that the peace will not continue after they leave, an arrest will be made. "Someone is going": police slang for making an arrest.

Functions of Evidence

An investigator will sift through and identify many types of evidence that serve different functions during an investigation. An investigator may have little evidence or many types. Evidence can be either inculpatory, which is evidence that shows involvement and tends to establish guilt, or exculpatory, evidence that can exonerate by eliminating them from contention.

The law enforcement community has an obligation to hand over all the evidence, especially exculpatory evidence, discovered during an investigation to the suspect's defense, even if it means putting the case at risk. The U.S. Supreme Court decided in *Brady v. Maryland* 373 U.S. 83 (1963) that prosecutors must disclose all exculpatory evidence. If they don't, they violate the suspect's due process rights covered under the Fourteenth Amendment. On a recent case in San Francisco on June 23, 2009, *Tennison v. San Francisco*, No. 06-15426, the appeals court applied *Brady v. Maryland* to the police. The police are mandated to disclose exculpatory evidence.

CI Tip Sheet

INculpatory Evidence = **IN**cludes
EXculpatory = **EX**cludes or **EX**onerates

Depending on the type of evidence, it would be wise for an investigator to make an appointment with **DR. Corpus CAB**.

Direct
Real

Corpus Delicti

Circumstantial
Associative
Behavioral

Direct Evidence

Direct evidence is any evidence that demonstrates an existence of a fact. No inferences or presumptions are necessary with direct evidence. Examples of direct evidence are an eyewitness's testimonial account, video surveillance, statements made by witnesses, victims and the perpetrator. A victim points to her bruise and states, "My husband punched me in the eye," or a bank video camera taking pictures of the individual robbing the bank are examples of direct evidence. Direct evidence is the opposite of indirect or circumstantial evidence. The law does not make a distinction between direct or circumstantial evidence in terms of importance. Either one can be used to convict someone of a crime.

Real Evidence

Real evidence is also known as Physical evidence. Physical evidence is anything that has real properties, can be touched, seen, and collected as the result of a criminal act. For example, a person was bludgeoned to death with a heavy object and blood spatter can be seen on the walls and ceiling. The blood spatter is real (physical) evidence. Other important examples of real evidence are: biological fluids, fibers, bite marks, ballistic, soil, tool marks, teeth impressions, shoe impressions, fingerprints, etc.

Corpus Delicti Evidence

Latin for "body of the crime," Corpus Delicti Evidence establishes that a crime occurred. It is any material evidence of a crime. For example, the police respond to a location and find a woman with multiple stab wounds in the back. For the investigators, suicide would seem unlikely. This would be corpus delicti evidence that a murder occurred. The term corpus delicti does not mean the body itself! Remember, the medical examiner is the only person than can classify the manner of death as a homicide.

In an extreme example of Corpus Delicti Evidence, a California gang member was arrested and convicted based on the crime scene tattoo that he had on his chest. Therefore, the body of evidence that a crime was committed was on his body (ABC News Radio).

Circumstantial Evidence

Circumstantial evidence, also known as indirect evidence, is evidence that makes an inference that a person is responsible for a crime. The USlaw.com website defines Circumstantial Evidence as, "a collection of facts that, when considered together, can be used to infer a conclusion about something unknown." Circumstantial evidence does not establish guilt in the straightforward sense. For example, the police execute a search warrant on the home of a man whose girlfriend was found shot to death. During the search the police recover the firearm. Believe it or not, the firearm is physical evidence, but still circumstantial—it could have been put there by someone else, unlikely; but remember the prosecution has the burden of proof. Ballistics will tell us if the gun was the one used in the murder. However, further investigative methods might prove it to be direct evidence by recovering fingerprints off of the gun or bullets, identifying gunshot residue (GSR) from the boyfriend's hand or clothes or a witness statement saying she saw him with the gun in the hallway. Circumstantial evidence alone may be used to convict someone. However, in most cases, an investigator identifies direct evidence to corroborate the circumstantial evidence.

Associative Evidence

Associative evidence originates from contact with **POP**:

People
Objects
People and Objects

Associative evidence establishes linkage between suspects and victims, suspects with crime scenes, a tool with tool marks, etc. Associative evidence is closely tied into the Locard's Exchange Principle. Anyone who has a dog or cat is well aware of associate evidence. Just look at your pants! Other examples of Associative Evidence are: semen from a sexual assault, paint transferred from an accident, impressions from tool marks, saliva from a cigarette, etc.

Associative evidence in criminal investigations is often represented by a Linkage Diagram. The most-often used diagram is that of the Criminal Enterprise. The Criminal Enterprise diagram shows the leader on top and then all the suspects that work underneath them and at what capacity. It can also be used to show the events that took place before and after a crime, show telephone calls between individuals, financial transactions and other data that can establish a link. These diagrams can help establish Direct Evidence in a case for the jury, but are labeled as illustrative evidence.

Behavioral Evidence

Behavioral evidence has to do with the psychological state of the offender and is used to build a profile. The basics of behavioral evidence are the Modus Operandi (MO) and the Signature. The MO is the "method of operation" that the crime was committed and the signature is the part of the crime that provides emotional satisfaction to the perpetrator (Turvey, 2008, p. 198). Think of MO and signature in this analogy: The MO is the restaurant you prefer, signature is the type of food you eat in that restaurant.

The Investigation Flow Chart

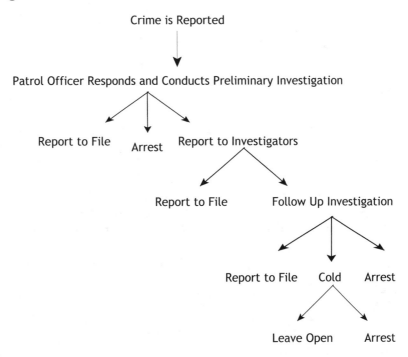

A criminal investigation is broken down into two (2) main parts:

(1) the *Preliminary Investigation* and
(2) the *Follow-Up Investigation.*

In this section we are going to tackle the preliminary investigation.

After a crime is reported, radio communications will dispatch the call for assistance to a uniformed patrol officer. The patrol officer responds to and begins the preliminary investigation at the scene. The first responsibility of the responding officer is to protect life. Even if the bad guy is climbing out of the window when they arrive, their first priority is to the injured person. In that case it would be perfectly acceptable to broadcast a description of the perpetrator and a direction of flight. If necessary, patrol officers will detain witnesses, establish a crime scene and make notifications. The actions of the first officer on the scene often makes or breaks the case.

STOP!	*Patrol officers should remind EMS personnel, if at all possible, to not cut through stab wounds or gunshot wounds in the clothing.*

The first officer on the scene must do some **C**rime Scene **PREP** for the investigators and their follow up investigation:

Check on the status of the victim and render first aid if required

Protect the scene to keep it as it was found
Restrict access to the scene
Ensure the safety of all that enter or remain near the scene
Protect the evidence until it can be collected

The preliminary investigation is a brief probing for facts and to identify evidence. In some cases it includes the arrest of the perpetrator. If no crime was committed, or if it was a civil matter, the officer will take the report, make referrals if necessary, close the case and file the report with the station house clerk. The report must have the most number of facts and follow a logical approach to solvability. The officer will attempt to answer the following Six (6) Basic Investigative Questions: When, Where, Who, What, How and Why.

If the report has at least one (1) solvability factor, such as the nature of the crime (felony), named perpetrator, physical evidence, eyewitness or biological evidence, the officer will leave the case open and refer it to an investigator. In cases of murder, rape, shootings/stabbings and pattern crime cases that referral and notification will be made directly from the scene whenever possible.

A thorough preliminary investigation and a prompt notification to an investigator are the keys to solving and clearing cases.

Among the many tasks that an investigator does, there is one that is often overlooked, but is very important. The training function that investigators take on may help improve future clearance rates. Because the preliminary investigation plays such a pivotal role in closing the case, investigators must train patrol officers in the proper steps of handling the preliminary investigation and most importantly tell them what and how you want it done. Investigators can build strong relationships with the patrol cops by talking to them and sharing information, especially on limiting crime scene contamination.

Internet Resources for Investigators

Police Careers and Job Listings
http://www.policeone.com/careers/

Criminal Justice Schools and Degrees
http://www.myonlinecriminaljusticedegree.com/

Questions for Discussion and Review

1. Who is responsible to conduct the preliminary investigation?

2. In your opinion, when would be a good time to execute an arrest warrant?

3. Is it true that circumstantial evidence is not admissible in court? Explain.

4. Real evidence is also known as _____ .

5. What are the three (3) exceptions to obtaining an arrest warrant?

6. Why is it so important for the police to determine if a crime was even committed before moving forward?

7. This type of evidence originates from contact between people and objects.

8. If convicted of a felony, how long can you be sentenced to?

9. Should the patrol officer have a more expanded role in the overall investigation? Why or why not?

10. What is the difference between circumstantial evidence and direct evidence?

11. The level of suspicion that a police officer must have before making an arrest is?

12. Provide two (2) examples of inculpatory and exculpatory evidence.

13. Would the theft of a car spark an immediate investigation? Why or why not?

14. Can the police arrest a dead person? Why or why not?

15. To make an arrest, the police must always have an arrest warrant. True/False

16. Opinion: What day of the year would be a good one to look for a suspect that has been on the run?

17. What is an Accusatory Instrument? Name some examples.

18. Of the five (5) qualities of an investigator discussed in this chapter, which one do you think is the most important? Why?

19. Which type of evidence is Locard's Exchange Principle associated with?

CHAPTER 2 — CRIMINAL IDENTIFICATION SYSTEMS

"One can only see what one observes and one observes only things which are already in the mind."

— Alphonse Bertillon

KEY TERMS

Anthropometry	CODIS	Buccal Swab
Dactylography	AFIS	Nuclear DNA
DNA	Frye Standard	Familial DNA
mtDNA	Daubert Ruling	Touch DNA

CHAPTER OBJECTIVES

At the end of this chapter, the student should be able to:

- List and explain the three major systems of criminal identification.
- Recall the three types of prints found at a crime scene.
- Recall the three distinct fingerprint patterns.
- Discuss the three ways that investigators can lawfully obtain a DNA sample.
- Explain the significance of Familial DNA for investigators.
- Describe what Touch DNA is and how it is used in investigations.

Over the last 125 years and counting, progress has been made on ways the police identify individuals who are responsible for committing crimes. As the means of identifying criminals developed, new technologies surfaced and proved more useful and reliable than their predecessors. These identification systems are extremely important in ensuring that the police apprehend the right person. Not only can these systems be used to convict a guilty person, but they can also exonerate an innocent person. It should be known, however, that generally an identification of an individual through one of these systems will not be the sole factor in determining guilt or innocence. It will be used by the prosecution in conjunction with other factors such as: physical evidence, victim statements, eyewitness identification, statements made, other forms of direct evidence, circumstantial evidence, etc.

Recently, investigators and prosecutors have been handed a setback in single eyewitness identification cases in *People v. LeGrand* 8 N.Y.3d 449 (2007). This case allows the use of experts in the field of misidentification to present the problems of eyewitness identification to the jury. More than ever, investigators must painstakingly search for and identify physical evidence instead of relying on a single eyewitness.

There are (were) three (3) major systems of criminal identification that have been developed over the years. Investigators must take their time processing crime scenes so evidence can **ADD** up.

Anthropometry
Dactylography
Deoxyribonucleic Acid

ANTHROPOMETRY (BODY MEASUREMENTS)

Anthropometry, or body measurements, was developed by a French anthropologist, Alphonse Bertillon (1853 – 1914). Bertillon believed that taking and recording measurements of the skeletal system was an accurate means of identifying criminals. Bertillon calculated that there was a 270-million-to-one chance that two people could have fourteen identical measurements (height, length and width of head, length of left forearm, ears, etc.). He felt that anthropometry would be an accurate identifier because once a person reaches a certain age the bone structure will remain the same (NYC.gov). However, like most investigators, Bertillon did not rely solely on one factor to identify a suspect. He used a combination.

The Bertillon method of identifying criminals was adopted all over Europe and eventually made its way into the United States. It was used for about twenty years before it was replaced by Dactylography (fingerprinting). Alphonse Bertillon was in the vanguard of criminal identification as well as criminal photographs. He was the first person to add his foresight and devotion to the topic, Bertillon has become known as the "Father of Criminal Identification."

DACTYLOGRAPHY (FINGERPRINTS)

Dactylography, better know as fingerprints, was first suggested by Dr. Henry Fauld in the late 1880s as a means of identifying criminals. Even though fingerprinting had early successes, it was not adopted for over two decades, when it officially replaced Anthropometry as the standard in identifying criminals.

Other contributors to the identification of criminals with fingerprints are:

- Francis Galton—wrote the seminal book, *Finger Prints*—which had a set of his own prints on the cover
  - o Established three distinct fingerprint patterns: Arches, Loops, and Whorls (see Figure 2.1)
    - Loops are the most common fingerprint pattern
    - Arches are the rarest fingerprint pattern
    - Within these three patterns exist different variations
  - o Established that friction ridge skin was unique

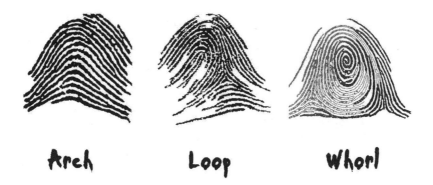

Figure 2.1 Fingerprint Patterns

© 2012 Anne Frances Clinton www.anneclinton.com

- Edward Henry established the classification system to file finger-prints, known as the Henry System, which is still used today throughout the world and in the Automated Fingerprint Identification System (AFIS)

Fingerprints are formed by the mixture of perspiration, dirt and the oil from our skin. There are three types of fingerprints that can be found at a crime scene that can lead us to our **VIP**:

Visible
Invisible
Plastic

VISIBLE

Visible prints, also known as Patent prints, can be seen with the naked eye and require no other process to make them visible. They can be found in blood, paint or any type of thick liquid.

INVISIBLE

Latent or invisible prints that can't be seen by the naked eye, require another process, like dusting or an alternative light source (ALS), to make them visible. The light source can be from a simple flashlight. Once it is visible, the investigator will ensure that it is photographed, without and with a ruler, before any attempt is made to lift it. This is done in case the print gets destroyed during the lifting process.

CI Tip Sheet

The proper order to secure fingerprint evidence is to:
Dust
Photograph
Lift

Fingerprint powders do not interfere with serological analysis; however, some of the chemicals used to develop prints may interfere with DNA and serological examinations.

PLASTIC

Plastic prints are also visible to the naked eye and can be formed in clay, tape, gum or glue. Patent and plastic prints will also be photographed in the same manner as latent prints, but the investigator should make an effort to see if they can take the entire object with them.

Today, the system of filing fingerprints has become an electronic forensic database called the Integrated Automated Fingerprint Identification System (IAFIS pronounced: Eye-A-Fiss), which is maintained by the FBI. Each state has its own database called SAFIS, which is linked to the FBI's IAFIS database. An unknown set of prints are loaded into the system and run against the known database. IAFIS and SAFIS contain prints not only from criminals but everyday citizens who have already been fingerprinted for a license, job, passport, etc.

AFIS can be helpful in identifying **LSD**:

Liars
Suspects
Deceased and missing persons

If the computer database gets a "hit (match)," then a fingerprint technician will retrieve the prints for the file and make a physical inspection by eye, magnifying glass and microscope. Then another technician will conduct similar tests to back up the AFIS hit and the human match. The human element is never eliminated because a computer says it's a match.

Fingerprint evidence admissibility was first challenged in the landmark case, *People v. Jennings* 252 Ill. 534 96 N.E. 1077 (1911) in Illinois. In this case, fingerprints were discovered at the crime scene and tied to the suspect, Thomas Jennings. Four fingerprint experts testified that the prints belonged to Jennings. Jennings appealed the decision to the Illinois Supreme Court but the Court upheld the conviction and therefore established the admissibility of fingerprints as evidence against a defendant.

Deoxyribonucleic Acid or DNA

Deoxyribonucleic Acid, or DNA for short, is the genetic blueprint that determines everything from our hair color to our disease vulnerabilities. The DNA "fingerprint" was discovered in England in 1984 by Dr. Sir Alec Jeffreys, who determined that each person has a unique DNA makeup, with the exception of identical twins.

In the village of Enderby England, 1987, DNA quickly became a reliable method of identifying individuals when Dr. Jeffreys's technique combined with old-fashioned police work was used to exonerate one suspect and identify another, Mr. Colin Pitchfork, for the rape and murder of two young women (Connors, Lundregan, Miller & McEwen, 1996, p. 4). Known as the Enderby Case, this was the seminal point that ushered in a new era for criminal investigation. The United States quickly put to use this new technique in November 1987 by securing a genetic match to a serial rapist and murderer, Tommie Lee Andrews, in Orlando, Florida.

There are two (2) types of DNA, (1) Nuclear DNA (cell has a nucleus) and (2) Mitochondrial DNA (mtDNA) (cell has no nucleus). Nuclear DNA is derived from both parents and mtDNA is derived only from the mother. Every cell, tissue, organ, etc. in our bodies has the same DNA. A hair follicle has nuclear DNA in the bulb, but not in the shaft. A shaft of hair recovered at a crime scene will have testing limitations due to the fact that it only contains mtDNA. There is a greater chance of finding mtDNA than nuclear DNA because it contains hundreds of copies of the genome as compare to only two (2) found in the nucleus (The DNA Initiative, DNA.gov). MtDNA can also be found in fingernail scrapings and teeth. Nuclear DNA can be found in all of the following: White blood cells, tooth pulp, spermatozoa, bone marrow, hair roots, saliva, cheek cells (buccal, pronounced "buckle," cells), sweat and skin cells. Nuclear DNA is not found in red blood cells.

Mitochondrial DNA played a big role in identifying victims of the World Trade Center. Some pieces that were recovered were the size of a quarter, but with mtDNA, they could be positively identified. To get a match of mtDNA, the investigator found a donor derived from the mother: a victim's brother, sister, maternal grandmother, and had it compared against a local DNA database. Some victims were identified years later after their remains were recovered during the cleanup and new construction. Because of the scientific advancements and the use of mtDNA during the identification process of the WTC, mtDNA has become a court accepted method of identifying people.

CI Tip Sheet

Mitochondrial is derived from Mom

The main database run by the FBI is called CODIS or the Combined DNA Index System. CODIS allows federal, state and local crime laboratories to exchange and share DNA profiles electronically (NIJ, Issue 249, 2003). CODIS is composed of two (2) databases: The Forensic and the Offender Databases. The Forensic (Unknown) Database includes DNA profiles from unknown individuals that were recovered from crime scenes. The Offender (Known) Database contains the DNA profiles of individuals who were convicted of certain crimes. Each state has different statutes that trigger taking a sample from a convict. There is much talk and current pending legislation that would require a person that is arrested to provide a DNA sample. DNA found at a crime scene is uploaded into CODIS in the hopes of identifying a known subject. CODIS is to DNA as IAFIS is to fingerprints and IBIS is to ballistics.

What happens if we (investigators) have obtained DNA evidence at a crime scene and we really "like" a particular individual for the crime? How can the investigator legally obtain a DNA Exemplar from the "suspect"? An investigator can obtain a DNA sample legally from an individual by using the three **C**s:

Consent
Court Order
Covertly

For example, a woman is brutally stabbed to death in her home. There are no signs of a forced entry or of a struggle. The victim was found in the back bedroom, fully clothed. The investigators suspect the ex-boyfriend who was observed on the block at the time of the incident. Fingernail scrapings from the victim were taken and a profile of a male donor was able to be extracted. However, the profile does not match any profile in CODIS.

In the above event, the only viable way to obtain a DNA sample from the ex-boyfriend would be to do it covertly. You do not have probable cause to obtain a warrant and if you ask for consent, you may frighten him away. So obtaining a sample covertly is your only viable option. You can accomplish this by following the individual and waiting for them to spit, drop a cigarette or chewing gum, or he can be brought in to "help" with the investigation and an attempt would be made to secure an abandonment sample. It could be in the form of a tissue, chewing gum, can of soda or bottle of water. The exemplar would be collected, packaged and submitted for DNA testing against the unknown sample from the crime scene.

What is a DNA Exemplar? An exemplar is an example from individuals who may or may not have anything to do with the crime. For instance, fingerprints are found at the scene of a murder inside of a home. The police would take exemplars, or elimination samples, in this case fingerprints, from all individuals who had lawful access to the location. Elimination prints will be compared to the prints found at the scene, instead of uploading them into AFIS. This applies to DNA Exemplars as well and saves both time and money. There are four types of exemplars that the police can come across during an investigation.

The investigator must **SAVE** the following:

Suspect sample
Abandonment sample
Victim sample
Elimination sample

How to Obtain a DNA Exemplar from an Individual

Obtaining a DNA Exemplar from an individual is very easy; however, the investigator must make every effort to prevent the sample from becoming contaminated. This is the main concern when taking the sample. The investigator must remember to follow their department guidelines on the proper methods of obtaining, securing and documenting a DNA Exemplar. By now, most police departments have bought a pre-made Buccal Swab Kit, which contains **RICE**:

Rubber or latex gloves
Insert for Cotton-Tipped Swab Applicators
Cotton Tipped Swabs (two)
Envelope with evidence tape

Here is a simple and effective way to obtain a DNA Exemplar from a person and to avoid contamination. The entire process is fast and should take no more than five minutes.

Step 1: Before anything else, the area where the swab is to be taken should be cleaned to avoid contamination.

Step 2: The investigator should don the pair gloves that were contained in the kit.

Step 3: Write on the envelope the date, name of the investigator taking the swabs, individual's name, case number and any other identifying information that is needed.

Step 4: Hand the individual the unopened swab applicator and ask them to remove it from the packaging.

Step 5: Ask them to rigorously rub the cotton swab on the inside of their cheek.

Step 6: Collect the swab from the person by holding the bottom of the applicator.

Step 7: Air dry the sample.

Step 8: Place the swab into the plastic insert and pull it through from the bottom of the applicator.

Step 9: Place the swab inside of the preprinted envelope.

Step 10: Seal the envelope with evidence tape. DO NOT LICK THE ENVELOPE!

Step 11: Collector signs his/her name across the evidence tape.

Familial DNA

Familial DNA is a new tool that cold case squad detectives are arming themselves with in California, Colorado and New York. It is the process of identifying suspects by generating a list of people whose DNA closely resembles the genetic makeup entered into the Combined DNA Index System (CODIS). Familial DNA does not provide an exact match but a family relationship. The list generally consists of parents, children and siblings and unlike mitochondrial DNA (mtDNA), it is not just limited to the mother.

At the Crime Scene: The Grim Sleeper Case

The use of familial DNA has already proven to be effective but controversial. LAPD Cold Case detectives arrested an alleged serial killer, who was dubbed the "Grim Sleeper" in July 2010 based on familial DNA. In that case, the DNA submitted from crime scenes was uploaded into CODIS and produced a potential match, but not a direct "hit." Then, detective work took over. Considering dates of the crimes, the suspicion quickly fell on the close match's father. The detectives conducted surveillance on the subject in an attempt to covertly obtain the man's DNA. Their persistence paid off when the subject discarded a piece of pizza. The DNA recovered from the pizza was a direct match to the profile found at the crime scenes (Miller, 2010). The man, Lonnie David Franklin Jr. was subsequently arrested and convicted of ten murders.

In addition to the LAPD example, investigators can use this technique in other ways. For example, a familial DNA match provides a person who has a brother close in age. Detectives can then attempt to satisfy the elements of **MOM**, **M**eans, **O**pportunity and **M**otive, which are needed for a suspect. Armed with this information, the brother can be asked to come to the station house to answer some questions or his photo can be used in a photo array. The photo array may prove to be the path of least resistance.

With this new tool, we may see an increase in clearance rates of old homicide statistics as well as help in missing person and found body cases. Even if jurisdictions do not allow this method to be used to identify suspects, no one can argue about using it on found body cases. This technique can provide closure for those families that have been haunted by the disappearance of their family members.

Familial DNA may prove to be a great tool for very difficult cold cases because it may provide a springboard to launch an old investigation and at the very least a way to identify found bodies. As the list of crimes that require a DNA sample on conviction grows, we may see a rapid expansion of the technique throughout the nation. Its potential cannot be ignored for very long.

Touch DNA

As the uses of DNA in criminal investigation expand daily, new techniques will be discovered, used and overused by investigators. Touch DNA is one of the relatively new techniques. Touch DNA is aptly named for how DNA is left at a crime scene: the perpetrator "Touched" something.

It wasn't that long ago when investigators were out of luck unless a decent amount of blood or other significant amount of body fluid was left and recovered at the scene. Now, with Touch DNA, investigators are hoping to find six to eight cells to be recovered. That is all that is necessary today to develop a DNA profile.

DNA testing provides a new means of solving cases, but like every new toy that the police get, they often break it. In the hopes of solving a greater number of cases, especially those tough property cases, police departments are swabbing everything at the scene with the hopes of getting lucky. This fishing expedition, no matter how good the intentions were, has created an even larger backup of cases that require DNA testing. According to the National Institute of Justice, the backlog doubled from 2005 to 2009. For this reason, investigators must search the right areas where DNA is most likely to be found and avoid swabbing everything. Collecting Touch DNA is easy when you know where to look for it at the crime scene. Investigators should concentrate on entry and exit points (including the walls), light switches, obviously moved items, and the following:

- Recovered firearms: hammer, trigger, cylinder or magazine, cartridges, slide
- Steering wheel, rearview mirror, windows and door locks, shifter (GLA cases)
- Recovered cell phones—number pad, screen
- Sink faucets, towels, flusher on toilet (think sex crimes)

Here is a scenario on how Touch DNA can prove to be invaluable. A perpetrator has just raped and murdered a young woman in her apartment. He goes into the bathroom, removes the condom and flushes it down the toilet with a towel, washes his hands and wipes them off on a paper towel. He thinks he has outsmarted the cops because he used gloves to enter the apartment and used a condom. He may however, have made one big mistake: wiping his hands on the paper towel. Drying your hands removes many skin cells, more than the required six to eight to develop a profile.

There are two generally accepted methods of collecting Touch DNA evidence: (1) Cut Method and (2) the Swab Method. The Cut Method involves the cutting or removing a piece of the item for testing, and the Swabbing Method uses a cotton-tipped applicator to swab harder surfaces.

The Role of DNA in Criminal Investigations

DNA has many uses in criminal investigations but most importantly it can help the police catch **PERPS**:

Place a suspect at the scene/or a weapon in their hand
Exonerate the innocent
Refute a claim of self-defense
Prove or disprove an alibi
Seal a conviction

DNA does have some limitations for criminal investigations. No matter what the television shows tells us, DNA analysis cannot determine:

The age of the suspect
The race of the suspect
How the DNA sample was left at the scene

Admissibility of DNA Evidence

Advances in DNA typing appear to be limitless. No one knows for sure how far or how fast DNA typing will develop in identifying criminal suspects. What we do know is that it is very reliable. The question is will the new scientific techniques be admissible in court? and if not, how long will it take? When DNA is introduced as evidence at a trial, an expert (forensic scientist, criminalist, etc.) will testify about what examinations were done and how they were done. This testimony will be affected by two (2) court decisions, depending on what state you live in: The Frye Standard and the Daubert Standard.

The Frye Standard (*Frye v. United States* 293 F. 1013 (1923)) states that in order for a scientific technique to be admissible, the technique must be sufficiently established to have gained general acceptance in its particular field to which it belongs. The Frye Standard is tougher to prove because some new methods have not been accepted yet and it takes longer to convince scientists.

In *Daubert v. Merrell Dow Pharmaceuticals, Inc.* 507 US 904 (1993), the Supreme Court stated that the trial judge will make an independent assessment of expert reliability as well as the processes and procedures used in a pretrial hearing. The Supreme Court was trying to limit the amount of courtroom showdowns between experts. The Daubert decision applies only to cases within the federal court, but this standard has been adopted by several states.

Internet Resources for Investigators

The President's DNA Initiative
http://www.dna.gov

FBI Combined DNA Index System (CODIS)
http://www.fbi.gov/about-us/lab/codis

The NIJ Fingerprint Sourcebook
http://www.nij.gov/pubs-sum/225320.htm

FBI Integrated Automated Fingerprint Identification System (IAFIS)
http://www.fbi.gov/about-us/cjis/fingerprints_biometrics/iafis/iafis

Questions for Discussion and Review

1. Why is it important to don gloves before obtaining a DNA Exemplar?

2. Which season of the year are investigators most likely to obtain fingerprints at a crime scene? Why?

3. What are the three (3) ways that the police can legally obtain a DNA exemplar?

4. Should everyone at birth be required to submit a DNA sample for the CODIS database? Why or why not?

5. What are the three (3) types of fingerprint patterns? Which one is the most prevalent?

6. In your opinion, which system of identification, DNA or fingerprints, is more reliable and why?

7. How many chromosomes does the average human have? Is there any difference between men and women's chromosomes? Animals?

8. What are the four (4) types of DNA exemplars discussed in this chapter?

9. What are some of the things that DNA cannot do for investigations?

10. Why are buccal cells (cheek cells) an excellent location to retrieve nuclear DNA?

11. What is Familial DNA? Should law enforcement be allowed to use it? Explain.

12. Which parent is mtDNA derived from?

13. Where can investigators most likely recover Touch DNA?

14. Which standard, Frye or Daubert is the toughest on the Criminal Justice System and why?

15. Which crime(s) do you think that DNA can be used to exonerate the innocent as well as convict the guilty?

16. What are the three (3) types of fingerprint types discussed in this chapter?

17. Which standard, Frye or Daubert, does your state follow?

18. What is the main concern for an investigator when obtaining a DNA Exemplar?

CHAPTER 3 — SEARCH AND SEIZURE

"The police must obey the law while enforcing the law."
— Chief Justice Earl Warren

KEY TERMS

Search & Seizure   Fruits of the Poisonous Tree
Fourth Amendment   Silver Platter Doctrine
Exclusionary Rule   Consent
Search Warrant   Emergency Exception
Hot Pursuit   Plain View

CHAPTER OBJECTIVES

At the end of this chapter, the student should be able to:

- Discuss what the Exclusionary Rule is and what it means for Law Enforcement.
- Recall how Search Warrants are obtained.
- Recall the Exceptions to a Search Warrant.

What is Search and Seizure? A search, as the term suggests, is a methodical and purposeful activity that looks to secure evidence that will be used to prosecute the perpetrator. A seizure is the confiscation of evidence, goods or persons found during a search for the purpose of securing it and using it against the perpetrator in a court of law.

Investigators know that during an investigation many constitutional issues come into play. They must be careful not to infringe on anyone's rights or risk being sued and losing the case. There are two important court cases that provide the history behind search and seizure and law enforcement. The student must understand "where we were" in order to get a grasp of "how we got here." Next to custodial interrogation, the topic of search and seizure is a highly contested subject among civil libertarians and crime control advocates.

I am only providing you a basic outline of what occurred in these cases; they are more involved than what I wrote. The student is encouraged to research these cases in depth. Here is an easy way to research a Supreme Court decision: For example, take a look at the following fictitious citation:

P   D
Smith v. Jones — 123 U.S. 456 2010

- Smith is the Plaintiff
- Jones is the Defendant
- 123 is the volume number of the law report where the decision is published

- U.S. — United States Report
- 456 is the page number in volume 123 where the information can be obtained
- 2010 is the year in which the decision was rendered

Here are the search and seizure cases that you should be familiar with:

1. *Weeks v. The United States,* 232 U.S. 383 (1914)

   Quick Case Synopsis:

   Freemont Weeks of Kansas City Missouri, was accused of sending lottery tickets through the mail, a federal crime. Federal agents entered Weeks's home and seized papers and other evidence against him. Later on that day, more federal agents entered his home and retrieved more evidence. Both times the agents did not possess a warrant. The evidence was subsequently used to convict him of the crime.

   Results of the Case:

   - The U.S. Supreme Court overturns Weeks's conviction by a unanimous decision (9-0) citing a violation of the Fourth Amendment
   - The decision gave birth to the Federal Exclusionary Rule
     o   Any evidence obtained in violation of the Fourth Amendment will be inadmissible in Federal Court
   - This led to the "Silver Platter Doctrine"—The Federal Exclusionary Rule did not prevent state officials from handing over evidence obtained in violation of the Fourth Amendment to federal agents on a "Silver Platter."

   Famous quote from the case: Justice William Rufus Day

   "If letters and private documents can thus be seized and held and used in evidence, the protection of the Fourth Amendment is of no value and might as well be stricken from the Constitution. The efforts of the courts are not to be aided by the sacrifice of those great principles established by years of endeavoring and suffering."

2. *Mapp v. Ohio,* 367 U.S. 643 (1961)

   Quick Case Synopsis:

   Cleveland Police Officers knock on the door of Dollree Mapp in search of a bombing suspect. Mapp is told by her lawyer not to let the police in without a warrant. The police eventually force their way past Mapp and enter the home. Mapp requests to see the warrant. The police flash a piece of paper that Mapp grabs and stuffs down her shirt. The police retrieve the "warrant" and handcuff Mapp. They then proceed to search everywhere for the suspect. During the search they find a chest that contained what amounted to pornographic materials—a crime in Ohio at the time. She is charged with the possession of obscene materials, convicted and sentenced even though the police never produced a copy of the "warrant."

Results of the Case:

- Mapp appeals to the State of Ohio
- The Ohio Supreme Court upheld her conviction, which is later overturned by the U.S. Supreme Court
- The Supreme Court applied the Federal Exclusionary Rule to the States
- Any evidence obtained in violation of the Fourth Amendment will be inadmissible in any (Local, State or Federal) court

Famous Quote from the case: Justice Thomas Clark

"We must close the only courtroom door remaining open to evidence secured by official lawlessness."

FAST FACTS ABOUT SEARCH WARRANTS

- The police must have PROBABLE CAUSE (PC) in order to obtain a search warrant (PC is also needed to make an arrest or to get an arrest warrant)
- The officer prepares a written affidavit
- The affidavit is sworn to before a judge and becomes a written order
- It must list the location to be searched and the persons or property to be seized—"The Elephant in the Ashtray"—the police can search anywhere that the object may fit. If I'm looking for a person, can I look in your sock drawer? No. But can I look under the bed, closet or chest? Yes.
- The following are examples of the type of property that can be seized via a search warrant:
  o Stolen Property
  o Property that was possessed unlawfully
  o Contraband
  o Property used or possessed to commit or conceal a crime
  o Evidence that points to an offense that was committed or that a person committed the offense
- In most jurisdictions search warrants must be executed within ten (10) days and between the hours of 0600 and 2100
  o Unless a Nighttime Endorsement is provided

- The police must announce their presence by knocking on the door
  o   Unless a No-Knock Endorsement is provided
- The police can break in if necessary

To avoid confusion about search warrants and arrest warrants, because they are similar, here is a quick breakdown:

Arrest Warrant	Search Warrant
The officer must have probable cause	The officer must have probable cause
The officer prepares a written affidavit	The officer prepares a written affidavit
The officer swears in front of a judge	The officer swears in front of a judge
**Executable any time	**Executable between 0600 and 2100
**No expiration date	**Valid for ten (10) days

Exceptions to a Search Warrant

"The young man knows the rules, the old man knows the exceptions."
— Oliver Wendell Holmes

Every American has protection against "unreasonable searches and seizures," as per the Fourth Amendment to the U.S. Constitution. The Fourth Amendment states the following:

> *"The right of the people to be secure in their persons, houses, papers, and effects, against unreasonable **searches** and **seizures**, shall not be violated, and no Warrants shall issue, but upon **probable cause**, supported by Oath or affirmation, and particularly describing the place to be searched, and the persons or things to be seized."*

A simple interpretation of the Fourth Amendment would be the following: A police officer develops probable cause that certain evidence exists at a certain location, swears to a judge who will determine if the officer has probable cause, the judge signs off on the warrant and the officer will then execute the warrant. Unfortunately, the practical application of the Fourth Amendment, as written, has little to do with any other types of interactions with the authorities outside of one's home. As you know, things such as cars did not exist when Thomas Jefferson wrote the Constitution. So case law decisions over the years have supplied law enforcement with the tools necessary to effectively do their jobs and balance the rights of citizens.

These court decisions, known as stare decisis, defined as the principal that the precedent decisions are to be followed by other courts, have lead to what law enforcement officers know as the exceptions to a search warrant. Searches without a warrant happen far more than those with a warrant as you will plainly see over the next few pages. These exceptions to a search warrant have also created strife between crime control advocates and civil libertarians. Crime Control Advocates view these decisions as a victory by allowing police to do their job and arrest criminals more effectively. Civil libertarians view them as eroding the foundation of an individual's civil rights and freedom.

The court decisions can be easily remembered with the help of the following acronym:

CHIP'S PEAS

Consent
Hot Pursuit
Inventor
Personal Garbage
Search Incidental to Lawful Arrest

Plain View
Emergency Exception
Automobile Exception
Stop, Question and (Possibly) Frisk

CONSENT

A person can waive their rights and give permission to an officer who does not have a warrant or probable cause, the authority to search their premise, person or vehicle. The person must have custody and control over the property. For example, your visiting friend cannot give the police permission to search your home, nor could your 9-year-old son. There are three (3) elements that must be present in order to have a legitimate waiver: the person must give up their rights: **VIK**

Voluntarily
Intelligently and
Knowingly

To effectively control false allegations, investigators should provide a preprinted department consent to search form that requires the individual to sign it. Remember that the police cannot use trickery, intimidation or make threats to obtain the waiver. If they do, all the evidence acquired will be thrown out.

HOT PURSUIT

The police can chase an individual wanted for a crime anywhere they go (even someone else's home) as long as they maintain continuous sight. If the police lose sight of the subject and later develop information on where the person is, they must obtain a search warrant for that location. For instance, the perpetrator runs into a building with the police close behind. The perpetrator runs up a few flights of stairs and the police officer falls behind. The officer then hears a door slam, but doesn't know which apartment it was. The officer cannot start knocking down everyone's door. Even if a neighbor points to the door that the suspect ran into, the police would have to obtain a search warrant for that location or persuade them to give up voluntarily. In either case, the police would have to secure the perimeter of the building so that the individual cannot escape while they are applying for a warrant.

INVENTORY

To protect against allegations of wrongdoing, theft or damage, police departments have established verifiable procedures on what to do with property that comes into their custody (*South Dakota v. Opperman* 428 U.S. 364 (1976)). This procedure covers automobiles as well as other types of property that comes into the possession of the police department. Any contraband that is recovered during an inventory will be accounted for and criminal charges will be added to the docket. Even closed containers, such as a knapsack, briefcase, luggage, etc., can be opened and inventoried. The police cannot use this procedure to circumvent the establishment of probable cause. It is solely an administrative procedure.

PERSONAL GARBAGE

In the case *California v. Greenwood*, 486 U.S. 35 (1988), it was decided that once a person abandons property by putting it in a location that everyone has access to (the curb), they forfeit their expectation to privacy. However, the police cannot come onto your property and search your garbage. Even though a homeowner must maintain the sidewalk and curb, they do not own it.

SEARCH INCIDENTAL TO LAWFUL ARREST

Once a person is arrested lawfully the police can search their exterior and inside of their clothes. This is done for three main reasons: (1) officer safety, (2) prevent the destruction of evidence and 3) prevent escape. The police can also search the "lungeable" or "grabable" area surrounding the person as well as any containers on or near the person (*Chimel v. California*, 395 U.S. 752 (1969)).

PLAIN VIEW

An item that is observed by the officer and can be interpreted as being unlawfully possessed can be seized without obtaining a search warrant, as long as the officer has a lawful right to be at the location (*Coolidge v. New Hampshire*, 403 U.S. 443 (1971)). For example, the police are called to a home where a domestic violence dispute took place. As the police are conducting the preliminary investigation, the officer sees a firearm on top of a nightstand. If it is an unlicensed firearm, the homeowner will be charged accordingly.

The Plain View Doctrine also applies to "open fields." An open field is any open, undeveloped land that is not used for a dwelling or a business. Even posted trespassing signs or fencing cannot stop the police from entering "open fields" if a crime is suspected.

EMERGENCY EXCEPTION

The police can enter a location where an emergency is or may be occurring. The belief is that if the officer does not enter immediately a life can be lost, evidence can be destroyed or a suspect can escape (*People v. Mitchell*, 39 NY 2d 173 (1976)). The officer can search for additional victims or perpetrators and can seize anything in Plain View during the emergency, but cannot conduct a full search for evidence. In addition, officers are allowed to make a protective sweep of the location to ensure their safety by searching the house for additional people (*Maryland v. Buie*, 494 U.S. 325 (1990)). However, once the emergency is over, the officers will have to vacate the premise, secure it and obtain a warrant.

The courts also decided that there is no such thing as a "Murder Scene" exception. Three (3) decisions over the last thirty-plus years, *Mincey v. Arizona*, 437 U.S. 385 (1978), *Thompson v. Louisiana*, 469 U.S. 17 (1984) and *Flippo v. West Virginia*, 528 U.S. 11 (1999), have stated that once the emergency is over, or if a person of interest has an absolute right to privacy at the location, the police must obtain a search warrant. If not, any evidence obtained will be suppressed. Because most people are murdered by someone they know, it is always a good decision to obtain a search warrant for the location unless you know for sure that the victim lived alone.

STOP!	*If it appears that the suspect has an absolute right to privacy (or you do not know) at the location then obtain a search warrant! When in doubt, fill it out!*

Automobile Exception

In *Carroll v. United States*, 267 U.S. 132 (1925), the court decided that a warrantless search of a vehicle stopped in transit could be searched if the officer had probable cause to believe that the vehicle (including mobile homes) was transporting contraband or evidence. Because an auto is "mobile," evidence can be disposed of quickly while the officer attempts to get a warrant. An individual does not have the same right to privacy with their vehicles as they do their homes. In a recent Supreme Court decision in the case *Arizona v. Grant*, 143 p.3d 379 (2006), the "police may search a vehicle without a warrant only when the suspect could reach for a weapon or try to destroy evidence, or when it is 'reasonable to believe' there is evidence in the car supporting the crime" (*Newsday*, April 22, 2009).

Also, a police canine can sniff a vehicle as long as the officer had probable cause to stop the vehicle (*Illinois v. Caballes*, 543 U.S. 455 (2005)).

STOP, QUESTION AND (POSSIBLY) FRISK

Also known as the "Terry Stop" (*Terry v. Ohio*, 392 U.S. 1 1968), this decision by the courts was to protect an officer who may encounter a suspect with a weapon. The Terry Stop is a brief investigatory stop based on **reasonable suspicion** that criminality is afoot. Note that I wrote possibly frisk. It is not automatic. An officer has to develop articulable facts that will allow them to pat down and reach into a suspect's clothing. Examples of an articulable fact can be the close proximity of a recent violent crime (murder, rape, robbery, felonious assault), clothing worn (heavy jacket in the summer) or a bulge.

State courts have made different rulings on what items can be searched for and/or removed. For instance, in New York, an officer can only reach into a suspect's clothing if they believe what they felt during a pat down was a weapon. Even if they know it is drugs, they cannot remove the item from the person's pocket and arrest them.

There are many case law decisions that changed the way the police deal with searches and seizures and the protections of the Fourth Amendment. Crime Control advocates view these court decisions as dealing with the impractical and/or unsafe circumstances that police officers found themselves involved with everyday.

Internet Resources for Investigators

U.S. Constitution
http://www.archives.gov/exhibits/charters/constitution.html

U.S. Supreme Court Decisions Lookup via Findlaw.com
http://www.findlaw.com/casecode/supreme.html

Questions for Discussion and Review

1.   Why would the police want a Nighttime or No-Knock Endorsement?

2.   What Amendment to the Constitution protects citizens against unreasonable searches and seizures?

3.   The police obtain a search warrant for a home belonging to James Smith. The police have purchased drugs from the home on several occasions. When the police execute the warrant, they find more narcotics and arrest James Smith and his 80-year-old mother Mary Smith. Why was Mary Smith arrested?

4.   Can the police use ordinary citizens to obtain evidence for them? Why or why not?

5.   What court case gave us the Federal Exclusionary Rule?

6.   On January 10, 2007, the City of Jay obtained a search warrant for a known drug location based on probable cause. The City of Jay Police Department executed the warrant at 0700 hours on the morning of January 21, 2007 and recovered six (6) kilos of cocaine, three (3) handguns and one (1) semi-automatic machine gun. Should the Police Chief congratulate these officers for doing a fantastic job? In a sentence or two discuss your reasoning.

7.   What court case applied the Federal Exclusionary Rule to the states?

8.   Is an arrest a seizure and therefore covered under the Fourth Amendment? Explain why or why not.

9.   Are the police allowed to chase an individual who went through a red light across state lines?

10. If a police officer observes a bullet in the back seat of a car, can he/she search the entire car?

11. In order to give consent, an individual must do it _____, _____ & _____.

12.   Do you feel that "exceptions" to a search warrant erodes the value of the U.S. Constitution?

13.   The police respond to a house about a lost child. While they are inside of the house, one of the officers opens a cabinet and finds an unregistered pistol. The homeowner is arrested. Would the pistol be admissible in court? Why or why not?

14.   In order for a Plain View seizure of evidence to be admitted in court, the police must be there how?

15.   List the nine (9) exceptions to a search warrant detailed in this chapter.

16.   When the police have probable cause on a vehicle, they can search it because the court case *Carroll v. the United States* said it was _____ .

CHAPTER 4 — THE CRIME SCENE PROTOCOL

"Oh, how simple it would all have been, had I been here before they come like a herd of buffalo and wallowed all over it."
— Sir Arthur Conan Doyle
The Boscombe Valley Mystery

KEY TERMS

Gatekeeper	Zone Search
Rosario Rule	Grid Search
Rough Sketch	Strip Line Search
Chain of Custody	Locard's Exchange Principle
Individual Characteristics	Class Characteristics

CHAPTER OBJECTIVES

At the end of this chapter, the student should be able to:

- Recall the steps taken before responding to a crime scene.
- List the people who must be interviewed at the scene if possible.
- Understand the order in which a crime scene is processed.
- List the five (5) types of crime scene search patterns.
- Describe what a rough sketch is and why it is important.
- Understand the chain of custody and what role it plays in criminal cases.

If criminal investigation was an automobile, the crime scene would be the engine that powered it. Without a good engine, the car goes nowhere. A crime scene is the location where a crime was committed. They can only occur in two (2) locations: Inside and Outside. Inside crime scenes are easier to maintain because you can keep most people out by shutting a door or blocking an entrance. In my experience nearly 70% of the cases I investigated occurred indoors. The real reason cops love indoor crime scenes is that they offer protection against the elements. Outdoor crime scenes are more difficult to secure because of their sheer size and lack of physical boundaries. Mother Nature can be very unfriendly to the investigator.

Weather is only one of the many uncontrollable occurrences known as evidence dynamics. The concept of evidence dynamics is defined as, "any influences that adds, changes, relocates, obscures, contaminates, or obliterates physical evidence, regardless of intent" (Chisum & Turvey, 2006). An investigator must make allowances for evidence dynamics that occur before, during and after a criminal event. For example, the first police officers on the scene may step on, kick or destroy physical evidence unintentionally. Investigators must keep this in mind, especially when conducting the initial interviews with responding officers.

Crime scenes are extremely important to the investigator because that is where you will find your physical evidence. The investigator must keep in mind that other crime scenes, a secondary or tertiary, may exist. The location where the crime occurred is the primary crime scene, unless you are investigating a homicide, then it is where you find the body. For example, a body is found out in the woods with multiple stab wounds, but very little blood. The "dump" site becomes your primary scene even though the act was committed somewhere else. An investigator can reach this conclusion based on the seriousness of the wounds. If an individual suffered multiple stab wounds, one would find a lot of blood at the scene. Sometimes, you will never find the location where the incident took place. The area where the crime was committed, or where the body was found, will be labeled the inner perimeter and the area that surrounds the crime scene will be the outer perimeter (see Figure 4.1). Both have to be secured and cordoned off. No one but necessary personnel, the case investigator, the investigating supervisor and crime scene unit personnel will be allowed in the inner perimeter.

Figure 4.1: Inner and Outer Perimeter

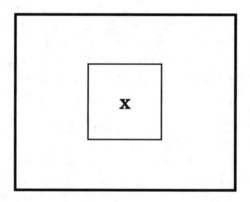

As you will see over the next couple of pages, a lack of crime scene control can have a disastrous effect on the outcome of the case. The investigator must take their time and process the scene properly—you get only one chance to do it right—there are no playground rule "Do Overs!"

My experience as a detective supervisor and instructor, has led me to create a crime scene protocol using the acronym, **CRIME SCENE**. Each letter stands for the basic steps the investigator needs to take (in order) during a major criminal event. Like them or not, police department lingo is littered with acronyms, and I believe ones that are easy to remember, work. Every department has a person locked in the bottom of headquarters whose sole job it is to discover new acronyms! I'm only kidding.

Collect all of the information you can before leaving the station house
Reassess the crime scene boundaries set up by the patrol officers on arrival at the scene

Initiate the crime scene walk-through with the first officer on the scene as your guide

Make extensive notes at the crime scene

Everything must be photographed

Sketch and search the crime scene

Collect and record physical evidence discovered at the scene

Evidence chain of custody is paramount to ensure a professional investigation

No stone is to be left unturned

Exit strategy

COLLECT ALL THE INFORMATION YOU CAN BEFORE LEAVING THE STATION HOUSE

Detective Smith is sitting at his computer typing a report when the phone rings. Sgt. Jones tells him that a woman was found dead in the park. What does Detective Smith do first? Det. Smith records the time of the notification and the identity of the person who notified him of the incident. Investigators can be notified of a crime scene in the following ways: (1) a direct notification from patrol officer or supervisor at the scene, (2) through the Desk Officer or (3) by police radio transmission. The notification to the investigator begins the investigation timeline. The investigator must prepare from this point on as if the case is going to court (Figure 4-2).

The investigator must find out if the victim is still at the scene. If not, what hospital were they transported to? An investigator should be dispatched immediately to the hospital in an attempt to interview the victim or to obtain a dying declaration. To obtain a valid dying declaration, the individual has to believe that he/she is about to die. The investigator at the hospital should obtain custody of the victim's clothes for future forensic analysis: body fluids, gunshot residue (GSR), physical evidence, Touch DNA, personal property, cell phone, identification, etc.

An all-out effort must be made to identify 911 callers and conduct basic computer checks on both the caller if known and any information they have received. For example, run the address to determine what types of calls for police service originated from the location in the past. Were there an unusual number of "gun runs" at the location or numerous calls regarding drug sales? Or is there a history of calls for domestic violence? Many cases have been solved before the detective ever left the stationhouse. Many times an investigator must obtain a subpoena for the phone company to obtain subscriber information.

The 911 callers play a pivotal role in the investigation because they are your eyewitnesses

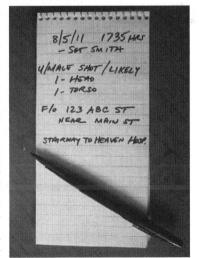

Figure 4.2: Sample notebook entry of the incidence notification.
© 2012 Joseph L. Giacalone

to the event in question. If someone made the effort to notify the police, they did so with trepidation. Therefore, interviewing them away from the scene is a good idea.

Armed with some background information about the case, the investigator must take some equipment with him to the scene. Business cards for leaving with witnesses or during canvasses, a digital camera, crime scene tape (you can never have enough of it), cell phone, a police radio, a flashlight and the new notepad you started in the squad room. The most important piece of equipment that the investigator must bring with him to the crime scene is his bullet-resistant vest. That suit you are wearing can't stop a bullet.

REASSESS THE CRIME SCENE BOUNDARIES SET UP BY THE PATROL OFFICERS UPON ARRIVAL AT THE SCENE

When the investigator arrives on the scene he must conduct a "sense" survey. A sense survey includes the use of sight, sound and smell. Patrol officers are the individuals who determine the overall size of the crime scene, not the investigator. Hopefully, they make the determination based on the information they received during the preliminary investigation. The rule is to make the crime scene as big as you can; it can always be made smaller. You have to ask yourself, "Is the crime scene big enough?" If possible, you, the investigator, will expand the boundaries. Next, ask yourself, "Is this the primary crime scene?" It may not be, so identify secondary or tertiary scenes and make sure they are properly secured. Fire escapes, back alleys or any egress that the perpetrator could have used to escape should be secured as "extended" crime scenes. Remember, a vehicle may also be part of the crime scene or act as an additional scene. Is the crime scene properly delineated so onlookers are kept out? Is this incident likely to attract media attention? Do we need to establish an area for the media? Where do we want to put the media? Ideally, we want to put them close enough so that they feel they are part of the investigation, but far enough away that they don't get in the way. The investigator should ensure that crime scene tape and other barriers are up to prevent any un-authorized personnel from gaining access to the scene.

The investigator must be observant of several conditions that may exist at the crime scene. For instance, were the doors locked or unlocked? Windows opened or closed? Lights on or off? Shades up or down? Were there any distinct odors in the air? What was the temperature of the room? What was the weather like?

The investigator should look for a location, away from the inner perimeter of the crime scene, to establish a temporary headquarters if one hasn't been set up already. The temporary headquarters can be used to plan how things will be conducted and provide a level of shelter from the weather. The crime scene is never a good location to set up a temporary command post. Many departments now have mobile temporary headquarter vehicles equipped with phones, wireless laptops, printers, fax machines and, most importantly, bathrooms.

In hours of darkness, request a support unit, i.e., SWAT, ESU, etc., that has movable lighting to help with the search. If necessary the police can ask a local utility or construction company for movable lighting. Flashlights alone will not be sufficient lighting for a crime scene investigation!

All crime scenes must have a patrol officer posted to act as the "gatekeeper." The role of the gatekeeper is to prevent access to the crime scene by unauthorized persons and nonessential personnel and to maintain a record of the identity of those who entered the scene. This record (Figure 4.3) must be secured and placed in the case file for possible use in the courtroom. Generally, police officers will stay out of the crime scene when their names are being recorded so they do not receive a subpoena to testify in court.

Figure 4.3: Sample Crime Scene Entry/Exit Log

Crime Scene Entry/Exit Log

Crime Scene Location: _____ Case #: _____

Officer Assigned: _____ Shield #: _____ Command: _____

Date	Time In	Print Rank/Name	Reason for Entering Scene	Time Out

ALL PERSONS THAT ENTER THE CRIME SCENE MUST **SIGN IN AND OUT** OF THIS LOG INCLUDING GATEKEEPER.   Page _____ of _____

The five (5) most destructible elements at a crime scene that the Gatekeeper must control are:

- Other police personnel
- Curiosity seekers
- Family members
- Fire personnel
- EMS workers
- Weather

```
┌─────────────────────────────────────────────────────────────┐
│                  Crime Scene Survival Tip                    │
│                                                              │
│  Always double your crime scene tape boundary with an upper  │
│  and lower "railing." Do this for both the inner and outer   │
│  perimeters. You ask why? So you can keep police personnel   │
│  out of your crime scene. They can decide if they should go  │
│  over it or under it. Unauthorized police personnel in a     │
│  crime scene can contaminate it and destroy valuable         │
│  physical evidence.                                          │
└─────────────────────────────────────────────────────────────┘
```

Once you are confident that the crime scene is secured, you must turn your attention to the many individuals who must be interviewed. In-person interviews at the crime scene should be conducted whenever possible. Here is a list of individuals who must be interviewed:

- First officer(s) on the scene
  o What were their observations on arrival at the scene?
    • Did they observe anyone/vehicle fleeing the scene?
  o Where did they enter the scene?
  o Did they touch anything at the scene?
  o Did they detain anyone at the scene?
  o Did they let anyone leave the scene?
  o Did they use the bathroom? Smoke at the scene? Use the phone at the scene?
  o Was anyone unnecessarily helpful on your arrival at the scene?
- Victim/Witnesses
  o Interviews must be conducted before the person's memory begins to fade or they get tainted by others
  o Separate victims/witnesses so they do not confer with one another
  o Properly identify each person interviewed
    • Pedigree information: name, address, date of birth, phone number, employment information, etc.
      • Use photo identification
- EMS personnel
  o Did they touch anything at the scene?
  o Did they move the body?
    • What was their reason for moving the body?
- Fire department personnel
  o Is the fire suspicious? Why?
- Medical Examiner/Coroner/Medicolegal Investigator (MLI)
  o What is their assessment of the situation?

At this time the investigating supervisor will make assignments. He/she will use a large flip chart or whiteboard to list the locations and the names of the investigators who will respond (Figure 4.4). It may sound a bit archaic, but a flip chart keeps everything right in front of everyone and makes it easy to read. In addition, when the supervisor is relieved, the next one doesn't have to guess where everyone is. Tight controls must be kept on who is where and doing what. This practice will prevent cross-contaminating scenes—a major problem in the O.J. Simpson case, for example.

Figure 4.4

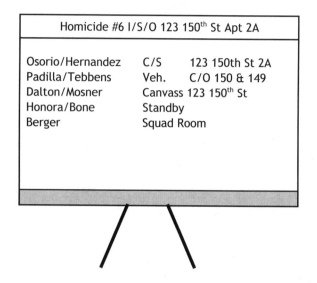

Homicide #6 I/S/O 123 150th St Apt 2A		
Osorio/Hernandez	C/S	123 150th St 2A
Padilla/Tebbens	Veh.	C/O 150 & 149
Dalton/Mosner	Canvass 123 150th St	
Honora/Bone	Standby	
Berger	Squad Room	

Crime Scene Management Tip

Use a flip chart to keep track of investigators and their assignments.

In the event that another crime scene is located, which two detectives will be excluded from it?

INITIATE THE CRIME SCENE WALKTHROUGH WITH THE FIRST OFFICER ON THE SCENE AS YOUR GUIDE

The investigator must make sure he follows the same path in and out of the scene that he originally used. If possible, think about cordoning off the pathway so all necessary police personnel can access the scene without destroying evidence. The goal of a crime scene walkthrough is to identify what physical evidence exists in the scene and to determine if there is a possibility that the evidence can be destroyed. For instance, you have an outdoor crime scene and it begins to snow heavily. The weather factor is your biggest threat to an outdoor crime scene. The investigator has to act quickly or risk losing the evidence forever. This is not the ideal situation when working with crime scenes.

Crime Scene Survival Tip

The goal of the crime scene walkthrough is to identify and preserve evidence!

After completion of the crime scene walkthrough, the detective should begin to formulate their investigative hypotheses. An investigative hypothesis is an assumption, or educated guess, of what is believed to have occurred based on the crime scene, the physical evidence, witness/victim statements and the preliminary investigation conducted by the patrol officer. I am a firm believer that generally investigators piece together what had occurred and who did it in the first five minutes, but spend the rest of the time proving it. The investigator begins to build his/her hypothesis on how and why the crime was committed at this point. Sometimes the "why" is more important that the "how." The "why" is the motive behind the crime. Identify the motive and you can establish a list of suspects. Investigators rely on the fact that most people are killed by someone they know. The closest people to the victim are always suspected first, so investigators must carefully choose to whom to speak with first and where they want to speak with them, i.e., the squad room, their home, place of business, etc. The investigator attempts to establish the elements of a suspect through the closet person in our lives: **MOM**

> **M**eans—Was the person physically capable of carrying out the crime?
> **O**pportunity—Was the suspect available to commit the crime? Do they have a rock solid alibi?
> **M**otive—Was it over what I refer to as the Homicide Triangle: Love, Money or Drugs? Why would somebody want this person dead?

The investigator needs to be careful not to marry the hypothesis. It is all right to be wrong, but be flexible. When the facts and circumstances lead you in another direction, do not fight it just to be right. Criminal investigations have no room for egos.

MAKE EXTENSIVE NOTES AT THE CRIME SCENE

Document the time you arrived at the scene for a continuation of the investigation timeline. What was the weather like? What were your observations? What information did you receive from your in-person interviews (see "Reassess the crime scene boundaries ...")? This information may prove or disprove a suspect's alibi in the future. In many jurisdictions these notes must be kept in the case folder according to the "Rosario Material" ruling (*People v. Rosario* 9 NY2d. 286 (1961)). In 2011, the State of New Jersey passed a similar ruling (*State v. W.B.*, NJ (April 27, 2011)). So it is always best to keep all of your field notes with the case folder. In addition, a new notebook should be used for each major investigation and preserved for a future criminal trial. Never tear any pages out of the notebook!

Crime Scene Survival Tip

Before using a new notebook, check how many pages are supposed to be in the book and then count them. If a page is missing, do not use the book!

At the Crime Scene: The Case for Keeping Notes

So you don't think keeping notes is important? A judge in Charlotte, North Carolina has suspended the death sentence for Demeatrius Montgomery who is accused of murdering two (2) police officers in 2007 because the detective discarded his notes. The judge has since barred prosecutors from seeking the death penalty at all. The detective was reassigned to desk duty and an inquiry is being made into all of his cases by Internal Affairs. To make matters worse is that the notes were discovered in possession of the detective who is now facing perjury charges (Smith, WBTV News, 8/30/10). In addition, the defense team has just been handed a gift in the entire case. The suspect may walk away after killing two cops. Do I hear a reasonable doubt claim?

Notes serve several purposes for the investigator. Notes for an investigator are indeed a good **CHAP**.

Create a written historical record of the event
Help write the initial investigative report
Act as a memory aid in courtroom testimony
Preserve information for statistical purposes

EVERYTHING MUST BE PHOTOGRAPHED AND DETAILED ON A PHOTOGRAPHIC LOG

Ideally, the scene should be photographed before any evidence is collected. In the real world this may not be such a reality. For instance, the likelihood of leaving a firearm on the street during an investigation may not be in your best interest. First, it can be used against you or another officer at the scene, or it can be easily stolen during the commotion and confusion that often takes place at a crime scene. If evidence is in danger of being stolen, have a reliable patrol officer stand near the object until it can be properly documented. This tactic works only if the department has ample personnel.

It is always best practice to take more photos then less. Photos provide an accurate historical record of the scene. Photos of the scene are taken in three steps:

1. Far away to give an overall view of the scene
2. A medium range and
3. A close up.

Also, the photographs should be taken using a reference point so that each photo can be strung together to form a landscape view. This is especially important in outdoor crime scenes. See the following examples of the landscape outdoor crime scene view (Figures 4.5 – 4.11).

Figure 4-5
Photos taken from left to right and framed by the
fence to the left and the lamppost to the right.
© 2012 Joseph L. Giacalone

Figure 4.6
The lamppost that was on the right
is now on our left. The next
lamppost is on our right.
© 2012 Joseph L. Giacalone

Figure 4.7
The next lamppost is now on our left
and the street sign is on our right.
© 2012 Joseph L. Giacalone

Figure 4.8
The street sign is now on our left.
© 2012 Joseph L. Giacalone

Figure 4.9
To the very next lamppost.
© 2012 Joseph L. Giacalone

Figure 4.10
Mid-range photos of the brush in the park and tire tracks.
© 2012 Joseph L. Giacalone

Figure 4.11
Up close of the brush.
© 2012 Joseph L. Giacalone

Photographing vehicles is another task of the crime scene technician. The following photographs should be taken of vehicles that are part of a crime scene or are the actual crime scene.

- All four sides of the vehicle
- Registration
- Plates
- Vehicle Identification Number (VIN)
- Interior of vehicle
- Odometer
- Trunk and its contents

Crime Scene Survival Tip

Do not take crime scene photos with investigators standing around in the background. The presence of investigators in the photos can be seen as a lack of crime scene management.

At least two sets of photos will be taken of physical evidence before it is collected. The first photo will be of the object *in situ* (Latin for "in place" (Figure 4.12)). The next photograph will have a scale or ruler placed near the object (Figure 4.13). The ruler gives us the accurate size and reference. The reason you take the photo without the ruler first is because you are altering the crime scene by introducing the ruler and also you eliminate the argument that the ruler was used to hide something.

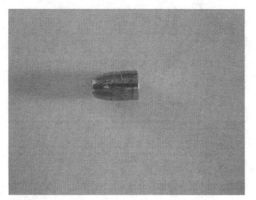

Figure 4.12
9MM bullet
© 2012 Joseph L. Giacalone

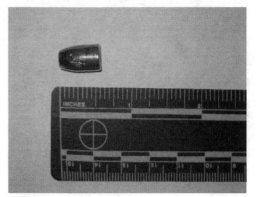

Figure 4.13
The same 9MM bullet with a scale.
© 2012 Joseph L. Giacalone

All photographs have to be accounted for on a Photographic Log or similar evidence collection form. The Photographic Log should have the following information:

- Name and department identification number of the photographer
- Address of the crime scene
- Case number
- Crime Scene Unit's number
- Time and date
- Weather conditions
- Photograph number(s)
- Type of film and camera used—state if digital camera

If possible, a videographer should be used to video tape the entire crime scene in addition to the taking of crime scene photos. Video can prove to be an invaluable piece of demonstrative evidence in the courtroom and provide investigators an opportunity to "revisit" the crime scene later. This can be extremely important when investigators are transferred, retired or when the case goes cold. Today's ever-changing technology makes this an easy option to use and store video evidence.

Crime Scene Survival Tip

When the crime scene unit is laying out the number markers, ensure that they are all facing in the same direction. This way they will all be visible in the crime scene photographs.

Sketch and Search the Crime Scene

There are two (2) categories of crime scene sketches: (1) the Rough Sketch and (2) the Smooth Sketch. You do not have to be Pablo Picasso to draw the rough sketch of a crime scene (Figure 4-14), but it is extremely important to the case. The Rough Sketch can be drawn in your notepad so that it is preserved forever. The sketch must have the day, date, time, location, case number, weather, page numbers (example: pg. 1 of 6) and the investigator's name.

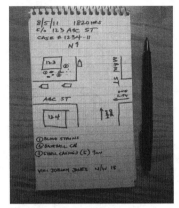

The Rough Sketch in a notepad should include:

- Locations of evidence
- Vehicles, furniture or other objects
- Finger, palm, tire or shoe prints
- Bullet holes

Figure 4.14
© 2012 Joseph L. Giacalone

The smooth sketch can be drawn either by hand or be computer generated. Most smooth sketches are done by computer and make great examples of demonstrative evidence. This is the sketch that will be used to demonstrate in court. So an artist or cartographer should be used from within the department. Make sure it is an accurate account and do not make any changes to it once you leave the scene. All sketches must have a legend explaining the sketch as well as a north compass point. Write the investigative report regarding the sketch and account for it as an attachment to that report, and file it in the case folder.

Crime scene sketches serve many purposes. If you want **PEACE** and quiet in your squad room, then make sure one is done. The following are benefits an investigator possesses from using a sketch:

Permanent record of the scene
Eliminates the clutter often associated with many photographs
Admissible in court as demonstrative evidence
Creates a mental picture for those who were not at the crime scene
    (jurors)
Establishes the precise location and relationship of object and evidence

STOP!	*Never change a sketch after you have left the crime scene!*

Once the location has been photographed and sketched, the investigator or crime scene technician will now employ the appropriate crime scene search method for the scene. There should be a specially trained member of the force whose sole job it is to process crime scenes. Even in smaller departments, it is worth the expense of properly training and equipping crime scene technicians. The "one hat fits all" program is not a good plan for processing crime scenes.

There are five (5) ways to search a crime scene; but in my opinion, two of them, the Spiral Search (Figure 4.15) and Pie/Wheel Search (Figure 4.16) are not practical or effective. The only thing missing in the Spiral Search is a blindfold and a pin the tail on the donkey. The Spiral Search is supposed to be used in the event that only one searcher is available. If a supervisor insists that a Spiral Search is used, the investigator will start at the outer rim and make their way to the core of the crime scene. The Pie/Wheel Search is not practical because it breaks the crime scene up into "slices of pizza," which makes it difficult to cordon off the area.

An investigator is better off using the Strip/Line Search (Figure 4.17) or the Grid Search (Figure 4.18). The Strip/Line search is conducted with a number of searchers "shoulder to shoulder" walking down a straight path. The Grid Search is more time consuming because the investigator redoubles the effort, but they also redouble the chance of discovering evidence. A Zone Search (Figure 4.19) would be more practical in large open areas, such as an open field or large park. A zone search should also be used for searching vehicles so that evidence is not missed. A zone is created and broken up into smaller more manageable scenes, usually four quadrants. Within each of the zones, the Strip/Line or Grid Search would be employed. In a vehicle search zone "A" should be the driver's area.

If a searcher comes across evidence during any of the above search methods, all searching will stop momentarily until a decision is made on how the evidence will be handled. The time of day, weather factors and the risk of loss, will play the dominant role in the decision-making process.

Figure 4.15   Spiral

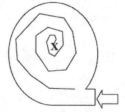

Figure 4.16   Pie/Wheel

Figure 4.17 Strip/Line Search

Figure 4.18 Grid Search

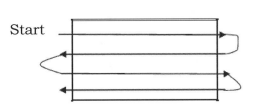

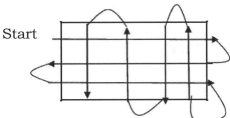

The Strip/Line Search has officers or searchers standing shoulder to shoulder down a lane—like a race track. The Grid Search is the most time consuming of all the methods, but you also have the best chance of recovering evidence.

Figure 4.19 Zone Search

A	B	Remember, one of the search methods will be used inside each of the "zones."
C	D	

Collect and Record Physical Evidence Discovered at the Scene

What is physical evidence? Physical evidence is anything that can prove that a crime was committed. It is also known as real evidence. Physical evidence is evidence that can be seen and held and can come in different forms such as solids, liquids etc. Physical evidence can come from **CVS**: the

Crime scene
Victim
Suspect

What is the value of physical evidence? Physical evidence comes in two (2) distinct categories of characteristics:

1. Class Characteristics
2. Individual Characteristics

The investigator has to realize that all objects have both class and individual characteristics. It will be the task of the investigator or forensic scientist to distinguish the two. Class characteristics are qualities that are shared by a group of objects. For instance, a group of .38 caliber firearms have class characteristics. They all hold the same size cartridge and they are all used to shoot the same size bullet. But is every .38 caliber the same? No. Individual characteristics are exactly as the word "individual" implies: that each piece of evidence has a unique characteristic, no two are alike. Fingerprints, DNA and the .38 caliber's barrel from the example above, will make unique striation marks on a fired bullet. Therefore, they have Individual Characteristics.

What can physical evidence do? An investigator, who knows the importance of physical evidence in a crime scene, **DRILLS** down to the truth! Physical evidence can do all of the following:

Determine whether a crime was committed
Reconstruct the crime scene
Investigate leads provided
Link a suspect to a victim and/or crime scene
Link serial crimes
Suspect & witness statement corroboration

Identifying physical evidence from the above sources falls under the theory of transfer known as Locard's Exchange Principle. In 1920, Edmond Locard suggested that when two objects come together, something is exchanged between and taken away by both objects (Turvey, 2008, pp. 8–9).

The following quote is taken from the seminal text on criminal investigation, entitled, *Criminal Investigation* by Paul Leland Kirk (p. 4). It sums up the importance of Locard's Exchange Principle and the importance of physical evidence:

> *Wherever he steps, whatever he touches, whatever he leaves— even unconsciously—will serve as silent evidence against him. Not only his fingerprints and his shoe prints, but also his hair, the fibers from his clothes, the glass he breaks, the tool mark he leaves, the paint he scratches, the blood or semen he deposits or collects—all of these and more bear mute witness against him. This is evidence that does not forget. It is not confused by the excitement of the moment. It is not absent because human witnesses are. It is factual evidence. Physical evidence cannot be wrong; it cannot perjure itself; it cannot be wholly absent. Only in its interpretation can there be error. Only human failure to find, study, and understand it can diminish its value.*

Locard's Exchange Principle is especially true in cases where a violent struggle took place. The chances of obtaining transfer samples in this type of event from the suspect are much greater. This is why proper controls at crime scenes are important so contamination can be avoided. For example, an investigator is inside of a crime scene conducting an investigation. During the investigation, the police develop probable cause to arrest the boyfriend. The investigator arrives at the boyfriend's house and arrests him. Do we see a problem? You should, because the investigator more than likely contaminated the boyfriend's house with evidence from the crime scene! A mistake like this could prove fatal in an investigation. This is why having a flip chart with everyone's assignments on it can be very useful (see Figure 4.4). The case investigator must retain the flip chart for future court considerations. It was part of the investigation.

Even though the case investigator is not the one who will collect and package the evidence, he should be aware of ways that evidence can be contaminated so that it can be avoided. The case investigator must be able to protect himself, protect the evidence and protect others. Evidence technicians should don a new pair of rubber gloves when handling different types of evidence as well as employ single-use tools to collect it. There is no eating, drinking or smoking allowed at a crime scene. Never! The techs should avoid handling the evidence unnecessarily and must avoid showing onlookers, AKA police supervisors, the evidence to satisfy their curiosity. This will help mitigate contamination. If you notice that something is not being done right, speak up.

Physical evidence that may contain physiological fluids (blood, semen, saliva, etc.) should be given the opportunity to air dry if possible before they are packaged. Because most of this type of evidence involves some sort of material or fabric, the investigator should take all layers of clothing or bedding as evidence. The biological evidence could have soaked through. Any evidence containing physiological fluids (therefore possible DNA) must be packaged in paper and *not* plastic and be stored in a cool dry place! The paper bags should also have a biohazard or similar type of sticker on it whenever you have skin, blood or other biological evidence. There are a variety of containers, bags and other packaging devices that will be used to collect evidence. Each one has a specific role. If the evidence is not packaged properly, you run the risk of destroying it. Most other types of evidence can be packaged in a suitable container or security-type envelope. DNA evidence must never be left in direct sunlight or inside of a hot vehicle.

STOP!	*All evidence that may contain biological evidence must be packaged in paper bags and never in plastic!*

It is not enough to ensure that you have the right type of container for a specific piece of evidence, but how it is sealed is also important. Many laboratories will not accept evidence that is not sealed properly. Again, anything that may allude to sloppy police work will be detrimental to the case and your career. Evidence containers should be sealed with tamper-proof evidence tape and not clear tape or masking tape. Also, evidence secured in paper must also be sealed with tamperproof evidence tape (Figure 4.20) and not staples, paper clips or binder clips.

Figure 4.20 is an example of a properly sealed paper bag using evidence tape. The packaging will also indicate the date and time the evidence was collected, who collected it, what agency is involved, the case number, victim's name and what type of evidence is secured inside. Some companies sell preprinted evidence bags.

Figure 4.20 Properly Sealed Evidence Bag
© 2012 Joseph L. Giacalone

Remember, the investigator is in charge of the scene. If you want something dusted because you believe it may reveal prints, ask the technician. It is not a good time to be shy; you may overlook a valuable piece of evidence. If you have a hunch, go with it. If the evidence is never recognized, recorded and packaged, it will be lost forever, or worse make you appear incompetent!

At the Crime Scene: The Amanda Knox Story

You would think by now that the law enforcement community would have its act together on the proper handling of crime scenes, but, no. Police in Perugia, Italy, have learned the hard way that there are no shortcuts when processing a crime scene. In the case against Amanda Knox, Rafaelle Sollecito and Rudy Guede for the murder of Meredith Kercher, there were many crime scene procedural errors including: packing biological evidence in plastic bags, using the same set of gloves to pick up different types of evidence, they used standards of identification of genetic material far below that of the international consensus and returned to the crime scene to collect evidence after forty-seven days! The police videotaped the crime scene process, which led to their courtroom demise.

There is a proper order to process the crime scene. Here is a quick reminder not to forget to hit the **ESC** key:

Everything must be photographed
Sketch the crime scene—then search
Collect the evidence for packaging

CI Tip Sheet

Photograph ➤ Sketch ➤ Search ➤ Collect

EVIDENCE CHAIN OF CUSTODY IS PARAMOUNT TO ENSURE A THOROUGH AND PROFESSIONAL INVESTIGATION

The chain of custody represents the written, chronological and unbroken history of who found the evidence and where it was found. The chain of custody begins at the crime scene and maintains the integrity of the evidence. It is all about accountability and therefore the chain of custody will be a part of the investigation that is attacked by the defense attorney. The chain of custody also records any changes in the evidence. For example, the lab may need to use some of the drugs recovered to conduct tests. Many cases have been lost because of poor or no chain of custody. You do not want to be the one on the witness stand trying to explain why evidence is unaccounted for.

Remember, each person that comes into contact with the evidence creates a new "link in the chain." Links should be kept to a minimum—the shorter the better, but some persons handling it are unavoidable. An evidence chain of custody could look like this: The Crime Scene Investigator ➤ An Evidence Property Control Officer ➤ The Police Laboratory ➤ The Medical Examiner's Office/DNA Laboratory (if necessary).

Not every police department is equipped with its own forensic laboratory. Therefore, the packaging and transmittal of forensic evidence is an important step in the chain of custody process. Many departments are required to submit evidence through the mail because the nearest lab is hundreds of miles away including the FBI Laboratory in Quantico, Virginia. Remember, the evidence is being sent to an outside agency, so it is important that the following information be contained on a transmittal form:

- Agency requesting the examination
- Agency case number
- County of commission
- Offense that was committed
- Date and time of incident
- Suspect (if known) and pedigree information
- NCIC number
- Victim information (if known)
- Case investigator's name and contact information (including e-mail)
- Description of evidence
- ***What type of examination is being requested?***

When an exigency exists, i.e., grand jury appearance, serial offender, investigative leads, etc., the submitting officer must make a note on the evidence transmittal form describing the exigency and why it is necessary to put a "rush" on the testing. Many forensic labs are overwhelmed with the amount of work that they currently have and backlogs are a problem. So only ask for a rush when it is absolutely necessary and not because your boss is in a hurry and under pressure.

| STOP! | *Before submitting any evidence to any laboratory for testing, ensure that you have requested a specific test: i.e., toxicology, DNA, etc.* |

No Stone Is to Be Left Unturned

Anything and everything can be evidence. If it caught your attention, it may be significant. When in doubt, "bag it and tag it," and never overlook the obvious. In addition, make sure that the body is thoroughly searched for identification. I have been an observer at the medical examiner's office when an unidentified body is delivered, only for the ME to reach into the back pocket and remove the victim's wallet. The investigator was very embarrassed. Do not let it be you!

Exit Strategy

Plan to release the crime scene only after a thorough search has been conducted and all debris left by emergency personnel is disposed of and removed. If possible have EMS police up their personal protective equipment (PPE). The case investigator should confer with the investigating supervisor before the final determination is made to release the scene. When necessary, conferrals should be made with the district attorney (police involved shootings), and other law enforcement entities.

If the crime occurred at night and there is a reasonable chance of good weather, it is best to wait until the morning to search the scene before releasing it. Daylight is better than any flashlight or floodlight.

Now that you have been introduced to the investigative techniques in CRIME SCENE that are used to secure crime scenes, preserve evidence and solve crimes, here is one more acronym to hammer the rules home. If an investigator has to, he/she must **CAMP** out at the crime scene to make sure that it is done properly.

    Conceptualize the scene
    Apply inclusiveness
    Maintain documentation
    Proceed cautiously

CONCEPTUALIZE THE SCENE

The investigator builds hypotheses on how the crime was committed, but always keep in mind the possibility of being wrong. When the evidence and information develop, your hypothesis may/may not have to be adjusted. It's OK to be wrong. The only fault you can make is not admitting it and continuing to push the facts to match the theory. The investigator should think of questions such as these:

"What is here?" — "What is missing?"
"What am I missing?" — "What is out of place?"

Take in the entire scene using as many of your senses as possible.

APPLY INCLUSIVENESS

Anything and everything can be important to the investigation. If you think it is evidence, treat it as if it was by collecting and packing it properly. No one is going to fault you if you took something that did not amount to anything, only if you didn't. You can't shout, "Do over!" Remember, not everything is what it seems to be.

Inclusiveness has to do with other matters as well. Don't be lazy. If another investigator or even family of the victim stated they did something, double check. Think of the Jon Benet Ramsey case where the father told the police he had searched the house, only to find the body hours later. The investigator should spare himself/herself and the department the embarrassment. Also, it is extremely important to obtain elimination print/swabs from members of the same household so you don't waste your time running prints through AFIS or DNA through CODIS. It is a waste of money, effort and, most importantly, a waste of valuable investigative time.

MAINTAIN DOCUMENTATION

Case documentation is like the old saying about buying a house, "Location, location, location." The same theory applies to criminal investigation: "Document, document, document." Even if you applied inclusiveness and identified, collected and packaged the evidence correctly, without proper documentation, you will lose the chain of custody, lose the evidence and therefore lose the case. The investigator is responsible for either completing or collecting **CAPE**:

Crime Scene Entry/Exit Log
Assignment Sheets
Photographic Log
Evidence Collection Log

PROCEED CAUTIOUSLY

Haste makes waste. Whoever said that must have been referring to crime scene investigation. Crime scenes take time if done properly. Weather conditions can cause angst for investigators, but items such as tents can mitigate damage from such an event. Preparation is the key. As a reminder when conducting the crime scene walkthrough, ask the first officer on the scene to show you how they entered, so that you do not destroy anything else.

It is human nature to be drawn straight to the body of a homicide victim. You have to fight that instinct because generally the area surrounding the body will have the most forensic evidence. If an investigator has tunnel vision, he/she may miss or destroy valuable evidence.

Here is a quick breakdown of the duties of a patrol officer (first responder) and the duties of an investigator at a crime scene. In many police departments across the country, lack of personnel may be an issue. In some cases, the first responder may also be the case investigator and the crime scene technician! Hopefully, as we learn more about forensic science, police departments will hire additional personnel so that they can let investigators do their job and crime scene technicians do theirs.

The Patrol Officer	The Investigator
Records time of notification & arrival	Records time of notification & arrival
Establishes the size of the crime scene	Expands the crime scene (if possible)
Enters scene through a single entryway	Conducts crime scene walkthrough
Primary function is to protect life	Primary function is to ID evidence
Establishes temporary headquarters	Establishes temporary headquarters if not done
Conducts the Preliminary Investigation	Conducts the Follow-Up Investigation
Detains witnesses/victims	In depth interviews with witnesses/victims
Secures the crime scene	In charge of the crime scene
Acts as the gatekeeper	Conducts the crime scene walkthrough
Maintains the crime scene log	Retrieves the crime scene log

Internet Resources for Investigators

USDOJ Crime Scene Guide for Law Enforcement
https://www.ncjrs.gov/pdffiles1/nij/178280.pdf

The FBI Handbook of Forensic Services
http://www.fbi.gov/about-us/lab/handbook-of-forensic-services-pdf/view

Questions for Discussion and Review

1.   Has physical evidence replaced the need for eyewitness testimony? Explain why or why not?

2.   Photographs from a crime scene are recorded on the _____.

3.   Why is it so important for investigators not to contaminate a crime scene?

4.   What is the correct order for processing a crime scene?

5.   Who is in charge of the crime scene?

6.   In order to properly document a crime scene, what are the four (4) logs that must be used?

7.   Explain the purpose of the gatekeeper.

8.   Why is a ruler/scale used in crime scene photographs?

9.   Explain the importance of an investigative timeline.

10.   What are evidence dynamics and what role can they play in the criminal investigation process?

11.   Name other occurrences that can become evidence dynamics other than the examples provided in the text.

12.   What type of crime scene search would you employ to search a vehicle? Why?

13.   When submitting evidence to any laboratory for examination, what is the most import piece of information that must be provided?

14.   Who makes the decision to release the crime scene?

15.   Why are crime scene sketches important to investigations?

16.   Make a list of physical evidence that an investigator can find at the crime scene and explain what individual and class characteristics they have.

17.   Why don't the police use chalk to outline bodies like they do on television?

18.   Where are the only two (2) locations where a crime scene can be?

19.   What are the three elements that must be established in order to have a viable suspect?

20.   What three things can contain physical evidence?

21.   List the three (3) steps that crime scene photographs are taken in.

22.   Discuss the difference between a line search and a grid search.

23.   Why is it a good practice to hold a nighttime crime scene until daylight?

24.   What are some of the ways that a crime scene and evidence can be contaminated?

CHAPTER 5 — THE FOLLOW-UP INVESTIGATION

"Joey, everyone is somewhere."

— Joseph Reznick

KEY TERMS

Canvass	NCIC Offline Search	Public Information Officer
911 Callers	Crime Stoppers	National Central Bureau
IBIS	Media Relations	Interpol
Timeline	Informants	
Social Media	Aguilar/Spinelli Test	

CHAPTER OBJECTIVES

At the end of this lesson, the student will be able to:

- Name the different types of canvasses employed at a crime scene.
- Recall steps in conducting canvasses.
- Discuss the role that police computer checks play in investigations.
- Describe the role Crime Stoppers can play in solving cases.
- Recall how investigators should deal with members of the media.

Depending on the incident, the follow-up investigation begins either directly at the scene or a few days later after the case has passed a solvability test. The follow-up investigation begins where the patrol officer's preliminary investigation left off. Sometimes, the leads are rare and sometimes the leads go dead real fast. An investigator has to develop new leads quickly. The follow-up investigation requires much digging, sifting and disseminating of information. Think of the investigator as an archaeologist who digs up the past, finds artifacts and puts together pieces of an ancient civilization.

Therefore, the investigator must perform immediate **CPR** on the case:

Canvasses
Police record checks
Reexamination of physical evidence

Canvasses

The ultimate goal of the canvass is to identify anyone who had eyes or ears on the street at the time of the incident. Investigators will begin canvassing the neighborhood shortly after their arrival to the scene and have been given a chance to confer with the first officer(s) on the scene. It is important to have the preliminary facts surrounding the case so the investigators know what questions to ask or what types of canvasses to conduct. When an investigator is prepared and knows the preliminary facts of the case they can identify any deception or an outright lie. Investigators can then zone in on a particular individual and why they lied. For instance, are they protecting themselves or someone they know? What benefit do they get for lying to us?

Canvasses should always begin at the crime scene (X) and spiral outward, starting with the areas that have a direct view of the crime scene (arrows). Spiraling outwards ensures inclusiveness. In Figure 5.1 the apartments facing the courtyard would be canvassed first. The nice thing about conducting canvasses is that the same rules apply to both apartment buildings and private homes. So it doesn't matter if the crime happened in a rural or urban area, they are both conducted the same way.

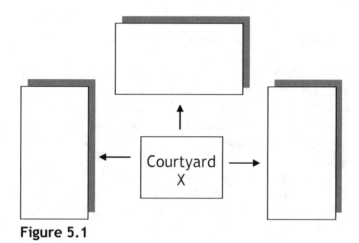

Figure 5.1

During the canvass, investigators will speak to anyone and everyone who will listen. They will speak to letter carriers, construction workers, dog walkers, homeless people, prostitutes, confidential informants, parolees, delivery workers and even at times drug dealers. No one can be left out, no matter how undesirable their position in society is. Who better to talk to than those who live with an ear and eye on the street?

Where do investigators start canvassing in a building? There are no rules for starting at the bottom and working your way up or vice versa. You can just pull up in front of the building and wait for the first curtain to move. That is the LOL. LOL is not what you guys know it as. The nosey Little-Old-Lady (LOL) who just moved the curtain may have also witnessed the incident. Every building and every neighborhood has one, so start there.

If an LOL does not live in the building, you can try the next best individual to speak with, the superintendent. The super of the building is attuned to the comings and goings of people in the building and can usually provide you with an apartment or family history. The super may also be able to provide you with a layout of the apartment including any changes made to the layout, which can prove to be extremely helpful in developing a tactical plan to execute a search or arrest warrant.

Conducting a canvass is not always about knocking on doors and requesting information from people. There are other types of canvasses that exist and are sometimes overlooked during the commotion of a major criminal investigation. These canvasses, when conducted properly, can be extremely important to your case.

> ### CI Tip Sheet
>
> An artist paints on a canvas,
> an investigator conducts a canvass.

Proper canvassing techniques will help investigators **SHAVES** hours off the investigative process (Giacalone, 2009, pp. 8–9).

Surveillance Camera Canvass
Hospital Canvass
Additional witnesses
Vehicle Canvass
Evidence Canvass
Social Media Canvass

SURVEILLANCE CAMERA CANVASS

The use of surveillance cameras by both commercial and privately owned properties offers an investigator an invaluable source of information. The next best thing to being there when the incident happened is to get it on tape. Investigators must also think of obtaining video surveillance footage from bridges, tunnels and other crossings when the suspect is believed to be fleeing by way of a vehicle. Video evidence can identify perpetrators, identify witnesses, key physical evidence and may assist in processing the crime scene. An added benefit of video evidence is that it can be used to develop and assist in the interrogation of suspects.

The investigator should be aware of the following potential problems: proprietary software—the tape may not work on your equipment, a lack of knowledge by the end user (i.e., store clerk), the tape/video is recorded at another site, and the famous, no video/DVD in the machine. Competition has made the technology much cheaper now and investigators are finding video surveillance evidence in residential properties as well. All departments should have specially trained individuals that deal solely with this issue.

STOP!	*Do not allow anyone to touch the video evidence or machine that is not trained for or qualified to do so. Every police department has a resident "expert" who knows how to "do everything." Don't do it. You risk losing everything!*

CI Case Study

All video has "value." No matter how dark, fuzzy or blurry the video is, the perpetrator can still be identified. It may be by a piece of clothing, hat, jacket or piece of jewelry; or, in one case I had, one of the perpetrators in a vicious murder was identified by a security officer by his discernible limp!

HOSPITAL CANVASS

It is quite possible that your suspect, or witness who does not want to be identified, has sought some sort of medical attention after an incident: a brawl, shooting, stabbing, gang fight, hit and run, etc. Often these individual(s) will drive to a hospital in another jurisdiction to throw off any suspicion. Therefore, it is a good idea to expand your search beyond the immediate area.

Hospitals are required to notify the police whenever an individual enters the emergency room seeking assistance for a bullet wound, knife wound or any wound that is suspicious, i.e., chemical burns, explosives, a nexus to terrorism, etc. Each investigative squad should have a preprinted "Hospital Canvass" form that can be faxed to all the local area hospitals. The form should have the preliminary facts of the case, the types of injuries that may have been sustained and the investigator's contact information. Hospital Canvass forms (Figure 5.2) should also specify if the squad is looking for a missing person or a victim. For those departments that are out of the Stone Age, an e-mail sent to those contacts or through social media can get the job done faster. There is no follow-up call necessary to see if they "got the fax." Many hospitals have their own Facebook and Twitter accounts and each can be sent direct messages that no one else can see. It is an avenue worth exploring because social media isn't going away anytime soon.

The day of the incident should not be the day that investigators are scrambling for contact information for hospital administrators/emergency room desks. When there is a lull in the action in the day-to-day workings of an investigations squad, investigators should seek out those who are in charge at area hospitals. An in-person meeting is always best to establish a rapport and to explain to them what is needed. Often this two-way conversation is not done and in my experience the relationship between hospital staff and the police department is tenuous at best. In-person meetings was what I used to mend fences and bring the conversation and cooperation to a professional level.

Figure 5.2

Hospital Canvass Form

Anytown Police Department Squad
Main Street, USA
Phone
Fax
E-Mail

On (Day of the week), (Date) at approximately (Time), the Anytown Detective Squad is
investigating the following situation and requires your assistance into this important matter:

Missing Person: Name: _____ Gender: _____ Race: _____
          DOB: _____ SSN: _____ Height: _____ Weight: _____
          Address: _____
          Last Date Seen: _____ Last Time Seen: _____
          Clothing Description: _____
          Scars / Marks / Tattoos Y / N Location(s): _____
          Requires Medication Y / N Condition: _____

Suspect: Name: _____ Gender: _____ Race: _____
          DOB: _____ SSN: _____ Height: _____ Weight: _____
          Address: _____
          Clothing Description: _____
          Scars / Marks / Tattoos Y / N Location(s): _____

Victim: Name: _____ Gender: _____ Race: _____
          DOB: _____ SSN: _____ Height: _____ Weight: _____
          Address: _____
          Clothing Description: _____
          Scars / Marks / Tattoos Y / N Location(s): _____

Account of the incident:

If this person is located, please contact the following investigator immediately:

Detective: _____ Office: ( ) _____ Cell: ( ) _____
Case #: _____
Police Report #: _____

CI Case Study

After a multiple shooting at a nightclub, one of the perpetrators was shot in the foot and driven to the hospital by one
of his friends. The friend drove up to the emergency room,
dropped him off and then fled the scene. A careful
examination of the surveillance tape revealed the license
plate of the vehicle, which led to an additional arrest.

ADDITIONAL WITNESSES CANVASS

Locating additional witnesses is the main reason to conduct a canvass.
Even though eyewitness identification is constantly under attack, investigators must endeavor to locate them. Remember, you are looking not only
for eyewitnesses but ear witnesses as well. An investigator should start at
the scene of the incident and spiral outward. This affords a chance of
inclusiveness. The skilled investigator interacts with and builds rapport to
extract information from people who may otherwise be unwilling to provide
it. The investigative canvass puts the community on notice that the police
are seeking help to solve the crime. The canvass may also generate a call
into the squad or the Crime Stoppers Unit. In addition, a follow-up canvass
is extremely important and should be conducted 24 hours, seven (7) and
twenty-one (21) days after the incident when the case is still active. This
way you can include individuals who may not visit or make deliveries every
day.

When investigators identify potential witnesses, they must be separated
to avoid interview contamination. If people are unwilling to speak in public,
ask to go into their apartment, to meet you at the station house or other
neutral location or at the very least walk them down the block away from
the scene. Investigators should have an ample supply of official business
cards with them that contains their contact information. The official business card should also contain the phone numbers to Crime Stoppers, the
Drug Hotline or any other anonymous reporting tip line. People may be
unwilling to speak with you in person, but provided with the opportunity
to call, will do so anonymously, especially if reward money is involved.

When conducting additional witness canvasses, the investigators must
employ smart tactics. First, a bullet-resistant vest must be worn. Remember, you do not know who is on the other side of the door. That is why it is
extremely important to "run" computer checks on the entire building. It
may reveal some interesting characters that currently live there and
sometimes the perpetrator(s) that you are searching for! Investigators must
avoid standing directly in front of any door. They should be off to the side
so that the door jamb provides them some protection. I used to reach out
with my flashlight and knock on the door to give the illusion that I was
standing on the left side of the door when I was on the right.

> ### CI Tip Sheet
>
> Canvasses are to be conducted:
>
> 1. As soon as practical upon arrival at the scene
> 2. 24 hours later
> 3. 7 days later
> 4. 21 days later
> 5. 1 month later

VEHICLE CANVASS

The vehicle canvass is a simple task that requires noting the license plates of vehicles in and around the area of a crime scene. A thorough review of a properly conducted vehicle canvass can prove or disprove a suspect's alibi or it can be used to find out where your target is laying his/her head. In addition, law enforcement officials have a tool called a License Plate Reader (LPR). The LPR records all the license plates in the target area and provides a printout of the registered owners. They also provide GPS coordinates. License plate readers have been mounted on stationary poles on main roads and highways. LPRs can help an investigator identify witnesses and/or place a subject at the scene of a crime—or at least their vehicle. This information is discoverable for defense purposes and can provide additional witnesses or suspects.

> ### CI Case Study
>
> Are you working on a case that did not have a vehicle canvass conducted? Then try this. Some municipalities allow you to pay your parking ticket online by punching in your plate number. If you know your target's vehicle information, enter it into one of these sites. This search can provide an investigator with the time, date, infraction, and most importantly, the location.

EVIDENCE CANVASS

An investigator should never take for granted that all evidence has been identified and properly collected by the police in a criminal investigation. If possible, respond to the original location and conduct a search of the area. Have a plan for how and what you are going to search. If you find something that may be evidence in a criminal investigation, photograph it in place (in situ) and notify the proper authorities so it can be "bagged and tagged."

SOCIAL MEDIA CANVASS

Before doing the traditional canvasses, investigators have a new tool at their disposal, the Social Media Canvass. The Social Media Canvass allows investigators to follow the conversations about the incident via social media. A couple of clicks or swipes and investigators are "listening to the chatter on the electronic street" (Giacalone, 2011, ConnectedCops.net). The two most popular social media venues are Twitter and Facebook.

For instance, the investigator arrives at the scene of a homicide on Main Street in Anytown. They step over the yellow tape and into the hot zone. Before the investigator whips out his reporter's notebook and starts knocking on doors, he will pull out the department issued wireless tablet, laptop or smartphone and start searching. This is a better strategy than deciding what door to knock on. Within seconds of an incident, people in the neighborhood, and sometimes those that are involved, are tweeting or posting on Facebook.

Here is how a search could work. The investigator goes to the Twitter.com search box and uses the hashtag (#) and types what they are looking for. In this scenario, the shooting occurred on Main Street in Anytown, so the separate searches would look something like this: #MainStreet, #MainSt, #Anytown, #ShootingMainStreet or any other combination. Based on the information they see, a better canvass strategy can be developed. Recently while searching for information on a past shooting incident, I found a Tweet that stated in sum and substance, "the cops just showed up at 'Bill's' house be careful of what you post."

Catching conversations on Facebook is challenging because the investigator needs an account to start searching. That account should be an authorized department account, and not their personal one. As easy as it is for law enforcement to track suspects, they can track us!

Because there are over 700 million users on Facebook there is a good chance that your suspect has an account, especially if he is in the young adult age range. Before signing onto Facebook with the department's password, the investigator should conduct a few general searches to narrow the focus. Most, if not all, investigators will go straight to Google, but that is not the best search for Facebook. Microsoft's Bing is Facebook's default search engine. Another free site that provides an individual's social media page information without signing up for an account is http://pipl.com.

Once the page is discovered it may be public, which means limited information, such as a photo, street name, etc., can be viewed without being friends. However, if the page is for friends only, look at the lower left hand part of the screen. It often provides friends of the target's page. Click on the target's friends because one of their sites may be public, which would allow the investigator to enter their world.

As the use of social media by police investigators increases in the short term, there will be many court challenges regarding it's use in the future. It is important for investigators to follow the policies and procedures set forth by their departments. Do not do anything that can jeopardize your career, the case or your personal safety.

Canvasses, if done properly, can yield the information required to successfully close a case or resurrect an old one. Each type of canvass should receive a separate investigator's report and be indexed for easy reference. Remember, the best investigative efforts will be lost if the information is not properly documented and recorded.

Police Record Checks

When a violent crime occurs, investigators have a series of tasks that they must perform. Today's investigator has a tool that wasn't available to them less than twenty years ago, the personal computer. Computers have replaced the typewriters and filing boxes and even the "paper case folders." The computer has allowed police departments to access an array of databases, both public and private. These databases allow investigators to develop leads and establish linkage between people, places and things.

As discussed in the Crime Scene Protocol lesson, the investigator will retrieve information from the computer before leaving the station house. Computer checks for 911 callers, on victims, perpetrators and possible suspects are an important investigative tool that may provide a lead in the case before they even start investigating! Databases also play a significant role in the hunt for a known perpetrator. When an individual is in trouble, who do they turn to? Yes, mom first then a girlfriend or relative. Wouldn't it be nice to have this information before traipsing all over the city or countryside for them? Investigative work is a lot like playing chess. You have to think two to three moves ahead of your opponent. Hopefully, your suspect is playing checkers.

Computer checks are designed to aid investigators with establishing links between three (3) broad categories: (1) People, (2) Places and (3) Things.

(1) People

First and most importantly are the people involved in the incident. Because we are victimized by people we know most often, it is in the investigator's best interest to properly identify all of the players involved in the incident. In order to have a violent crime, you need a victim and a perpetrator. Each half makes the whole. Know the victim, and maybe you will identify the perpetrator.

Sometimes the victim cannot tell us what happened for obvious reasons, i.e., deceased. Even if they could speak with us, they may leave out some pertinent artifact that they don't want anyone to know about. For example, hiding a certain person they are dating from their parents, an alternate lifestyle, a mistress, illicit drug use, gambling problem, nightclubs visited, etc. I think you are developing the picture. This is why the police will seek out family, friends, hair stylists and coworkers of the victim, especially if the victim is dead. People aren't too worried about passing along information that was held as a "secret." There may be even a little guilt. Remember the famous quote from Benjamin Franklin, "Three people can keep a secret as long as two of them are dead." As an investigator wouldn't you like to speak with the victim's best friend?

Contemplate a moment and think what type of information you shared in confidence with your best friend. Is it information that could land you on the front page of the papers? If so, you better be real nice to them!

The investigator will begin to create a cursory investigative timeline (Figure 5.3) of the incident and begin to input facts discovered during the investigation. Some investigators will plot the timeline of events on a flip chart or spreadsheet for easy reference. Just remember what ever medium you use to create your timeline may have to be kept for discovery purposes. It is easier to keep an electronic file in your case folder than a flip chart. The next step is to complete a series of computer workups on the victim. To an investigator this is known as the Victimology, or "why this person was chosen to be the victim."

Figure 5.3   Sample Investigative Timeline

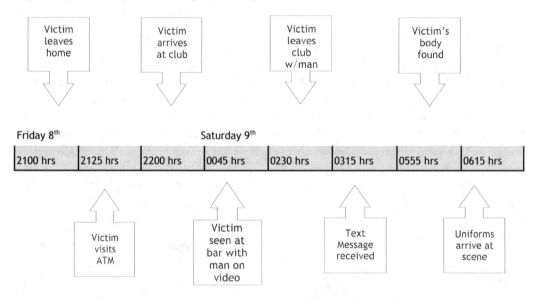

The investigator will attempt to complete at least a 24–48 hour time frame backwards from the incident in the hope of piecing together who the victim was with or where they went. The main focus of a victimology is to learn more about the victim than they knew or wanted to know about themselves. This two-part process is accomplished through (1) computer inquiries and by (2) interviewing family, friends and coworkers. Is there anything in the victim's background that made them vulnerable?

Here are some questions you want answered about victims and witnesses through police computer inquiries:

- Did the victim have any previous contacts with the police?
  o Is there a current photo of the suspect available?

- o Previous arrest records can provide information about the background of the victim
  - • Were they ever arrested for assault?
  - • Were they ever arrested for dealing narcotics?
    - • Who were their codefendants?
    - • Any gang affiliation?
    - • Could the incident be narcotics related?
      - o Can narcotics units provide some background on the subject(s)?
  - • Were they in a fight?
  - • Were they ever arrested for possessing a firearm?
  - o Did they ever file or have filed against them a Domestic Incident Report?
    - • Did they have marital problems?
    - • Were they in an abusive relationship?
      - • Was there an order of protection? Valid? Expired?
    - • Were any photos vouchered regarding domestic violence incidents?
  - o Does the victim have an active warrant?
  - o Was the victim wanted in connection of another crime?
  - o Have they been a victim of a crime recently?
    - • Harassment/Stalking?
    - • Robbery?
    - • Burglary?
    - • Sexual assault?
  - o Have they filed a report of lost property?
  - o Have they received any summonses?
    - • Moving violations?
    - • Criminal Court Violations?
      - • What were the locations of these violations?
  - o Do they possess a valid pistol license?
- • Was the victim ever an aided (person requiring medical attention—no crime) case?
  - o What types of injuries, if any, were reported?
    - • What hospital were they transported to?
- • Was the victim the subject of a Stop, Question and Frisk Report?
  - o What was the alleged crime?
  - o What was the location?
  - o Was anyone else stopped with them?
    - • Conduct background checks on them

Here are some questions you want answered about perpetrators (if known) through police computer inquiries:

- • Has the perpetrator ever been a victim before?
  - o What contact information did they provide back then?

CI Tip Sheet

When bad guys are victims they tend to provide accurate information including their correct name, date of birth (DOB) and address—including the elusive apartment number.

- Do they have any nicknames?
  o Are records kept of nicknames?

STOP!   *If your squad does not currently have a nickname database, now is a good time to start one. Investigators should ask patrol officers to capture tidbits of information like this—it's invaluable.*

- What previous arrest record does the perpetrator have?
  o What type of crimes are they "in to"?
    - Street robberies or commercial robberies?
    - Burglary?
      - Burglars have been known to escalate to sexual predators
  o Do they have a violent background?
  o What contact information did they use on previous arrest records?
    - Phone numbers called?
    - Addresses and Apartment numbers used
    - Aliases
    - Social Security Number(s) used
    - Nicknames used
    - Tattoos, marks and scars
    - Gang affiliation
  o Have they been arrested in other states?
    - Similar crimes?
      - Who were their associates?
      - Who bailed them out?
      - Who did they call from jail?
    - Check with NCIC and conduct an Offline Search (see below)
- Have you pulled records from Central Booking (also known as the ROR report)?
  o What information was taken down there?
    - Contact information or notification information?
      - You'll be surprised at the different information received at intake

---

CI Tip Sheet

An NCIC Offline Search (also known as the NCIC Transaction Log Search) provides information on individuals that have been stopped by the police and either run in the system, summonsed or arrested. An Offline Search can track down an individual located in another state or to keep tabs on an individual while the investigator establishes probable cause to obtain an arrest warrant. NCIC Offline searches can also provide information on vehicles, partial plates, firearms and boats.

The Offline Search can also give you information based on the ORI numbers for a specific date/time range. For instance, you can ask for every person and vehicle queried by the Chicago Police Department between 2359 hours and 0400 hours during the time leading up to a specific incident: i.e., police involved shooting, sexual assault, kidnapping, etc. It can also be used to identify associates by asking for a query of 10 minutes before and 10 minutes after of all persons stopped within the same jurisdiction

Investigators must use an official police department e-mail address to request the Offline check to IOAU@leo.gov or they can call the Criminal Justice Services staff at 304-625-3000.

---

o   Have they received any criminal court summons for violations (non-crimes)?
   • What were the locations?
o   Was the perpetrator ever stopped, questioned and frisked?
   • Days, times, locations
     • Any location near the date and time in question?
o   Do they have any active warrants?
o   Are they wanted for other crimes?
   • Is any other law enforcement agency looking for him/her?
     • Make a coordinated effort and share information
o   Do they have any gang affiliation?
   • Which gang?
     • Is there any gang intelligence information?
o   Did they ever have a Domestic Incident Report filed against them?
   • Was an Order of Protection filed?
     • Criminal or Family Court?

> **CI Tip Sheet**
>
> Investigators count on relationship changes. Remember the
> old adage, "Hell hath no fury like a woman scorned?"
> Ex-significant others can play a vital role in capturing your
> suspect.

"OTHER" PEOPLE

The following people can also be found in police computer database
searches:

The investigator's eye and ear witnesses to a crime are 911 callers and
are sometimes overlooked during the initial chaotic stages of a major
incident. Next to physical evidence, they are your most important pieces of
the investigative puzzle. Eyewitness identification, however, is increasingly
under attack, so investigators must identify, locate and thoroughly debrief
all the callers so their valuable information is not lost.

The investigator understands that they are not going to track down
every caller all the time, but an effort must be made and the hunt
documented. Once the callers are located, the interviews must be done in
person whenever possible. An investigator can never get the real sense of
the incident from the person when they speak to them over the phone. The
individual's body language, eye contact and other methods that investigators use to test the veracity of the callers information cannot be seen
when talking on the phone. There is nothing more gratifying than asking
the right question and seeing the "Ah ha" moment in the person's eyes that
would be otherwise lost. There are too many distractions in the person's
house to keep them focused while the investigator conducts the interview.
Another reason to conduct interviews in person is that often the individual
who called 911 is the perpetrator. A little pro-activeness can go a long way
in solving the case quicker than the investigator first imagined.

Not everyone is going to be cooperative and thrilled to see you when you
show up at their doorstep either. This is where the investigator's professionalism, preparedness and rapport-building skills spring into action.
Prior to conducting any interviews, the investigator should obtain and
listen to the recordings. This can provide the investigator with an idea of
what occurred based on the calmness or lack thereof in the caller's voice.
It may also provide other details such as background noises and other
onlooker's comments. Investigators can then be prepared to ask a series of
open- and closed-ended questions that can accomplish three (3) things: (1)
establish the facts of the case, (2) corroborate or debunk eyewitness or
suspect's statements and (3) provide additional leads.

Each person interviewed should appear on a separate report, this way
indexing and referencing will allow for quick access to the information. In
some jurisdictions the investigator is required to keep all notes taken

during the course of an investigation. The following information should be obtained for the report:

- Name, address, date of birth—through positive identification
- Were they an eye or an ear witness to the incident?
- Where were they positioned in relationship to the incident?
- What did they say exactly?—use quotation marks when appropriate
- What did they see?
- Who else was present at the time of the incident?—cultivate potential additional witnesses

There is one more thing you can do with 911 callers. If possible, take them back to the scene and ask them exactly where they were standing or sitting. When you are convinced they are at the right location, snap a few photographs from that perspective. It may be helpful to spur the witnesses' memories if the case takes years to go to trial.

Documentation of these interviews is mandatory as well as securing the recorded media with the case folder. In cold case investigations the 911 callers will be on cassette tape. Before you lose the information forever, have them converted to electronic files by a department qualified technician. If the case goes to trial, those interviews will be cross-examined and picked apart to discredit the eyewitness testimony.

Remember, if the investigator fails to document the interview, it never happened; if he does not secure the recordings, it opens the door to reasonable doubt that other information exists that would exonerate the suspect.

CI Tip Sheet

Investigators must positively identify people with whom they are speaking. It is a terrible feeling to find out that the person you interviewed was the actual perpetrator and you failed to ID them!

- Parolees are an excellent source of information for one main reason, they must speak with police. If they refuse to cooperate, their parole can be violated, which means they will be sent back to prison
  - o Parolees can also be a subject of the investigation themselves based on their previous crimes
    - For example, the police department may have a spike in sexually related crimes in the area—has anyone with that type of background been released back into society?
      - Certain levels of sex offenders must register with their local police precinct
- Active bench warrants from the area can be a source of information regarding the incident under investigation or the whereabouts of a known perpetrator. A bench warrant is issued when an individual fails to show up for their court date. Sometimes investigators have

to "shake a few trees" to get the fruit to drop. Re-arresting persons wanted on bench warrants are "low hanging fruit," which means they are easily attained. But make no mistake about it, individuals wanted on active bench warrants can provide critical information.

- Confidential Informants (CIs) can act as the investigator's HUMINT (human intelligence) tree by providing information in real time. Generally, they help the police without anyone knowing. Their life depends on it.
  - o The first thing any investigator must find out is why this person is willing to help me out. The two (2) main reasons people become informants are for (1) court consideration (time off or charges dropped) and (2) money. However, another motive exists that could be detrimental to your case, revenge. The investigator has to know what an informant's motivation is before they are used.
  - o An informant and their information have to pass a two-prong test in many states, called the Aguilar-Spinelli Test (*Aguilar v. Texas* 378 US 108 (1964) and *Spinelli v. the United States* 393 US 410 (1969)). The first prong, is the informant reliable? and the second prong, is the information reliable? In *Illinois v. Gates* 462 US 213 (1983), the Supreme Court abandoned the two-prong test for a "totality of the circumstances test," which was adopted by several states. Depending on what state you work in, informants and their information are handled quite differently.

(2) Places

The location where the event occurred, either inside or outside, has to be examined as if it were a person. What type of location is it? Is it an apartment building or private house? Parking lot? Nightclub? etc. If we take a location such as a nightclub, what can that tell us? Information regarding the location can tell us what type of individual likes to frequent it and it tells us about the lifestyle of the victim. Besides lifestyle issues, it can also provide the motive behind the crime.

Here are some questions you want answered about commercial locations through police computer inquiries:

- Any previous calls for police service?
  - o Robberies?
  - o Fighting?
  - o Illegal narcotic sales/use?
    - Is it a known drug location?
    - Is there currently an active narcotics investigation?
      - Did they have any under covers inside of the location at the time of the incident?
      - Are we able to identify the packaging, color of caps, etc. to a known dealer/gang?
  - o Prostitution?
  - o Gangs?

- Colors displayed or identifiable?
- Gang graffiti at or near the scene?
o Underage drinking?
o Street parking conditions?
o Loud music?

CI Tip Sheet

Many nightclubs and bars have installed driver's license scanners at their establishments to prevent underage drinking. These scanners can provide a list of everyone that entered the location as well as provide a photo, client ID number and pedigree information.

- Who is the owner?
  o Do they have any arrest background?
    - Are they affiliated with anyone?
- Has the location been the subject of enforcement?
  o Does the location have a liquor license?
    - Contact the State Liquor Authority (SLA)
- What is the capacity limit?

Here are some questions you want answered about residential locations through police computer inquiries:

- Who owns the property?
- Who lives at the location/house/apartment(s)?
  o Are there any active warrants or wanted people attached to the address?
  o Any parolees currently living at the location?
  o DMV inquiries can provide a list of registered car owners
- Are there any past calls for police service?
  o Any similar crimes occurred in the past?
    - Robberies?
    - Burglaries?
      - Does the homeowner have a residential burglary alarm permit?
    - Sexual assaults?
      - Check patterns
      - Any past search warrants executed at the location?
  o Fighting?
  o Drug sales?
    - Any open drug cases?
    - Drug paraphernalia on the scene?
  o Domestic violence?
- Utility Company/Cable Company Law Enforcement checks
  o Can provide you the information on who is paying the bill at the location
    - It may provide additional person(s) of interest

(3) Things

This last category is a catchall for other objects that may be attributed to, used to escape with or linked to a specific person or place.

- Does the victim/perpetrator have any current/past vehicles registered to them?
  - o What vehicles are registered to the home/apartment's address?
    - Any vehicle accidents in the past?
    - Do the vehicles have any summons activity?
      - Caught in red light camera traps?
        - o What are the locations that summonses were issued?
- Are there any lawfully possessed pistols/long arms registered to the location?
  - o Any reported lost/stolen?
  - o Domestic violence history?
- Are there any phone numbers attached to anyone involved?
  - o Were phone numbers ever used on police department records?
  - o What locations do they come back to?
    - Subpoena records if necessary
      - Incoming and outgoing calls
        - o Text messages
        - o Photographs
        - o Videos
- Electronic Toll records
  - o Do Electronic Toll records support or discredit an alibi?
  - o Do toll records establish the opportunity to commit the crime?
    - Subpoena records if necessary
- Train/Bus/Cab/Airplane Manifests (or any other means that could facilitate flight of your suspect)
  - o An alert can be put on the individual with the appropriate law enforcement agency, i.e., Port Authority, Customs Border Patrol (ICE), etc.
    - ICE can conduct a check (formerly known as a TECS—Treasury Enforcement Communications System), which shows passport issuance/usage (a list of contact numbers of all 20 CPB Field Offices is located in the Internet Resources for Investigators at the end of this chapter)

CI Tip Sheet

Electronic Toll programs have installed readers along many major highways that track vehicles from point to point. If the perpetrator's vehicle has an electronic toll device, there is a good chance investigators can subpoena the information. It can also prove/disprove a suspect's alibi.

Reexamination of Physical Evidence

When the case hits a snag, or there wasn't much information to go on to begin with, the investigator will sit down and take a fresh look at the following items: Crime scene photos/video, the evidence log and the requests for lab testing (evidence submitted).

The investigator should find a quiet location and sort out the crime scene photos. The photo series should have begun with the front door (if inside) and walk you through the house, eventually landing where the body was located. The investigator thinks, "Did we miss anything?" If he is fortunate enough to have a video of the crime scene, he will ask another investigator who wasn't at the location to watch it in order to obtain an unbiased observation. If you don't have a video of the crime scene, take a drive to the location to see if you can get a "feel" for it.

As the investigator views the photos/video, they will make a list of physical evidence as well as examine the scene for behavioral evidence. Sometimes a fresh look or a different theory on how/why the crime was committed is all that is needed. Do victim/witness accounts of the incident match up to what is observed in the crime scene? Perhaps some re-interviewing may be necessary.

Other than the case officer in a major case, investigators from other precincts and sometimes even different jurisdictions write reports for the case. The case investigator must ensure that those reports are accounted for, indexed and read. Was a lead developed by someone else and then lost in the confusion? Was a person that was spoken to now become of interest? A conferral must be made with those investigators to avoid missing critical information as well as avoiding duplicating efforts.

The evidence log is a chronological list of physical evidence that was recovered at the crime scene. It lists what type of evidence it is, who found it, who packaged it, who vouchered it and where it went (police laboratory, medical examiner's office, etc.). Can the evidence in the crime scene photos/video or sketch be accounted for on the evidence log?

Not all evidence is going to require special examination and testing. After perusing the evidence log, the investigator must answer the following three (3) questions about the physical evidence recovered from the crime scene: (1) What type of evidence is it? (2) Where is it? and (3) What stage of analysis is it in?

There are several categories of physical evidence that require special laboratory testing. However, three (3) categories appear quite often: Fingerprints, DNA, and Ballistics. Fingerprints are loaded into AFIS, DNA into CODIS and Ballistics into IBIS (AFIS and CODIS were covered in Chapter 2). IBIS stands for the Integrated Ballistics Identification System, which is coordinated by the Bureau of Alcohol Tobacco and Firearms (ATF). The goal of the IBIS database is to establish linkage between fired bullets (striation marks) and shell cases (firing pin locations) recovered from crime scenes to firearms and to link firearms removed from individuals to fired bullets and shell casings.

Figure 5.4
Striation Marks on recovered bullet.

Figure 5.5
Firing pin location on shell casing.

© 2012 Joseph L. Giacalone

© 2012 Joseph L. Giacalone

CI Cheat Sheet

AFIS - Fingerprints
CODIS - DNA
IBIS - Ballistics

It is the responsibility of the investigator to track down where evidence is, i.e., the police lab or ME's office, and find out what stage of analysis the evidence is in. For example, was the DNA submitted to the local or national CODIS database? Is there a delay? Why is there a delay? Backlogs are not an uncommon problem. Is there an urgent need to have the DNA tested immediately? Crime labs can stop testing other evidence to work on an "emergency" request. What constitutes an emergency? A perpetrator that is on a crime spree, serial cases, cases in which the perpetrator may flee the country, police officer involved shooting, etc.

Releasing Information to the Media

An indispensable part of the follow-up investigation is releasing information to the media. Each department should have a Public Information Officer (PIO) or Public Information Bureau by now if they are following the National Incident Management System (NIMS). The PIO should be the only one that speaks to the media regarding investigations unless they OK a specific person to do so. Supervisors must ensure that information isn't leaked to the media from the inside. However, the frontline managers are not the ones with the cameras and microphones in their faces. If the department wants to ensure good media relations and to avoid leaks, each department should train their patrol officers and investigators on how they want them to deal with the media. Another simple idea is for each department to disseminate a guide for the media on who to contact and how.

There are two types of investigators concerning the media, those who have had a bad experience with them and those who will have a bad experience. Dealing with the media is often more difficult than dealing with the armchair detectives downtown. You will more than likely be misquoted, so if you have been authorized to speak with the media be very careful. Investigators should always behave as if they are on camera, because they probably are. Just because you don't see the official news truck that doesn't mean that reporters, bloggers or freelance photographers/writers are not on the scene.

Here are some simple hard-and-fast rules that you can use when dealing with the media:

- Provide them their own space (Media Pen) in the cold zone at an outdoor crime scene. This makes them feel as if they are part of the scene and have "special" privileges.
- Always direct them to the Public Information Officer or Public Information Bureau.
- Never say, "No comment"—simply say you are not authorized to speak on the matter, but you can call (provide them with the PIO's number). They already know what they are supposed to do and what the procedure is, so why are they asking you? Yes, to get a sound bite!
- Never talk "off the record." Nothing is ever off the record, including the media and of course the courtroom.
- Don't call, e-mail, Tweet, Facebook or text reporters; it is too easy to discover the "unnamed source."

Every department should have "A Request for Media Attention" procedure so that what goes on television and in print is controlled. It also prevents the Chief from being embarrassed and it prevents the release of information that could be detrimental to the case. Never release information to the media that only the perp would know about, i.e., method of operation (MO), specific locations of wounds, number of wounds, use of bindings, etc.

Crime Stoppers

Crime Stoppers Units play an integral role in solving crimes and is part of releasing information to the media. The offer of a reward, generally up to $2,000, for information that leads to the arrest and indictment of the person(s) responsible for a particular crime is all that it takes. One of the ways that police departments can combat the "No Snitching" campaign is to offer money. The most beneficial part of the Crime Stoppers program is that it allows the caller to remain anonymous throughout the process. During the initial canvass for additional witnesses is the perfect time for the investigator to hand out his/her business card with the Crime Stoppers information.

Many times the person calling knows the suspect very well. Here is the scenario: You are sitting in your Squad or staffing the Crime Stoppers Line and you get "the call" that will help you solve the case. What should you do? Beyond the basic information you seek: name, address, apartment number, date of birth (age), where he/she attends school (if applicable), here are some other suggested questions and tips:

1. *Don't interrupt*—let the person finish telling you what/how they remember the incident
2. *Listen attentively*—no TV, conversations, newspapers, etc.
3. *Be patient and polite with the caller*—they are trying to help you!
4. *Don't ask compound questions* (more than one question at a time)
5. *Establish rapport with the individual to keep them talking*
6. *Ask the caller if they know the perpetrator's street name, nickname, etc.*
7. *Ask the caller if the perpetrator has a Facebook, Twitter or some other social media site*
8. *Ask the caller what media they saw this on, news, paper, poster, etc., and which one.* You may have to follow this up with the PIO
9. Before ending the call, *ask them if they remember anything else*—or anything they would like to add
10. *Always ask the caller to call back if they develop more information on the whereabouts of your subject*
11. *Provide the caller with your name to keep the rapport*
12. *Have a list of referral numbers for the caller if not crime related*—don't dismiss them—they may know information in the future

The goal is to put the money out on the street when practical. Information disseminated through the Crime Stoppers Unit is generally by a poster or flyer. However, many departments with Crime Stoppers Units have police vans that are capable of broadcasting the information and the toll-free tip line. This is another consideration. Whenever possible, photographs of the individuals should be put on the poster when you have Probable Cause to Arrest.

Crime Stoppers posters are not for field information requests; it is for wanted perpetrators. For field information requests, investigators should use Requests for Information Posters (RIPs (see below)). Investigators should flood the area of the crime with the flyers in the hopes of getting the call. It is always a good sign when the investigator finds that the posters have been torn off the walls, mailboxes and poles of the suspect's neighborhood—someone is protecting them. Don't forget about using social media and the web to get Crime Stoppers information out. Many departments are using Facebook, Twitter and/or have their own webpage. Take advantage of this medium.

There are some caveats when using Crime Stoppers posters/flyers/van/website:

•   The tip line should be answered by investigators who know how to ask questions and gather intelligence
•   Don't get to fancy with the poster campaign—the simpler the better

- Each department should have a standardized poster—this avoids any "freelancing"
- Don't place them on the glass of local business storefronts. Sympathizers may boycott the store or break the glass.
- Never put the address of the victim of a sex crime on a poster/flyer. Use "confines of" or "vicinity of" for the location instead. Their identity is protected by law.
- Posters/flyers should be numbered so that they are easily identifiable and searchable (large police departments should have them broken down by borough, county, jurisdiction, parish, etc.)
- Use the Crime Stoppers van so that it doesn't annoy people, i.e., after 0900 hours and before 2300 hours. You are looking for help, not to turn people off.
- Don't have too many people on the website at one time—it can be overwhelming for the user
- The webpage should be searchable by zip code

Request for Information Posters (RIPs)

RIPs are used to request information from the public other than the whereabouts of wanted perpetrators—that's what Crime Stoppers Posters are used for. Examples of what RIPs are used for: pictures of jewelry taken in a burglary, requesting the identity of an unknown dead body or missing person. Reward money is not offered on these types of requests—they are to obtain information only. On the bottom of RIPs should be the complaint/report number, the squad investigating and the assigned investigator's contact information.

Conducting Surveillance

There have been books and volumes written on how to conduct surveillance, and investigators should take the time to do some homework on the subject. I am only going to lay out a quick summary and some tips on what to do/or not do while conducting surveillance.

When the location of a perpetrator has been established, investigators may have to conduct surveillance at the location. There are many purposes of surveillance: to obtain information that can corroborate what the investigators already know, or to obtain additional intelligence, locate suspects/witnesses, learn about associates of the suspect, recover stolen property, verify witnesses' statements, develop information for interrogations, etc. There are three (3) broad categories of surveillance that investigators can use:

1. Mobile (foot/vehicle)
2. Fixed (stakeout)
3. Electronic

No matter what type of surveillance is deployed by investigators the main themes are preparation, patience, alertness, versatility, good observation skills and a good memory. The most important of these themes is preparation. Investigators must have the facts of the case and know who they are watching, what they are watching and most importantly why. If this basic information isn't communicated the investigators lose interest and therefore the operation will not be successful. Ground rules on what to do or what not to do should be explained before conducting any surveillance. A reconnaissance of the location must be made so fixed locations can be optimized for a direct line of sight if possible. Investigators can also use web based tools such as Google Earth to map out the location, but nothing can replace a "drive by."

Supervisors must confer with other units within the police department, gang squad, narcotics, other precincts, etc., or with other law enforcement agencies (state police) to ensure that they are not watching the location or have an ongoing long-term investigation.

Here are some common sense surveillance tips for investigators:

- Vehicles should be nondescriptive, have a full tank of gas and should be switched up each tour
- Each surveillance team should have a picture of the perpetrator, the house, residence, hotel/motel, place of employment, etc.
- Information if the suspect is armed and dangerous (if unknown treat as such)
- Equipment should be checked before leaving for the location
- Batteries should be fully charged or have a car charger, i.e., cell phones
- Because most surveillance is conducted at night, investigators should have night vision equipment
- Do not read newspapers, books, play video games or watch DVDs
- When videotaping the surveillance, shut off or cover the microphone or the investigator's conversations will be recorded. This can be very embarrassing in a courtroom!

One important aspect of surveillance is to have a plan if something goes wrong. Remember you are sitting outside of a location of a wanted suspect who is probably armed and very dangerous. Investigators must have on (not in the backseat) their bullet-resistant vests. They must maintain their situation awareness and look into the rearview mirrors and side mirrors to make sure no one sneaks up on them. Supervisors must create a tactical plan—which should describe exactly who is where and what their role is. One of the teams should be designated as the "Hospital Car" in the event that an investigator is seriously injured. The team should be familiar with the location and fastest route to the hospital as well as have the emergency room phone number readily available.

International Wanted Persons

During the follow-up investigation you may discover information that your perpetrator has fled the country. If so, law enforcement officers have a central location located in Washington, D.C., The U.S. National Central Bureau of Interpol, that acts as the liaison between local law enforcement and Interpol. Investigators can ask for a "Red Notice" which states that an arrest warrant has been issued by the local government and the United States is asking that the country with the help of Interpol to locate, arrest and extradite them back to the United States. A "Blue Notice" can also be requested when probable cause does not exist and no arrest warrant has been issued. A "Blue Notice" is processed to identify, locate or obtain information on a person of interest in a criminal investigation. There are also other types of notices that can be issued. Check out the links in the Internet Resources to learn more about them.

Very few departments have a liaison with the National Central Bureau, so investigators can reach directly them at 202-619-9000. An investigator should always confer with their supervisors before reaching out to an outside agency.

Hunting for a Known Perpetrator Checklist

- ☐ Driver's License/Registration Information
- ☐ Records as the victim
- ☐ Arrest Records
    - ☐ Codefendant Information
    - ☐ Court Reports
    - ☐ Warrant Information (Past/Present)
        - ☐ Where they were located last time?
    - ☐ Summons Information
- ☐ Domestic Incident Reports
- ☐ Cell Phone Records
- ☐ Department of Probation/Parole Information
- ☐ Depart of Corrections Information
- ☐ Utility/Cable Subscriber Information
- ☐ Social Media Site Checks

STOP!

Did you submit a BOLO Alert for your known perpetrator?
Did you submit an alarm on your suspect's vehicle?
Did you ensure that both are in the system?

Internet Resources for Investigators

Crime Stoppers International Program List
http://www.csiworld.org/index.php?q=programs

Customs Border Patrol (CPB) Field Offices
http://www.cbp.gov/xp/cgov/toolbox/contacts/cmcs/

Law Enforcement Online
http://www.leo.gov/

Interpol Notices
http://www.interpol.int/INTERPOL-expertise/Notices

Social Media for Law Enforcement
http://ConnectedCops.net

U.S. National Central Bureau of Interpol
http://www.justice.gov/usncb/programs/international_notice.php

VINELink Nationwide Prison Inmate Lookups
https://www.vinelink.com/vinelink/initMap.do

Questions for Discussion and Review

1. What type of information can family members tell an investigator about the victim?

2. Why is it important to identify previous locations where a wanted perpetrator was arrested?

3. What is a social media canvass?

4. Why is it important to find out if the perpetrator we are looking for was once a victim?

5. What is the significance of identifying parking summons activity on a particular vehicle?

6. Should the use of confidential informants be banned? Why or why not?

7. What type of information can be gotten from an NCIC Offline Search?

8. What is the most important theme of surveillance?

9. How should investigators deal with the media?

10. Why is it a good idea for departments to train all of their personnel on how to deal with the media?

11. This type of canvass is the "door-to-door" request for information.

12. Why can some states not follow a Supreme Court ruling like in *Illinois v. Gates* (use of informant's information) and use their own standard?

13. Why do the police count on changes in people's relationships?

14. Computer checks are designed to aid investigators with establishing links between what three (3) broad categories?

15. What can past calls for police service tell an investigator?

16. Canvasses should start at the incident and spiral _____.

17. What were the three (3) broad categories of surveillance named in this chapter?

18. What is Interpol?

19. What role can a license plate reader (LPR) play in a criminal investigation?

20. What goal do the databases AFIS, CODIS and IBIS have in common?

21. What are the two (2) types of witnesses discussed in this chapter?

22. How is a Hospital Canvass conducted? Why are they conducted?

23. Why identify individuals wanted for warrants in a residential building that have nothing to do with the crime currently being investigated?

24. List and explain what occurs in the five types of canvasses discussed in this chapter.

25. What is the difference between a "Red Notice" and a "Blue Notice"?

CHAPTER 6 — EYEWITNESS IDENTIFICATION PROCEDURES

"You did it because I said you did it!"

— Mom

KEY TERMS

Due Process
Show-ups
Photo Arrays
Lineups

Sequential Lineup
Double Blind Lineup
Fourteenth Amendment

CHAPTER OBJECTIVES

At the end of this lesson, the student will be able to:

- Define what a show up is and how it is used.
- Define the term photo array and discuss the procedure of how they are used.
- Define the term lineup and discuss the procedure how they are used.
- Discuss attorney issues during eyewitness identification procedures.

Eyewitness identification is an important tool of the investigator. However, they must take special care to ensure that a misidentification does not occur. No one wants to send an innocent person to jail, but according to the Innocence Project, "the most common element in all wrongful convictions later overturned by DNA evidence has been eye-witness identification" (Innocence Project, 2011). Investigators must ensure that they follow their department's policies and procedures to avoid a travesty of justice. Eyewitness identification still plays an integral part of the investigation process and weighs heavily with a jury. Investigators must be even more prepared to defend the identification process when cross examined at trial.

Section 1 of the Fourteenth Amendment to the U.S. Constitution states the following:

> ...nor shall any State deprive any person of life, liberty, or property, without due process of law; nor deny to any person within its jurisdiction the equal protection of the laws.

The Due Process Clause is what protects the citizens of the United States from unfair police identification procedures that are too suggestive. Investigators must be mindful of these issues when using eyewitness identification procedures.

After a crime is committed the police attempt to bring the victim to a particular location to view a stopped person or to the station house to view photographs. The idea is to use the person's memory of the event quickly before it fades. Eyewitness identification has been under attack now for several years, citing all types of experiments that showed that eyewitness accounts are not reliable. That is why it is extremely important to identify physical evidence of the crime and to seek out additional eyewitnesses who can corroborate what was observed. Single eyewitness cases with little or no physical evidence are extremely difficult to prosecute.

Unfortunately, the police have to rely on eyewitness identification because most of the time the victim is the only person who saw the perpetrator commit the act. They must depend on the reliability of the victim's perception, memory and communication. These are the crimes where the identity of the suspect is the issue. More often than not, the victim never even gets a chance to see the perpetrator. Victims often do not see the perpetrator for the following reasons: the victim was approached from the rear, tunnel vision, victim was not paying attention (talking on phone, listening to MP3 player, etc.), out of fear, poor eyesight and even the weather can be a factor. Therefore, an investigator will make every attempt to identify physical evidence (see Chapter 2) and obtain surveillance camera footage when available (see Canvassing in Chapter 5) from the crime scene to corroborate or disprove eyewitness accounts.

An investigator will employ **SAL** to help them with the three (3) eyewitness identification procedures: **S**how-ups, **A**rrays and **L**ineups. SAL is also the proper order in which eyewitness identification procedures should be conducted.

Show-ups

A show-up is a prompt, on the scene viewing of a suspect one-on-one by the victim/witness. A show-up is often confrontational because the police detain a suspect based on a physical description broadcasted by the police from the victim/witness. The legal question that always arises is, "Do I take the suspect to the victim or do I take the victim to the suspect?" There is no answer to this question because it depends on the circumstances. Taking the victim to the suspect is far less suggestive than vice versa. A show-up is suggestive enough. The victim/witness should always be taken to the suspect absent extenuating circumstances. What happens if your victim is seriously injured and likely to die? Then you have no choice but to bring the suspect to the victim, even if it is in a hospital (*People v. Johnson* 81 NY 2d 828 (1993)). A show-up should never be conducted at the station house.

When a show-up is used, there are some things that should be avoided at all costs. The police should never tell the victim/witness that the "Perpetrator has been caught," nor should they ask, "Is this the guy?" when the victim views the person stopped. In addition, the suspect should not be sitting cuffed in the rear of the police car or being held unnecessarily when showed to the victim/witness.

The idea of the show-up is to capitalize on the freshness of the incident in the victim's/witnesses' memory, if they have the wrong person that they can be released without unnecessary delay and continue looking for the perpetrator.

Some of you may ask, "What gives a police officer the right to stop someone?" My question to you is, "What level of suspicion do the police have in that case?" Here is a review of previous material. A person matching a description provides a police officer with reasonable suspicion. What can the police do at reasonable suspicion? They can stop, question and (possibly) frisk. Not only does the person in this case match a description, but they are in proximity of a violent crime. Would a reasonable person conclude that criminality was afoot? The only constraint is that a show-up must be conducted within a reasonable amount, generally a few minutes, from the time of the initial incident (*Stovall v. Denno* 388 U.S. 293 (1967)).

CI Tip Sheet

The proper use of a show-up can do two (2) things:
(1) it can identify a suspect quickly
(2) it can exonerate an otherwise innocent person

A show-up would never be used when a victim knows the suspect or if the suspect is already under arrest. When the victim knows the perpetrator it is fine to show a single photo to the victim in order to confirm the identity—known as a Confirmatory Identification.

Arrays
(AKA: Photo Arrays, Photo Lineup, Six-Pack)

An array, or photo array, is a procedure used when the police have an idea who the perpetrator is, or have a detailed description or the suspect has a certain modus operandi (MO). A photo array can be used only when the suspect is *not* in custody. If the suspect is in custody, the police must use a Lineup. If the victim/witness identifies the suspect in the array, the police now have probable cause to go out and make the arrest. On his/her arrest, the individual will then be put in a live lineup even though he was chosen in the array. However, if the victim/witness fails to pick the suspect out of the lineup, he/she will be set free and the investigation will probably be over.

With the arrival of technology, constructing photo arrays has never been easier. Computer programs now exist that allow the user to input a description and create electronic arrays for viewing by the victim/witness almost immediately. When creating arrays the investigator must try to make it as fair and impartial as possible.

The police can use photographs from the **MOD S**quad's **FAVS**:

Mug books
Online mug books
Driver's license photos
Sex offender databases

Family photos
Arrest photos
Video cameras
Sketch artist

- ***Guidelines for preparing an Array:***

  - Photo arrays are not to be used for "fishing expeditions"
  - Sealed photos cannot be used (*United States v. Crews* 445 U.S. 463 (1980))
  - A minimum of 6 photos (more can be used) will be used: one (1) suspect and five (5) fillers
  - Each of the five (5) fillers will be of the same gender, age, race, physical makeup (*Grant v. City of Long Beach* 315 F. 3d 1081 (2002))
  - Nothing in the suspect's photo can make them stand out: i.e., he/she is the only one wearing eyeglasses, has a big scar, mustache, bald, different colored background, etc.
  - All arrest numbers or other identifying police information must be covered in the photos
  - The identity of the other photos used in the array must be recorded

- ***Guidelines for showing the Array:***

  - Instruct the person that they are about to view a photo array
  - Hand the array to the person so nothing can be suggestive about the array
  - The investigator must explain to the victim/witness that the photos are in random order and that the perpetrator may or may not be included
  - If the victim/witness "picks" the suspect, the investigator will have them sign their name under the photo: Identification = Probable Cause
  - In instances where multiple victims/witnesses exist, each one will be shown the array separately (Not the same one!). Also, the police must make every effort to ensure that the victim(s) or witness(es) do not speak to one another
    - o Additional arrays should be created with the perpetrator in different locations
  - Never assist the victim/witness to pick anyone

- Never tell a victim/witness that they chose the "right" or "wrong" person
- The photo array used will be vouchered as evidence and kept with the case folder

SEQUENTIAL PHOTO ARRAYS

Some states are now adopting Sequential Photo Array procedures. The major change is that the victim/witness will be shown one photo at a time and they have to make a decision (yes or no) on the photo before they receive the next one (Mecklenburg, Police Chief, October 2008).

The investigator must prepare a report on the results of the photo array including any statements made by the victim/witness, if they had difficulty picking someone out or if they picked anyone at all and how long it took. Be prepared for these questions on the witness stand from the defense attorney!

Lineups

(AKA Investigatory Lineup, Live Lineup, Simultaneous Lineup)

Lineups are used when a suspect is under arrest. The lineup procedure is very similar to the photo array, except that the individual is in custody. There are different types of lineups and there may be issues that the police must deal with in regard to a suspect's lawyers. Both will be addressed later in this section.

The lineup will be conducted in a room that has a one-way mirror, with a shade, so that the victim/witness can view it without fear of being seen. Also in the room with the victim/witness, the lights will be turned off. If the light is on, you can see through the one-way mirror. To avoid problems, the perpetrator and fillers should be kept somewhere away from the viewing room so that they can see the victim/witness and vice versa. For the very first viewing (in multiple victim/witness cases) the victim/witness should be brought into the viewing room first and the door should be closed. If not, you run the risk of blowing your lineup.

- Guidelines for conducting Lineups:

    - If necessary, the victim/witness can wear a mask to hide their identity
    - If the suspect is going to be interrogated before, during or after the lineup, the investigator must read the Miranda Warnings to them
    - The investigator should inform the suspect that he is being placed in the lineup and why
    - The case investigator, investigating supervisor and the assistant district attorney (ADA) will be present
        o A lineup will never be conducted without a conferral with the ADA

- A minimum of six (6) individuals (more can be used) will be used: one (1) suspect and five (5) fillers
  - o Police officers can be used as fillers as long as they are not wearing a uniform or other article of clothing that would identify them as the police or if they had contact already with the witness/victim, i.e., drove them into the station house
  - o If juveniles are needed, the police must obtain permission from a parent or guardian before using them
- Each of the five (5) fillers will be of the same gender, age, race, physical makeup and have similar dress
  - o Investigators usually have a collection of white T-shirts, black ball caps, etc., to make everyone "look" the same
  - o Each filler will also be instructed not to do anything that may single out the suspect
    - Directing eyes toward them
    - Head nodding
    - Finger pointing
- Nothing can make the suspect stand out: i.e., he/she is the only one wearing eyeglasses, has a big scar, mustache, bald, etc.
- The suspect is allowed to choose his/her place in the lineup: 1 through 6
  - o Each person will be given a placard with their number on it
  - o In multiple viewings, the suspect can choose a different position each time
- Before the lineup begins a series of photos will be taken of the lineup to disprove claims of unfairness
- In instances where multiple victims/witnesses exist, each one will be shown the lineup separately. Also, the police must make every effort to ensure that the victim(s) or witness(es) do not speak to one another
  - Never assist the victim/witness to choose anyone
- Never tell a victim/witness that they chose the "right" or "wrong" person
- The investigator fills out a lineup report, which is signed by the investigator, supervisor and in some jurisdictions the ADA too
  - o The lineup form records the identity of all who where present—including the names and pedigree information of the fillers
  - o The lineup form is secured with the case folder along with the photos and names and pedigree information of the fillers

Once the investigator is ready to start, he/she will say to the victim/witness, "You are about to view a group of individuals and that the suspect may or may not be in the present. If you recognize anyone, tell us who you recognize and where your recognize them from." After that is said, the investigator will knock on the glass and another investigator will open the shade. The police can also make each individual in the lineup say a phrase that the perpetrator used, "Your money or your life," for the purpose of voice identification.

When the viewing is over, the investigator will knock on the glass again so that the shade can be drawn. The lineup report will be completed as well as an investigator's report detailing the events that transpired during the lineup and if the victim/witness identified the suspect or not. A negative report will also be written. "On (date, day of the week) at (time), the victim, known to this Department, was unable to identify a suspect in the lineup conducted at (location). The following persons where present...."

CI Cheat Sheet

Number of Fillers in both an Array/Lineup = 5
Number of Suspects in an Array/Lineup = 1
Total = 6

Lawyer/Legal Issues

When we deal with eyewitness identification procedures, we have to be concerned with three Amendments: the Fifth, Sixth and the Fourteenth. Parts of the Fifth Amendment and the Fourteenth Amendment's deal with due process, which simply state that the procedure be fair. The Sixth Amendment deals with right to counsel issues. A suspect *does not* have an absolute right to counsel at an investigatory lineup (*Kirby v. Illinois* 406 US 682 (1972)), only at a post-indictment lineup (*United States v. Wade* 388 US 218 (1967)). However, if a lawyer calls the police and states he/she wants to be present at the investigatory lineup, the police can grant them the request if practical. The lawyer will only be granted a reasonable amount of time, generally an hour, to arrive at the lineup location. If present, the lawyer can make suggestions regarding the lineup, but the police do not have to make any changes. The defense attorney cannot interview victims or witnesses but must be allowed to confer with his client. Remember, the ADA will also be in the room, so the investigator will let the lawyers argue over it.

In a post-indictment lineup, the suspect is already represented by counsel, so he/she must be present at the lineup. A post-indictment lineup is usually scheduled on a prearranged date and time between the ADA and the suspect's lawyer.

STOP!	One caveat about a post-indictment lineup, the police *cannot* question the suspect on anything unless his lawyer is present!

Sequential and Double Blind Lineups

Other types of lineup identification exist than the one described above. Double Blind and Sequential Lineups have been adopted by different states throughout the nation. These different lineup procedures were designed to lessen the likelihood of a misidentification or police misconduct.

A Sequential Lineup is set up similarly as the investigatory lineup: the room, five (5) fillers and the suspect, but the victim/witness does not view all six (6) individuals at the same time. Each person is brought into the room alone, one at a time. This is a harder identification process, but it can mitigate misidentifications.

A Double Blind Lineup is the same as the investigatory lineup, but the investigators that are conducting the lineup do not know which person is the perpetrator as well as the victim/witness. In April 2001, the state of New Jersey became the first state in the Union to use the double blind lineup and photo array whenever practical (Cronin, Murphy, Spahr, Toliver & Weger, 2007, p. 44).

CI Cheat Sheet

Here is a quick formula reminder on when to use
an array or a lineup:

NOT in custody = Array
IN custody = Lineup

Internet Resources for Investigators

National Institute of Justice: Eyewitness Evidence: A Guide for Law Enforcement http://www.nij.gov/nij/pubs-sum/178240.htm

IACP: Eyewitness Identification: What Chiefs Need to Know Now http://www.policechiefmagazine.org/magazine/index.cfm?fuseaction =display_arch&article_id=1636&issue_id=102008

Questions for Discussion and Review

1.   In order, name the three (3) types of eyewitness identification procedures employed by the police.

2.   Should a suspect have an absolute right to counsel at an investigatory lineup? Why or why not?

3.   Why can't the police interrogate a suspect at a post-indictment lineup?

4.   If a suspect's lawyer requests to be at his client's lineup, how long do the police have to give him/her to arrive at the station house?

5.   Should either a Sequential or Double Blind Lineup be mandated for all police departments across the United States? Why or why not?

6.   Can the police force a suspect into a lineup?

7.   If a victim said, "I'm 99% sure it's #4," would that be a positive identification? Why or why not?

8.   Why aren't eyewitness identification procedures used to identify a perpetrator that the victim knows?

9.   How can the police prevent witness contamination?

10.   In what type of cases would it be a good idea for your victim/witness to wear a mask before viewing a lineup?

11.   Why do you think the police can't use a photo array if someone is in custody?

12.   What are some factors that can make eyewitness identification suggestive?

13.   What is the minimum number of fillers that can be used in an array?

14. What is the minimum number of individuals that must stand in a lineup?

15. Which Amendment(s) of the U.S. Constitution deals with lawyers?

16. Which Amendment grants protection against impermissibly suggestive identification procedures?

17. What are all the rights which are protected under the Fifth Amendment?

18. Can the police use a photo of a "filler" that makes it stand out against the rest? Why or why not?

CHAPTER 7 — INTERVIEW AND INTERROGATION

"There're only two people in this world you should lie to, the police and your girlfriend."

— Jack Nicholson

KEY TERMS

Lie	Admission	Confession
Interview	Miranda Decision	Active Listening
Rapport Building	Open Ended Question	Statement Analysis
Interrogation	Closed Ended Question	Control Question

CHAPTER OBJECTIVES

At the end of this lesson, the student will be able to:

- Identify the reasons why people lie.
- Explain the two (2) ways that people lie.
- Differentiate between an interview and an interrogation.
- Recall the steps in preparing to conduct an interview.
- Recall the steps in preparing to conduct an interrogation.
- Name the two (2) goals of interrogation.
- Discuss the proper set up of the interrogation room.
- Restate when the Miranda Warnings are necessary during an interrogation.
- Discuss the process of Statement Analysis.

The Liar's Puzzle

Why do people lie? The answer to this question is simpler than you think. From my own experience, human beings are taught at a very early age that there are good lies (white lies) and bad lies. But aren't they still lies? Of course they are. So it's all right to tell your aunt with a mustache that she looks good, so you don't hurt her feelings? In fact we even lie to ourselves! We also learn that lying is a way of escaping punishment. For example, "Did you break the lamp because you were playing ball in the house?" "Yes, I did." Your response is then followed by either a smack or a "wait till your father gets home" threat. You say to yourself, "boy I'm never gonna admit to something like that again." Naturally, all future responses to "interrogations" by your parents will be full of denials followed by demands for proof. I can hear kids everywhere saying, "Hey, Ma, you got that on videotape?"

Learning how to be a better liar doesn't end in childhood. By the time we are young adults we have begun to understand the technique of deception and get better at it. Some even become masters of deception. This practice prepares us for marriage and the famous, "Does this make me look fat?" question. "You know it does, or you wouldn't have asked me in the first place." Could you even imagine what would happen if you said that? You would be sleeping with one eye open for sure! We lie to our parents, loved ones, teachers, friends and strangers. No one is immune to this phenomenon; some spouses would say they lie for survival reasons. So why be shocked that someone will lie to us in the interrogation room?

We begin to see how the pieces have developed and fallen into place in our lives. Lying is like putting a puzzle together. Some only have just the edges completed, some the middle, while others have the entire puzzle mastered. We encounter people who are very good liars and who lie for the sake of lying without even benefitting. Generally, there is a benefit of lying for most people. Some want out of a relationship, "It's not you, it's me," some want to get out of work, "I'm not feeling well today," and some don't want to go out with you, "I'm dyeing my hair tonight." In police work the stakes are much higher. People lie to stay out of jail, prison and in extreme cases the electric chair. They have nothing to lose and everything to gain by lying. It's up to you, the investigator, to identify lies and deception and somehow get to the truth of the matter. Easier said then done.

How does the Liar's Puzzle affect police work? Well, your first step to completing a regular puzzle was to dump all the pieces on the table and sort them by type: edge and interior pieces, and generally start with putting the edges together first to create the framework. The liar does the same thing with the facts of the incident because they are editing from their imagination and not their memory. They dump the facts in their head; separate the types of facts/lies (pieces) and starts with peripherals (edges) of the incident. Gradually, a skilled investigator asks the right questions and begins to push the individual to put the pieces of the puzzle (incident) together. This is why the technique of asking someone to tell the story backwards or to pick it up from the middle is so effective. Liars can't do it.

For example, ask your spouse, boyfriend, girlfriend, friend, etc., to tell you everything they did from the moment they woke up. You will see a natural progression of events: the alarm went off, I got out of bed, I went to the bathroom, I got dressed, I ate, etc. Why? Because they are editing from their memory. After they're done, ask them to tell you the same story backwards. You will notice that the story flows just as well backwards as if you were depressing the rewind button on the DVD player. It is an effective technique to use.

The two main ways individuals lie are by hiding and by making things up. Which one is worse? They are both forms of lying, but if it makes you feel better, much of hiding would fall under the "white lie" category. Lying by hiding is rather easy, because the individual is not actually telling any lies, he/she selectively tells you (or omits) what you want or what they think you want to hear and leaves out the information that may implicate them. Hiding information is not lying you contend? All right, then ask yourself this question, "If I told (fill in the blank with spouse, boss, detective, etc.), would I be in big trouble?" If the answer to this question is yes, then you lied by hiding. Omitting is easier, so it is the most widely used.

A "Puzzle" of someone who hides information has the edges done, most of the picture completed, but they are missing a few key pieces. Therefore, hiding is more difficult, but not impossible for an investigator to detect. Preparation cannot be stressed enough in criminal investigations. It is the key ingredient in successful interviews and interrogations. Investigators must know the facts of the case and be familiar with each part of the investigation so they can detect if someone is hiding information from them.

An individual that hides information from an investigator may be a **CON** artist that:

Conceals
Omits
Not forthright

Making things up is a separate category. Someone that makes up information better have a good memory. Even a good memory pitted against a skilled investigator is no match, especially when they are prepared. When someone falsifies, their "Puzzle" pieces are scattered all over the place, lacking structure, and therefore making it easier to uncover. The pieces simply do not fit.

An individual that makes things up may be an **ELF**, or one who:

Embellishes
Lies outright
Fabricates

A skilled investigator has to be a convincing liar also—fight fire with fire. An investigator is allowed to trick and deceive a suspect in order to obtain a confession as long as if the methods used could not coerce an innocent person to confess. Several court cases, most notably *Frazier v. Cupp* 394 U.S. 731 (1969), have rubber stamped the verbal allegation by law enforcement that evidence or statements exist to prove the suspect's guilt. For example, the courts have accepted informing a suspect that his/her fingerprints/DNA were/was found at a crime scene, or that the codefendant implicated the other, when they did not or that a video surveillance tape existed depicting the suspect entering/leaving the location. Statements that make the suspect say to himself, "Do I call their bluff?"

For argument's sake, you cancel a night out with your girlfriend because you are not "feeling" well and therefore you are going to bed early. However, your intention is to go out to a sports pub with your friends to watch the football game. The next day she smugly asks, "how are you feeling?" "OK, I guess." "Are you sure?" That last question would leave you a little uneasy, no? Does she know something? Did a friend of her's see me at the bar? Your girlfriend will also slip in another tactic—silence. Silence is golden. When you ask a question, don't respond to his answer either verbally or nonverbally and watch what happens. The silence makes the person uneasy and he often fills that dead space with extraneous information. That extraneous information can be a potential windfall because quite often you say too much.

There are many ways that the investigator can create that, "Oh no" moment in the suspect's head. When someone does something wrong he begins to get his story together or have a prepared "statement" for the police, especially those who have been on the Criminal Justice merry-go-round before. Investigators must use this to their advantage. Remember, when the suspect is preparing a story he is in essence playing checkers—planning one move at a time. He has stock answers ready for the questions that are most likely to be asked. I always examined the situation and tried to catch a suspect off balance with that very first question. Think of the pitcher that throws a curve ball to the batter who is anticipating a fastball. What happens? His knees buckle. The investigator must think of his questions in the same manner. For example, during an interrogation of a rape suspect, I have used these as my first questions, "Do you know what DNA is?" or "Do you know where DNA samples come from?" These are the types of questions that suspects are totally unprepared for. Every investigator has to develop their own killer curve ball.

The grey area of deceit and trickery comes in the form of fabricating evidence. Appeals courts have given split decisions on the tactic of fabricating evidence in order to obtain a confession.

In the case, *State v. Cayward* 552 S.2d 971 (Florida 1989), the police presented a fabricated laboratory report specifically tying the suspect's DNA to a sexual assault and murder of a five-year-old girl. After seeing the report, the suspect confessed. The Florida Appeals Court decided that fabricated documents violate due process. In direct contrast to this decision, the Supreme Court of Nevada upheld the use of a fabricated laboratory report tying a suspect's DNA to a sexual assault in *Sheriff v. Bessey* 914 P.2d 618 (Nevada 1996). I would make an educated guess that the U.S. Supreme Court will eventually be asked to weigh in on this practice. Until they do, I believe that most police departments will avoid this tactic. I never wanted my name in a legal decision and neither should you.

Conducting Interviews

> *"It is an old maxim of mine that when you have excluded the impossible, whatever remains, however, improbable, must be the truth."*
>
> — Sherlock Holmes (Sir Arthur Conan Doyle)

An investigator spends most of his time speaking with people. Even with the terrific advancements in the forensic sciences, especially with DNA, the need for human interaction is critical to the investigative process. Generally, when an investigator or reporter conducts an interview their goal is to develop information and answers to questions that they do not know. Keep this in mind, because when we get to interrogation, the goal changes. During an interrogation the investigator/reporter attempts to validate the information they already know. An interview is *not* an interrogation.

Conducting interviews is not an easy task for some individuals. If you are shy or introverted, you may have a tough time making it as an investigator because so much of what you do depends on your interactions with others. Interviewing is a skill that an investigator gets better at the more they do it. An investigator will learn what works and what doesn't, and he also learns that the same techniques that he was successful with in the past are not guaranteed to work with everybody. This is what makes interviewing so difficult. An investigator has to read a person, determine his level of comprehension and decide what approach will work best all in a matter of seconds. Rarely will you ever get a second chance to make a good first impression.

When conducting interviews, investigators must remember that certain aspects of their behavior are important to use and control. Therefore, the investigator has to be patient and compassionate and stay focused, objective, on point and logical when talking to people.

If you ask investigators how they would define an interview, most would probably say, "A two-way conversation with an intention." The intention is to extract information. During an interview, the interviewer does a lot of listening and not so much talking. Interviews are noncustodial, which means no lawyers or Miranda Warnings are necessary. Interviews are not combative and should be conducted in a relaxed environment. It doesn't matter if you are conducting an interview or an interrogation, there are Six (6) Basic Investigative Questions that we need the answers to: When, Where, Who, What, How and Why. These six questions help us establish **MOM**.

The key to **GREAT** interviewing is:

Groundwork
Rapport Building
Elucidation of Statements
Active Listening
The Assessment

GROUNDWORK

Before conducting interviews, investigators must know what happened. For example, shortly after arriving at a scene of a major incident, the investigators should be gathered by the investigator supervisor and the case investigator. Additional investigators who arrive at the scene play a support role. It should start off with, "Here is what we know so far." The additional investigator must be brought up to speed regarding evidence that was found, who the victim was and what the circumstances were surrounding the crime, statements by the first officers on the scene including their observations. Investigators should be thinking about the type of questions they want to ask, not only to citizens but to the case investigator as well. This is the opportunity to strategize on what is being done and what needs to be done. This is not the time to be shy, and everyone at the meeting should be encouraged to participate. Somebody may have a good idea. For instance, it may be prudent to transmit an alarm for a wanted perpetrator or vehicle at this time.

At the very least the investigator should pull the job transmission of the incident, including 911 callers. If time permits, computer checks should be done on the suspect and the building/house the investigators will be canvassing. "Running" the location in computer databases can provide information such as: residents, persons wanted on warrants or other crimes, and parolees. The most important reason to conduct computer checks is for officer safety. I, personally, would want to know that the door I was about to knock on may be the residence of someone who is wanted for a crime. Armed with this information, the investigator can now start to canvass (see Chapter 5). The investigative canvass is a series of interviews conducted over a short period. The locations canvassed and the information obtained must be properly documented on an investigative report or it may be lost forever.

When the canvasses are concluded there should be a follow-up meeting to go over all the facts of the incident. An investigator may have picked up a vital piece of information or even that trifle—but according to Sherlock Holmes, "There is nothing more important than trifles." This is the stage where a "To Do" list can be drawn up.

STOP!	Do you know who is behind that door before you knock on it? Remember, officer safety comes first!

RAPPORT BUILDING

Building rapport is one of the most important, if not the most important, aspect of conducting interviews. Building rapport is not as easy as it sounds. There are four (4) types of people an investigator will encounter during police/public interviews: (1) those who hate the police, (2) those who are scared of the police, (3) those who distrust the police and (4) those who like the police. That means 75% of the people you come across will be less than willing to provide information. An investigator has one strike against them before knocking on the door, so rapport building is extremely important to win over the individual's cooperation. Looking the part is also important of the rapport-building process. A well-dressed investigator engenders a level of respect as well as presenting a professional image. In my experience, people are more willing to open up to a "suit" than to the uniforms.

Rapport building is an attempt by the interviewer to identify common ground between them and the interviewee. It may be a quick acknowledgment of a sports team shirt, or photos of children or a boat in the driveway. Anything to get the "two-way conversation" started. This works only if the investigators properly introduce themselves and make a quick statement as to why they are there. The introduction is often a critical step in the process that sets the tone for the rest of the interview. Unfortunately, investigators are reluctant to do so. Can you see the difference between these two "introductions"? "Hi, sir/ma'am, my name is Detective Magpie and I from the ABC Police, how are you today? I am here seeking information about the incident that occurred a few hours ago. Do you mind if I come in?" Versus, "It's the police, open up. We're detectives. Do you know who killed Johnny Jones?"

If you noticed in the first introductory statement by the investigator, he didn't request information when the person answered the door. This is done for one reason, some people do not want to be seen talking to the police in public. Make this error and the information will be lost forever. It may not be good for their health or "street cred." People will be reluctant to provide information based on where you are standing and not so much as what you say. The environment can play a role in obtaining information. Also, Detective Magpie referred to the situation as an incident and not what it really is, a murder, rape, robbery, etc. This technique downplays the severity of the situation and may put the person at ease. You never know if the person who you are speaking to knew the victim personally or may even be related to him or her. Keeping people comfortable about the topic can never hurt you.

What you say is important, but sometimes not as important as how you say it. A negative attitude or disinterested questions may turn the person off and send you packing. If the investigator is rude, discourteous or talks down to the interviewee, he will wind up with nothing. This defeats the entire goal of an investigator: to obtain information and evidence to identify perpetrators (Chapter 1). Remember the old adage, "You get more flies with honey than you do with vinegar." Think of yourself as a sales representative. We aren't selling a product for money, but we do want information from them instead. The person you are speaking to has to trust you and that is why rapport building is extremely important. Would you buy something from a salesperson that you didn't trust?

ELUCIDATION OF STATEMENTS

To elucidate is to make clear or clarify. An investigator cannot clarify statements if he is not aware of what transpired. That is why conducting the groundwork is the first and most important step. Investigators use a series of open-ended, closed-ended and follow-up questions to extract information from people. An open-ended question elicits a story from the individual and produces the most amount of information. Open-ended questions also spur leads and avenues to follow-up questions. "Tell me what happened?" would be an example of an open-ended question. Here the investigator is attempting to get a story. Interviews should be started with a series of open-ended questions. Open-ended questions cannot be answered with a simple, "Yes" or "No" and, therefore, provide more information to work with. Open-ended questions also allow the investigator to develop a baseline on how the interviewee reacts under normal questioning. Do they seem comfortable or uncomfortable with the topic or specific question? Are they able to talk about certain parts of the event without difficulty and then about other parts exhibit signs of distress? Do they answer some questions quickly and then stutter and stammer when pressed for specific information?

A close-ended question attempts to establish facts and/or lock a person into a statement. "What time did you get home last night?" "Were you home last night?" "Do you know Mary Smith?" are all examples of close-ended questions. A close-ended question can be answered with a simple yes, no or one word answer. Any additional information beyond those answers may prove to be critical. Unlike the open-ended questions, close-ended questions look to elicit specific details of the event. Pay close attention to any extraneous information that you receive from a close-ended question! "John, what time did you arrive home last night?" "I dropped my girlfriend off first and then I went home. I guess around nine." That response provides you with another lead or at the very least a possible additional witness. It may be a cold lead, one that does not solve the case, but still may provide intelligence information.

The best open- and closed-ended questions are useless without the investigator being able to properly form follow-up questions. Follow-up questions are designed to obtain additional information. For example, "John, you mentioned that you were in the parking garage at the time of the incident. Why were you there?" This may prove to be an important point in the case and you will never know if you don't know how to ask follow-up questions.

In the reference page at the back of the book is a link to the transcript of the O.J. Simpson case from *Star* magazine. Every investigator should read it and learn what happens when investigators fail to ask follow-up questions. Each semester for a term project, I require my students to read the transcript and identify five (5) instances where a follow-up question should have been asked, what should those questions be and what answers you would expect from the follow-up questions. I have yet to get only five questions.

CI Tip Sheet

Remember the following:

Open-Ended = Overview of the event - a story
Close-Ended = Specifics - facts

Before ending an interview, the investigator should paraphrase statements made by the individual to ensure accuracy and for clarification. This provides the interviewer a chance to check his/her facts and to lock a person into their statement. This is important because your witness may develop "amnesia" or change their story once they enter the courtroom. The prosecutor should be able to "refresh" their memory from a well-prepared and documented report.

STOP!	The investigator must beware of following phrases such as these when taking statements from victims/witnesses: "Maybe" or "May have" "Could be" or "I think" "Pretty much" or "I'm pretty sure"

Some jurisdictions require the police to audiotape and video record all/ some interviews and interrogations. Even though taping can cause an administrative nightmare for the police, an interview on tape can prove that the statement was not coerced from the individual. This can be very damaging to the perpetrator, especially when viewed by twelve people that don't know how to get themselves out of jury duty. Civil libertarians have been fighting for this a long time and I don't know why. They claim that it prevents the police from coercing confessions, but I think about how damaging a confession on video tape would be. There is nothing for a defense attorney to challenge or to use to plant the seed of reasonable doubt in a jury's mind. They just watched the perpetrator admit to the crime!

Investigators must avoid using foul language, police jargon or street language and the use of certain types of questions during both interviews and interrogations. Questions from **UCLA** must never be used by an investigator:

Unclear
Compound
Leading
Any question or statement that could disclose investigative information

UNCLEAR

An unclear question creates confusion for the interviewee because it is poorly constructed. "When you arrived home the day after yesterday and met your assailant, how did you know that he was your assailant and that he was about to attack you?" Huh? Here is another example, "So, you do not know if Jones went to the party last night?" How does the person answer this? If they say, "Yes," what does it mean? Do they mean that yes Jones was there or do they mean yes I do not know. Unclear questions cause delays and detract from the effectiveness of the interview/interrogation.

COMPOUND

A compound question should never be used because the interviewer asks at least two questions at the same time. The individual may answer both questions, but more than likely, they will answer only the last question. "What time did you come home last night and what did you see?" Seldom are you ever going to get a definitive answer when you ask a compound question. Ask one question at a time, get your answer, then move on to the next one. In the preceding example, the time the person arrived home may be the most important question that helps establish the timeline and therefore prove that the suspect had the opportunity to commit the crime!

LEADING

A leading question "leads" the interviewee to the answer or provides the answer and they often start with "Did you ..." and "Could you ..." For example, "Could you tell me if he was driving a white Chevy?" "Did you see Mark do this to you?" Instead, the questions should have been asked this way, "What color was the car he was driving?" and "Who gave you the black eye?" Any question that you ask that has an answer in it is a leading question and must be avoided at all costs.

ANY QUESTION OR STATEMENT THAT COULD DISCLOSE INVESTIGATIVE INFORMATION

The investigator must be careful not to disclose investigative information that may be detrimental to the case when speaking with potential witnesses and suspects. Rarely will the police disclose all the facts surrounding the case. Remember an interview was defined as a two-way street, so there is a chance that the investigator may leak information inadvertently. The police must "hold some things back" so that they can determine who is telling the truth and who is not. This type of information is saved for Control questions. A Control question is one where the person asking knows the information to be true and acts exactly like the control group in an experiment.

For instance, a "suspect" enters the station house and claims he was the guy who killed the female jogger in the park. Depending on the situation, a case like this will garner a tremendous amount of media, so the police may withhold the cause of death. An investigator will take the person to an interview room, read him his Miranda Warnings (more on this in Conducting Interrogations), of course, and ask some questions. After obtaining the man's pedigree information, the investigator may test the "confessor" right from the start, "How did you kill her?" "I strangled her." The investigator would then probably stand up, open the door to the interview room and shout, "Next!"

Active Listening

If you have ever been told, "You never listen to me!" your spouse is probably right. We don't listen as well as we should. It is a proven fact. An investigator has to listen and weigh every word used. An individual may make an incriminating statement or provide information that they shouldn't have, but only if the investigator is listening attentively will they hear it. The individual may choose words that will lead to additional follow up questions or make an inadvertent slip of the tongue. For example, investigators are conducting a canvass with an upstairs neighbor about a homicide that occurred in the building. The investigator asks, "Did you hear anything last night?" "I heard a scream and said to myself, that's Jimmy." That was an inadvertent slip. I personally wouldn't jump on it right away. I would save it for the right moment and ask, "Why did you think it was Jimmy?" or "How did you know it was Jimmy?" This was a true story. "Jimmy" was found stabbed to death and set on fire in a local park. The gentleman that made the statement to us knew it was "Jimmy" because he had given up his whereabouts to a local drug dealer who was looking for the person that ripped him off.

The investigator must fight the urge to interrupt the person when they are speaking. This is known as breaking the stream of consciousness. Have you ever had a great dream, where everything was going perfect or you were having a good time and then the phone rings? You try to find that exact place in your bed, fluff your pillow just right and what happens? Nothing. You can never regain that stream of consciousness. The same thing happens to people who are interrupted in the middle of their story. Let them speak, jot down notes and when they are done, now elucidate (clarify) their statements.

There are some things that the person who is conducting the interview can do to listen more effectively. First, and most important, is good eye contact. It is not a stare-down session, but good contact shows the person that you are interested in what they are saying. Also, the interviewer should lean forward toward the person and every now and then nod. This further makes the point that you are listening.

Taking notes is an important part of the listening process. The notes provide a chance to ensure accuracy and completeness. When two investigators are present for an interview, only one will do the talking and the other will take notes. This decision should be made before conducting the interview. The unwritten rule is that the case investigator will conduct both the interview(s) and interrogation(s) if practical. This is a good rule to follow because it makes it easier to testify in court when only one investigator conducted the interviews. However, there may be a good reason why someone other than the case investigator should do the interview. For instance, they have dealt with them in a previous case and therefore the rapport has already been established or the first interaction with the case investigator did not go well. The information that we are trying to retrieve can sometimes amount to giving up a "secret." Would you be willing to share a secret with a stranger if they treated you badly? I don't think so. You don't have to like them, but you must give the illusion that you do.

CI Tip Sheet

A quick guideline for note taking and to sum up the interviewing process is to catch a **LIAR**:

Listen Attentively
Intervene only if the interviewee loses focus
Add or correct information as needed
Review the notes with the interviewee before leaving

Remember, notes taken must be preserved as "Rosario Material" (*People v. Rosario* 9 NY2d. 286 (1961)) in many jurisdictions. To be on the safe side, investigators should be in the habit of saving and securing all notes in the case folder.

The Assessment

Have you ever left an interview and said, "Damn, I should have asked them ..." The assessment or evaluation is a self-critique conducted by the interviewer regarding their interview. It is a very important step in the interview/interrogation process, but it is seldom done. An assessment can prevent mistakes in the future and the techniques that were discovered can be used to train other investigators. The investigator must be honest with themselves. Did they ask the right questions? Would they have done something different? What worked? What didn't work? Was it easier or harder than first thought and why? These questions are a good starting point in the self-evaluation process.

In order for the assessment to be successful, the investigator must be honest with their own self. Self-evaluation is often difficult. If you are unable to evaluate yourself, ask one of your coworkers to do it for you. It may sting a bit, but take it as constructive and always look to improve.

Preventing Interview Contamination

An investigator has the difficult task of ensuring that the interview is not contaminated. Contamination can occur in many ways, but the worst kind of contamination occurs when witnesses/victims talk to one another. An investigator must keep witnesses/victims separated at all costs! Other contamination issues are distractions like phones ringing, babies crying, and televisions and music playing. An investigator has to be careful when they ask the homeowner to lower the radio/TV or put the children in another room. Remember, you are a guest that has a purpose. No one wants to be told what to do in their own home by a complete stranger.

Cell phones present an even bigger problem. Witnesses/victims should be strongly encouraged *not* to use their phones until all the interviews are completed and, if possible, ask them if the phone can be safeguarded for them until everything is done. If the resources exist, a uniformed police officer should stay with each victim/witness to help prevent interview contamination. They all do not have to be in the same room to talk with one another. Access to a cell phone allows individuals to text and e-mail one another. Remember, a television in the room poses another risk of contamination especially in high-profile media cases. Your witness may be contaminated by the news reports and/or the comments of experts interviewed for the particular piece.

STOP!	Do not transport witnesses in the same police vehicle. Preventing interview contamination starts at the crime scene!

Conducting Interrogations

"If you can't get them to tell you the truth, get them to tell you lies."
— Joseph L. Giacalone

You often hear this topic called the "Art of Interrogation." In a way, it is an accurate depiction of the process as long as the student understands that even famous painters started out drawing stick figures. I can't stress the fact enough that the only way to get good at interrogating suspects is by doing it. You are going to make mistakes and sometimes you will fail in achieving your goal (a confession), but you will also obtain some confessions even when you were not at your very best. Conducting interrogations is similar to professional sports. Sometimes calls will go your way and sometimes they won't. It all evens out in the end. There are two (2) dangers that are inherent to conducting interrogations: Believing the lie and disbelieving the truth. The investigator must make every effort to not commit either one. There is not one thing or one tool that can help you identify if someone is lying. I would be lying if I said there was. The investigator builds their case carefully with the collection and examination of physical evidence, conducting interviews and interrogations and taking witness statements.

Television has taken advantage of the "Art of Interrogation" and introduced the highly popular show, *The Closer* on TNT. All that I can tell you is that there are no specialists who come in at the end of your interrogation and obtain the confession for you. If you have been paying attention so far, you would see that a "closer" would be at a huge disadvantage in an interrogation room because they could not possibly know all the requisite information on the case, especially what has recently transpired in the room. Television is fantasy and entertainment, that's all.

Ideally, the last step of every criminal investigation should be the interrogation. The investigator must find out all the available information regarding the case so that he/she would know if a suspect is corroborating what the police already know or that they are lying. An interrogation is not like conducting an interview. An interrogation is custodial, adversarial in nature and the goal is to develop a certainty of guilt. Even with advances in DNA and physical evidence to aid in establishing guilt, the words from the perpetrator's own mouth are usually what sinks them. An oral, written or recorded confession is powerful evidence.

CI Tip Sheet

We interview victims and witnesses.
We interrogate suspects/perpetrators.

We are going to build on the keys to **GREAT** Interviewing that we learned from conducting interviews by carrying those principles over into the interrogation room. For instance, the interrogator must know the facts of the case and must employ active listening in order to hear what is being said or not said. They must also be able to follow up and press for answers. The main difference between an interview and an interrogation is the custodial nature of the event. By the time an investigator is ready to interrogate, a suspect's guilt has been reasonably established from the physical evidence, victim/witness statements and/or identifications. Therefore, before we learn about the basics of interrogation techniques, the student must understand the legal implications and/or ramifications of custodial interrogation.

Custodial interrogation is when the police have a person under arrest (they are no longer free to leave) and they are going to ask the questions that are narrowly related to the event. Here is a question for the reader, "do you believe that once you are under arrest, the police must read the Miranda Warnings to you?" If you said yes to that question, you are a victim of television. Only in Hollywood do they start with, "You have the right to remain silent ..." as soon as the cuffs are slapped on. In reality, when the cuffs go on, those deep, dramatic words are rarely used. The police do not have to read a suspect their Miranda Warnings unless they have custody and they are going to interrogate (Giacalone, Writing.com 2004). Not every perpetrator will be interrogated.

CI Tip Sheet

Here is a quick math formula to help you remember when the police must read the Miranda Warnings:
CUSTODY + INTERROGATION = MIRANDA

Who was this guy Miranda anyway? Ernesto Miranda was arrested in the state of Arizona in 1963, where he confessed to the kidnapping and raping of a mildly retarded teenager. Miranda did not know that he had a right to remain silent, a right that came about from a strict interpretation of the Fifth Amendment to the Constitution when he signed his written statement "full knowledge of his legal rights." His conviction for the crime, partially based on his confession, was overturned and Ernesto was granted a new trial.

Supreme Court Justice Earl Warren presented the following procedural Fifth Amendment safeguards for future custodial interrogations:

> *The person in custody must, prior to interrogation, be clearly informed that he has the right to remain silent, and that anything he says will be used against him in court; he must be clearly informed that he has the right to consult with a lawyer and to have the lawyer with him during interrogation, and that, if he is indigent, a lawyer will be appointed to represent him. (Miranda v. Arizona 384 U.S. 436 (1966)).*

The improperly obtained confession could not be used against him in the retrial. His girlfriend's testimony, however, could be used. He was convicted for the second time. Miranda served several years in prison for his horrific crime; he was subsequently released back into society. Justice however, would not be denied. In 1976, Miranda was stabbed to death during a bar fight. When the police arrested a suspect for the murder, the accused refused to make incriminating statements and invoked his Miranda Rights. No one in the bar at the time was willing to come forward and pick out the perpetrator. Without the proper identification, the suspect was released. The murder was never solved because this suspect invoked his right to remain silent. There's irony for you.

The Miranda decision is not a constitutional right but it has been given a constitutional setting in the Fifth and Sixth Amendments. The Miranda decision made it mandatory that law enforcement officers across the United States read the Miranda Warnings to any individual in police custody who will be questioned. If not, any incriminating statements will be inadmissible. The police should read the Miranda Warnings from a card word-for-word (Figure 7.1), but may use simple direct language if the situation calls for it (*Duckworth v. Eagen* 492 U.S. 195 (1989)). However, the investigator must document how and why he/she used other language to explain the individual's Miranda Warnings. The request for a lawyer must be unambiguous. In the case *Davis v. United States*, 512 US 452 (1994), the suspect says, "Maybe I should talk to a lawyer." The Supreme Court said the request for a lawyer must be clear.

The Miranda decision has been applauded by civil libertarians and disputed by crime control advocates since it happened. However civil libertarians shouldn't be that excited because according to statistics 80% of people in custody waive their Miranda Warnings (O'Neill, 2002). Over the years, like we saw with search and seizure, exceptions to the "rule" have been carved out from the Miranda decision. Crime control advocates have applauded these changes. Generally, these exceptions have been made to protect the lives of citizens and the police.

In the case *Rhode Island v. Innis* 446 US 291 (1980), any spontaneous utterance or statement made by a defendant in custody can be incriminating as long as it was not in response to a question posed by the police. For example, the police arrest a suspect for murdering his wife and put him in the interrogation room. The police are preparing a strategy for the interrogation when the suspect says, "I want my lawyer." The police stop planning the interrogation and start with the booking process. During fingerprinting, the suspect says to the investigator, "She was cheating on me. I did what I had to do. I killed her." This statement was a confession or a direct acknowledgment of guilt. It was used against the suspect in a court of law, even though he previously invoked his right to counsel.

In the case, *New York v. Quarles* 467 US 649 (1984), we see the "public safety" exception. This decision allows law enforcement to question a suspect in custody without the benefit of Miranda when an exigent circumstance exists that requires protection of the public; in this case a gun hidden in a grocery store (Giacalone, Writing.com (2004).

Figure 7.1. Sample Miranda Waiver Form

Any Police Department
City of Anywhere

Defendant: _____

Miranda Warnings:

You must understand your rights before we can ask you any questions:

You have the right to remain silent. Do you understand?   Yes/No_____ _____
                                                                          Initials

If you give up that right to remain silent, anything you say can and
will be used against you in the court of law. Do you understand? Yes/No_____ _____
                                                                          Initials

You have the right to speak with an attorney for advice before we
ask you any questions and to have them with you during
questioning. Do you understand?   Yes/No_____ _____
                                                                          Initials

If you cannot afford an attorney, one will be appointed to you
without charge before any questioning if you wish. Do you understand? Yes/No_____ _____
                                                                          Initials

If you decide to answer questions now without an attorney present,
you still have the right to stop answering questions at any time. Do
you understand?   Yes/No_____ _____
                                                                          Initials

Now that I have read your Miranda Warnings to you and knowing that you have these rights and are willing to waive these rights voluntarily, intelligently and knowingly without threats or promises of any kind, are you willing to answer questions and make a statement of the facts?

Signature of Defendant: _____ Date:_____ Time:_____

Witness Signature: _____ Date:_____ Time: _____
Witness Signature: _____ Date:_____ Time: _____

Does the Right to Counsel attach during other situations other than custodial interrogation? Yes. When the defendant's lawyer has **A CAR**:

Asks for a lawyer

Contacted by lawyer
Accusatory instrument has been filed
Retains a lawyer for the matter under investigation

ASKS FOR A LAWYER

If the suspect states unequivocally, "I want a lawyer," all interrogations must stop until his/her lawyer is present.

CONTACTED BY LAWYER*

If a lawyer contacts the police looking for his/her client, the right to counsel attaches. All interrogations must stop unless the lawyer is present. This presents a problem for big police departments because the lawyer doesn't even have to know what precinct his/her client is in. If the lawyer told one cop in the department, he told everybody. It would be incumbent on the precinct where the call was made to send out a message to all the other commands to notify them that this person is represented by counsel and that all questioning must cease.

*The Supreme Court decision in *Moran v. Burbine* 475 U.S. 412 (1986), stated that the Miranda Rights are personal and can be invoked only by the suspect and that the police had no obligation to inform an individual that voluntarily, intelligently and knowingly waived their rights that a lawyer had called the police and said he represented the suspect. However, state supreme courts in Michigan, Florida and Illinois as well as local jurisdictions, have ignored *Moran v. Burbine* and expanded suspect's rights requiring interrogation to stop once a lawyer contacts the police. Investigators must know what cases their jurisdictions follow. Ignorance will not be a defense!

ACCUSATORY INSTRUMENT HAS BEEN FILED

If an indictment (True Bill) has been handed down or an arrest warrant has been issued, an absolute right to counsel comes attached with it. This is why investigators don't like obtaining arrest warrants—they can't speak to the suspect about the case unless their lawyer is present.

RETAINS A LAWYER FOR THE MATTER UNDER INVESTIGATION

If a suspect is not in custody and has retained a lawyer for the particular matter under investigation and the police are aware of it, they cannot talk to him about that particular case. But, since he is not in custody, the police can talk to him about an unrelated matter without his lawyer being present. For instance, Johnny Jones was arrested for a robbery and is currently on bail. No matter if Johnny hired a lawyer or not, he was provided one free of charge at his arraignment. Johnny is released on his own recognizance and given another court date to show up. The police want to question Johnny about a murder they think he was involved in. Can they talk to him about the murder without his lawyer present? Yes. Would the answer change if he is in custody still on the robbery? Yes. If you are in custody and awaiting trial, the police cannot talk to you about any case, related or not unless your lawyer is present.

CI Tip Sheet

When investigators can speak to suspects that have lawyers:

Not in Jail on the related crime—No
Not in Jail on an unrelated crime—Yes
In Jail on an unrelated crime or not—No

It is difficult to defend the argument that the police "didn't know he had a lawyer" because if the investigator conducted the proper background checks, he would have found out. The lawyer's name is listed on the Criminal Justice records and other court records. If an investigator interviews or interrogates any suspect in direct violation of the Fifth Amendment, any information received will be inadmissible.

You may have never thought of it this way, but the oldest recorded interrogation is the Bible story of Adam and Eve. Adam and Eve's story contains valuable lessons for student interrogators:

- A separation of "coconspirators" before questioning
- The use of open- and closed-ended questions
- The use of base line questions to develop a normal pattern of answers
- The "Interrogator" knew the answers to the questions
  - o   He asked to test truthfulness

- The "Interrogator" used the suspect's nonverbal body language to decipher uneasiness with certain questions
- The "Interrogator" did not reveal information about the investigation to the suspects
- The suspects ultimately lied
  - o   Used emphatic denials at first
  - o   Finger pointing and alibi crafting to obfuscate the truth
- The "Interrogator" used questions and their answers to "get them" off their denials and to the truth
- The case ended in punishment

When the heat is on in the interrogation room, turn up the **AC**! The investigator's goal in an interrogation is to obtain either an **A**dmission or a **C**onfession. Ideally, a confession is the desired result.

An **admission** is a statement that self-incriminates, but falls short of owning up to committing the act. "I was there, but I didn't kill him." An admission can open the door to a confession. Further development of the admission may lead to the name of the perpetrator (if not the person you are interrogating). An admission could be used to charge someone for a crime, so it holds a tremendous amount of weight in an investigation. The idea is to get the person talking.

In cases where there were multiple perpetrators, the admission will more than likely be used as testimony against the main perpetrator. A thorough investigation can yield an admission by confronting the suspect with evidence of his/her whereabouts. For instance, video surveillance footage recovered from a canvass showing the suspect inside of the grocery store around the time of the murder, or cell phone records placing them in the area at a particular time.

A **confession** is when an individual acknowledges their guilt by incriminating oneself as the perpetrator of a crime. "Yes, I shot her." This is, of course, the ultimate goal of an interrogation, but not always possible. Sometimes you have to settle for an admission and develop the rest of the case around that by destroying the suspect's alibi, obtaining witness statements and recovering physical evidence.

The question is how do we find our way to the truth? You get there by doing what you do when you go someplace for the first time: you look it up on a map, or online, or you ask someone else who has already been there. You need a road map for where you are going because each interrogation is like a road trip that involves many traffic jambs, tie ups and U-turns. Sometimes, when things aren't going well, you have to get off the main road and take the back streets or a dirt road to get to where you have to be. It may be long and rough, but the goal is the same: arrive at the desired destination.

Most things begin with a planning and preparation phase before anything else. An interrogation is no different. The case investigator must thoroughly review the case and speak with other investigators that helped obtain information from canvasses. Sometimes, the case investigator is not the best choice to conduct the interrogation. There may be another investigator who has more experience or that may have struck up a good rapport with the suspect, an essential element of any interview or interrogation. This decision will ultimately be made by the investigator supervisor, unless a previous agreement has been reached. However, other factors such as culture and gender issues could come into play such as the nature of the crime. For instance, an individual has a long history of abuse on women and now he is the prime suspect in the brutal murder of his wife. The investigating supervisor may decide to have a male officer conduct the interview. But it may work to your advantage as well. Would a female investigator make the suspect even more arrogant and cocky that he may slip?

Investigators have to remember that their interrogation starts with the first interaction between you and the suspect. The term "you" also refers to your fellow officers/detectives. When the suspect is treated badly, it only makes your job more difficult.

In cases with multiple perpetrators the decision has to be made on who should be interrogated first. The decision can be based on at least three (3) choices:

1. **The individual who has the most to lose**—The person, who may be willing to "roll over" on the others to save their own skin when in a tough spot, may be the first choice. A three-time loser or someone who just violated their parole are examples of individuals who have the most to lose.
2. **The weakest link**—The person who has the most to lose.
3. **The person who has never been to prison before**—The individual who is new to the arrest process and hanging on the cell bars may be a good starting point.

As you can see, planning and preparation are important prerequisites to any investigation.

An investigator must ensure that their plan has an **EKG**:

Environmental/setting considerations
Knowledge of how and why
Ground work on all parties involved

ENVIRONMENTAL/SETTING CONSIDERATIONS

Where the interrogation takes place plays an important role in obtaining a confession or admission. There is no argument that the location is in the advantage of the police. The most important factor when preparing and planning an interview is officer safety. A complete and thorough search of the suspect must be made before they are put in the interview room, AKA "The Box." Anything that could aid in escape or cause injury must be removed from the individual. By now you have seen the video of the perpetrator placed in the interrogation room and removes a firearm from his pants and blows his brains out. Those San Bernadino officers were very lucky; he could have easily turned the gun on them. The moral of the story, don't take it for granted that the last detective searched the suspect. In addition, any electronic devices must be removed from the suspect. Investigators should never be armed in the interview room.

The room should be small, free from distractions (phones, newspapers, etc.), with no wanted posters on the walls and be equipped with a one-way mirror. Are you asking, why no wanted posters? Think about it for a moment. You are sitting in the interview room and you know what you did or didn't do. You are waiting for the investigators to come back into the room. You may be nervous and or bored. Your eyes start to dart around the room. Now you are looking at all of these photos of persons wanted for all types of heinous crimes. You start to think about the predicament you got yourself into. You'd probably dig your heels in and fight for your freedom. No?

The room should contain three (3) chairs, two (2) for the investigators (comfortable with wheels) and one (1) for the suspect (hard back no wheels) and a small table that should be off to the side. One of the investigators will play the role of note taker and will not participate in the interrogation unless asked to by the case investigator (Figure 7.2). Note takers are like children, they are seen and not heard.

The reason the investigator's chair has wheels on it is so that they can move in on the suspect when warranted to exert pressure (more on this later) and the suspect's chair is hard backed so it is easier to watch non-verbal body language. It is difficult to pick up any clues that the suspect is uncomfortable when they look as if they are watching television in their living room.

Figure 7.2   A look inside of the interrogation room, which is also called "The Box."

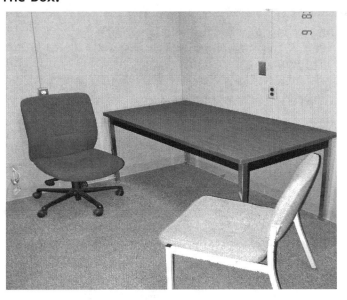

© 2012 This photo appears courtesy of Hudson County Prosecutor Edward J. De Fazio

If you examine Figure 7.2 carefully, you should have noticed three (3) things that aren't the norm for interrogation rooms:

1. ***The suspect has his/her back to the door***—There are two (2) reasons why you don't want the suspect looking at the door. First, it is easier for another investigator to grab your attention when warranted, but most importantly the suspect isn't staring at the exit thinking, "That's my way out!" The investigator has to be concerned about an escape attempt as well as a physical assault. When suspects get desperate they resort to desperate measures.

2. ***The desk is off to the side***—A desk between the suspect and the investigators is a barrier that benefits the suspect. It is something that they can "hide" behind. It also prevents the investigators from observing and identifying any nonverbal body cues given off by the suspect. Whenever possible, the desk should be pushed off to the side. Also, being close to the suspect causes them stress and anxiety. We all have our personal space that we don't want people in, especially strangers. The closer the investigator moves in the more uncomfortable it is for the suspect. According to Edward Hall, an anthropologist and the father of Proxemics, which is the study of comfortable distances between people (Figure 7.3), we have four (4) distinct zones of space: Intimate space—6" to 18"; Personal distance—18" to 4 feet; Social distance—4 to 12 feet; and Public distance—more than 12 feet (Rosenbloom, NYT, 11/16/06). Moving closer to a suspect is done gradually in stages as the investigator builds the case against the suspect. It gives the "we're closing in on you" feeling. However, if the investigator moves in too quickly, the suspect may shut down.

3. ***The suspect is not looking into the mirror***—You don't want the suspect looking into the mirror either. He/she may suspect that there is someone on the other side watching and listening, especially when they are in the room alone. Also, over time, those mirrors lose their sheen and you can see through them. You would never want the suspect to see the complainant right through the glass.

Figure 7.3.   Proxemics

© 2012 This photo appears courtesy of Hudson County Prosecutor Edward J. De Fazio

KNOWLEDGE OF HOW AND WHY

The investigator must know every investigative step taken and every fact that has been obtained. They will speak to other investigators, medical examiners, victims, witnesses and review lab reports and crime scene photos. This effort is to ensure thoroughness, accuracy and allow the investigator to establish the credibility of the investigation to the suspect. During the interrogation the investigator will drop "hints" on the quality of the investigation and the amount of information that the police already know. The investigator may be looking to find a few of the pieces of the puzzle that are missing and address the elements of **MOM** (**M**eans, **O**pportunity and **M**otive).

The investigator has to be able to ask the right questions to "kill" the eventual denial and/or alibi "person." Like a villain in the James Bond movies, the investigator has to understand that the suspect is going to drop **OIL** to evade telling the truth to the police:

Omit
Impede
Lie

The only way an investigator can overcome this is to make sure that they are prepared. Preparation keeps the interrogator focused, which allows them the opportunity to bring the suspect back to the conversation when they wander, leave out important facts and fabricate details of the incident.

GROUND WORK ON ALL PARTIES INVOLVED

Knowing who you are dealing with can give the investigator some insight on how to interrogate them. The individual's age, education level, job and experience with the Criminal Justice System are factors that must be considered before any interrogation begins. An investigator cannot interrogate an individual who has a rap sheet as long as his arm the same way he/she would a first-time offender. As previously stated, the investigator will decide who to speak with first in a multiple-suspect case based on their background.

Don't forget the obvious. The investigator should have obtained the 911 caller tapes and listened to them. There are three (3) questions that should be examined about the call: What was the call about? Who was the call about? and How was the call made?

The groundwork includes more than past interactions with the police, but also information about the suspect's whereabouts before and after the crime. This can play a pivotal role in the investigation. In provides critical timeframes for the investigator to prove/disprove alibis and statements. For example, it can help identify the approximate location of an individual via a subpoena of their cell phone GPS coordinates. It's hard to explain that you weren't "there," when your phone puts you there. To avoid the retort, "I lent my phone to a friend," I would have asked him if he had his phone with him or did he make any calls prior to telling him about the subpoena so I could lock him down into his statement. An investigative step like this takes time to develop and this is why you always want to interrogate last.

The investigator can also use the information retrieved from the Vehicle Canvass that was conducted in and around the crime scene. You wouldn't confront them with, "Can you explain why your car was around the corner from the scene?" "Yeah, I lent it to this guy" and then spend the next hour trying to find out who the "guy" is, when there never was one in the first place. Instead, you could ask "Do you know where your car is currently?" and followed up with, "John did you lend your car to anyone?" After you have established that his car is in his driveway and he hasn't lent it to anyone, now we hit him with the "Can you explain ...?" question.

The Interrogation Process

The investigator is now at the crossroads on when and where to start. Getting ready to conduct an interrogation is very similar to getting ready to act in a play. It's show time. You've memorized your lines, prepared the "stage," your supporting cast is in place and you're now ready to perform. The investigator will walk into the room and introduce themselves if it wasn't done already. This introduction is very important. The investigator should extend their hand, make eye contact and give the suspect a firm handshake. A firm handshake exudes confidence and sets the tone early.

The investigator must have a positive attitude before entering the room. No professional ball player takes the field thinking, "We're going to lose today" (unless they play for any of the teams that I like). So why would you ever go into the interrogation room saying, "I'm going to go in there and talk to this moron, but I'm never going to get him to confess. He is probably going to ask for a scumbag lawyer." Walk in with a bad attitude and you will lose. An interrogation is a battle of wits. I'm sure that the perpetrator is not saying, "I might as well confess because I really am guilty." After the initial greeting, don't blow it by saying something stupid, yelling and screaming and banging on tables. I've seen it and it doesn't work. "Listen you puke. I'm going to bury you under the prison. You're despicable. Now, tell me why you did it." A successful interrogation is like baking a cake. It all starts with preparation of the ingredients, in this instance the facts of the incident. Now you need the right choice of words, a little rapport building and mix in a little BS.

Remember, there is custody and interrogation, so what is necessary at this stage? Right. The investigator will read and/or explain the Miranda Warnings to the suspect. If the suspect wishes to answer questions, the investigator will have them initial each line of the Miranda Warnings and sign a department form. That form must be signed by the case investigator and an additional witness. A refusal to initial the paper or sign their name does not invoke their right to counsel. In order to obtain a valid waiver of one's rights, the individual must do so voluntarily, intelligently and knowingly. Silence can never be construed as consent.

CI Tip Sheet

In order to have a valid waiver for conducting a search
without a warrant or to waive Miranda it must be given:

Voluntarily
Intelligently
Knowingly

What can make a waiver of one's Miranda Rights invalid?

PAD can make a waiver invalid:

Promises or threats
- o   Promises of time off or other court consideration (only the ADA can do this!)
- o   Threats to deport them or their family
- o   Threats to arrest other family members

Any use of force to get the confession (self-explanatory)

Denial of essential accommodations
- o   Food, bathroom, breaks, sleep

Remember, in an interrogation the investigator will do most of the talking. There are four (4) parts of an interrogation that the student investigator can use as their **ROAD** map to help find their way to the truth:

Reduce resistance
Obtain an admission
Admission development
Documented on paper

REDUCE RESISTANCE

As stated earlier, an interrogation is adversarial in nature, so resistance will be evident from the very beginning. Do you think someone is really going to say, "Hi detective, I know you have to go to your kid's softball game, so I'll make this quick. Yes, I shot Johnny Jones because he encroached on my drug-dealing operation. Please lock me up and send me to jail the rest of my life. If you give me a piece of paper I'll be more than happy to write it all out for you." Sounds ridiculous, right? The stakes are very high for the suspect. He/she could go to jail the rest of their lives. As one would surmise, resistance will be the strongest at the very beginning of the interrogation, so an investigator must be careful not to push too hard at the onset of the interrogation. Remember, an interrogation is not a conversation. You start by accusing the suspect of a heinous crime! How do you think they are going to react? Have you ever asked the question, "Do you know why you are here?" as an opener? You may be surprised at the answers you get.

Resistance comes in the form of denials. There are two (2) types of denials: the emphatic denial and the explanatory denial. An emphatic denial is one where the suspect will refuse any knowledge or participation in the crime. "I don't know what you are talking about. I wasn't there," or the famous, "It wasn't me." An explanatory denial is one where the suspect will offer up an excuse why they couldn't be involved. I come from a very religious family. My mother always made sure we went to church (Zulawski & Wicklander, 2001, pp. 343–358)." "I'm married, why would I have sex with that girl?"

Denials can develop because the suspect wants some **PIE**:

Past experience with the Criminal Justice System
Interrogator's lack of experience, poor choice of approach and/or plan of attack
Environment is not conducive for interrogation purposes—timing, location, distractions

It is the investigator's job to identify who is telling the truth and who is lying. It is not that easy to do. If it were, we'd all be in trouble! How do people act, how do they talk/behave when they lie? Access to videos and newscasts over the Internet allows the student to train themselves to detect lies. Learn from those who have already done it and got caught! Choose from anyone that we know who, for a fact, lied and study his before and after statements as well as his non-verbal body language and tone of voice, such as: Richard Nixon, Bill Clinton, Mark Hacking, Susan Smith, Alex Rodriguez or Scott Peterson to name a few. Listen to what they said and how they did or didn't say it. Study the words they chose and their body language. An investigator in training could learn a lot from these simple clips.

The strength of a denial is also important to the astute investigator. They can come in two strengths: strong and weak. Bill Clinton's infamous speech to the American people would be a great example of a strong denial:

> *I want to say one thing to the American people. I want you to listen to me I'm going to say this again. I did not have sexual relations with that woman. Miss Lewinsky. I never told anybody to lie, not a single time, never. These allegations are false and I need to go back to work for the American people. Thank you.* (YouTube, posted on August 30, 2006)

We now know that everything he said, with the exception of thank you, was a lie. The idea behind using a strong denial is to shut the accuser down, which is exactly what the president was able to do. It can be very effective against anyone that is not sure of themselves. I want the student to play the video repeatedly and try to identify any signs of deception. They may not be recognizable at first, but you can pick them up as you train your eyes and ears to see and hear the lies. Former President Clinton appears that he is telling the truth. He makes good eye contact and points his finger as if he is annoyed at the allegation. However, there are some leaks. He has what I call "fake anger." He sounds angry, but his facial expressions don't show it—wrinkling of the forehead, narrowing of the eyebrows, etc. The ironic part is if you can find the video for the Nixon "Watergate" speech, it is eerily similar to Bill Clinton's "Monicagate" speech.

A weak denial is one that is given rather sheepishly. For example, listen to baseball superstar Alex Rodriguez's denial to Katie Couric about the use of performance-enhancing drugs (Gaines, 2009).

KC: "For the record, did you ever use steroids, human growth hormone or any other performance enhancing substance?"
AR: "No."
KC: "Have you ever been tempted to use any of those things?"
AR: [slight pause and head shake] "No."
KC: "You never felt like, this guy is doing it. Maybe I should look into this too. He's getting better numbers, playing better ball?"
AR: "I never felt overmatched on the baseball field. I've always been in a very strong, dominate position. And I felt if I did my work since I've done since I was, ahh, you know, a rookie back in Seattle. I didn't have a problem competing at any level, so, uh, no."

You can see the difference in the tone of voice, the inflection in the voice, the calmness and the words chosen as compared to Clinton's strong denial. However, he does not answer many of the questions right away. He stalls for time, which is another clue that the person may not be telling the truth. There are a few instances where the viewer can pick up changes in facial expressions when certain questions are asked; see if you can find them (see References for the link). This is a great video to watch because, like many interviews, the interviewee knows the questions ahead of time and he still had difficulty answering them.

STOP!	Did the suspect answer your question?
	Did he evade your question?
	Ask again until you are satisfied with the response.

The real crux of the situation becomes, "How does the investigator overcome a denial?" The investigator never wants this to turn into a schoolyard argument: "Did not," "Did to," "Did not," Did to," etc. An investigator can combat denials by presenting alternatives or excuses on why the person did the crime. An investigator can gain the advantage over the suspect by offering them a way out by allowing them to think that what they did was all right. It is an opportunity for the suspect to save face.

Excuses can take many forms, but it is always a good idea to a make a **BID** for an admission or a confession using one of these:

Blame game
Increase feelings of guilt or shame
Diminish the seriousness of the crime

Other excuses do exist, but these are probably the most popular ones employed by investigators. If you haven't noticed yet, an investigator must be good at the lying game too!

BLAME GAME

Have you ever noticed that when someone gets involved in a car accident it is *never* their fault? It is always the other guy's fault. Someone always came from nowhere, was driving too fast, or hit me, etc. The person telling you the story is never at fault because they are hiding much of the truth, probably from embarrassment. Individuals like to fix blame and do so quickly. For this reason, I believe there is no better way to get the perpetrator to feel okay about what he has done than to play the "blame game." The failure to take responsibility for one's actions has fueled the need for using the blame game. When an investigator places blame squarely on the shoulders of the victim, it allows the suspect to relax and feel better at the moment. It sounds harsh, but you don't actually believe or feel what you are saying. The investigator lies to the suspect to get him to open up about the event. For instance, in a rape case, an investigator can cast blame on the victim with any of the following questions or statements:

- "I know she came on to you, how could she resist a good-looking guy like you? You didn't do anything that any ordinary guy wouldn't have done."
- "Listen. I get it. You spent a lot of money on dinner and you expected something in return. I know I would. It's a guy thing."
- "I saw that dress she was wearing. I wouldn't be able to control my urges either."
- "The way she was dressed, she as asking for it."
- "It was a spur of the moment thing. It just happened."

In a murder investigation an investigator could use any of the following:

- "We have thoroughly investigated this case and discovered that you were only defending yourself. He (insert victim's name) would still be alive today if he hadn't attacked you first."
- "If I came home and found my spouse in bed with someone else, I would have stabbed him to death, too. Their actions and lack of respect for you in your own bed drove you to do it."

- "Listen to me. If she was so intoxicated and talked to you that way, she would still be here right now."
- "I know you really loved your wife. It was just the fact that your marriage was breaking up that really took a toll on you. It must be tough."

As sick as these statements/questions sound, the idea is to get the suspect to talk carelessly about the event. These statements/questions are so repulsive that it is difficult to say them. This is where your acting ability comes to play. Dissociate yourself from the reality of your statements and do it. If he/she is talking, then you are doing your job. Keep going. This is when you will find out if you established a good rapport with the individual. The investigator should watch for some nonverbal quest that the person is agreeing with you, such as nodding his/her head up and down. If the suspect feels he/she has to justify their actions then he/she will buy into the "blame game."

INCREASE FEELINGS OF GUILT OR SHAME

Religion and your mother are the greatest causes for feelings of guilt and shame. No one in my opinion does it better! Cultural or religious issues are easy to develop and can act as divine rationalizations.

- "Sam, Margaret is a very devout Catholic girl. She was saving herself for marriage. Now her life and her plans are totally changed by this event."
- "Fred. Do you know how upset your mom is right now? She's totally heartbroken. But I know she raised you to do the right thing. My mom is just like yours and she would want me to come clean too."
- "Who am I to pass judgment on you? I haven't done everything right in my life either."
- "Listen. I know how it is. I wasn't always a cop you know."
- "I know it's hard to be the 1%. Have you ever tried to support a family on a cop's salary? The company you work for is ripping off everyone, so why not get back at them?"

DIMINISH THE SERIOUSNESS OF THE CRIME

When you diminish the seriousness of the crime, you are providing an open door for the suspect to step in and explain their actions. The suspect believes that a diminished crime will equal diminished time. Shakespeare once said, "A rose by any other name is still a rose." It doesn't matter what words you use to diminish the crime. It is what it is. The investigator must be careful using the stark words of murder, rape, robbed, stabbed, beat, etc., to the suspect, especially when attempting to diminish the event. When you read the following statements pay close attention to the italicized words and phrases.

- "I know you had consensual intercourse with that young girl. You didn't force her like she claims."
- "You're not as bad as [fill in the blank] that did XY and Z."
- "When your wife got hurt, where were you standing?"
- "We know you got caught up in this whole thing and that you had nothing to do with planning the incident. But, someone passed away."
- "It was an accident. It could have happened to any one of us."

OBTAIN AN ADMISSION

The investigator is now at the stage where the suspect has been thoroughly convinced about the quality of the investigation and about the facts that the police have already laid out. An admission confirms the interrogator's assertion that the suspect was involved when he/she obtains one. It is an acknowledgment of their involvement in the incident. The investigator has listened to the **OIL** (Omit, Impede, Lie) the suspect has dropped so far and has digested the suspect's alibi. The suspect has presented excuses for their behavior and is now primed for the investigator to move in.

Obtaining an admission can be a lengthy affair. Is there any limit on how long you can interrogate somebody? The answer is no, as long as the person was given adequate bathroom breaks, something to eat and time to rest. These events must be documented on a department form (Figure 7.4), an investigator's report and, if possible, written in the suspect's final statement (see Documented on paper below). It would be extremely difficult for the suspect's attorney to mount a defense that the police coerced the confession from his client.

Figure 7.4

Person Interviewed: _____   Date: _____
Case # _____

TIME		LOCATION	OFFICERS PRESENT	ACTIVITY
FROM	TO			
1200	1215	54 Squad - Interview Room	None	Alone
1215	1315	do	Giacalone & Weaver	Rights & Interview
1315	1345	do	Giacalone	Bathroom / Refused food
1345	1500	do	Giacalone & Weaver	Interview / Confession
1500	1600	do	Alone	Lunch

| TIME | | LOCATION | OFFICERS PRESENT | ACTIVITY |
FROM	TO			
1600	1630	do	Sister: Joy Alleto	Chatting
1630	1700	do	Giacalone & Weaver	Written Statement
1700	1715	do	Alone	None
1715		Removal to Central Booking	Giacalone & Weaver	

If you noticed one thing about the example interview sheet above is that each minute of custody is accounted for. Initially, the suspect is left alone for only fifteen minutes. I am not a big fan of letting someone sit and contemplate why they are there for a long time. In my experience, I learned that the longer they stay alone, the harder their denials are in the beginning. Don't wait a long time before you go in especially if they have been through the routine before. When the person is in the room, take that opportunity to learn more about your subject through police computer checks.

The investigator will now begin to poke holes in the suspect's story. For example, the suspect denies ever being at the location. Getting them to come off of their denial and into an admission could be as simple as showing them a still photo taken from a video surveillance camera of the suspect at the scene or asking them, "If someone saw you in the area, how would you explain it?" Here is another example: The investigator is questioning a suspect about a rape and asks, "Do you know Mary Jane?" "I don't know the girl." The investigator then shows a photo of the victim. "Nope. Never saw here before in my life." "Have you ever had intercourse with Mary Jane?" "What's the matter with you man? I told you, I don't know her!" The investigator pulls an official report from the case folder and hands it to the suspect. "Do you know what this is?" "No, what is it?" "That (insert suspect's name) is a DNA report from the medical examiner's office. I want you to pay special attention to the second paragraph. Can you explain to me how your DNA ended up inside of the victim?" Then the Oh S*%$ light bulb goes off. "Ohhhhhhh, that Mary Jane."

An investigator obtains an admission by knowing the case, having the facts, crafting the right questions and choosing the right moments to drop them on the suspect. If you think that you have enough information, dig deeper! When investigators are ill prepared or lack the experience terrible things can happen to the case. Here is a small example of how not to conduct an interrogation. The following snippet was extracted from the O.J. Simpson statement (November 29, 1994 issue of *STAR* magazine):

Det. Vannatter: "So what time do you think you got back home, actually physically got home?"

Simpson: "Seven-something."

Det. Vannatter: "Seven-something? And then you left, and ..."

Simpson: "Yeah, I'm trying to think, did I leave? You know, I'm
                    always ... I had to run and get my daughter some flowers.
                    I was actually doing the recital, so I rushed and got her
                    some flowers, and I came home, and then I called Paula as
                    I was going to her house, and Paula wasn't home."

Det. Vannatter: Paula is your girlfriend?

"Paula is your girlfriend" would not have been the follow-up question I
would have asked. If you were the detective in this scenario, what would be
a good follow-up question(s) to O.J.'s answers? Remember, one of the
elements of **MOM** (Means, Opportunity and Motive) that must be established right away is the opportunity. Clearly, the detectives in this interrogation failed to establish the timeline by accepting "seven-something" for
the time.

The more you do this, the more you realize that the largest gaps in any
questionable story revolve around three (3) things: Time, People and
Details. Anytime you discover a gap in the story, the person may be
omitting important information. However, if you are not actively listening
to the story then you will never catch the gaps.

ADMISSION DEVELOPMENT

Once the investigator has obtained an admission, he has to develop it
into a confession. The hardest point to determine in an interrogation is
when a suspect is ready to confess. If the investigator moves too early, he
may back the suspect into a denial. If he moves too late, he may never
reach that point again. This is a good time to kill the suspect's alibi. "You
stated earlier that you were at home watching television on the night of the
incident. Is that correct?" "Yes, it is." "You also said that you ate pizza for
dinner. Is that correct?" "Yes, it is." First, a home alone, watching television
scenario is not a very good alibi, but you'd never believe how often it is
used. Here you can see the investigator is getting ready to kill the alibi by
locking his statements down. What part would you attack first? I'm almost
positive that most of you would start out asking questions about the
television: "What shows? At what time? What was the episode about?" are
not bad questions, but, you're rather limited to the number of questions
that you can ask. Don't you think he is ready for that? Now is the time to
throw him that curve ball. Let's take a look at the "pizza" instead and see
how many questions I can come up with:

1.   Did you make it yourself?
2.   Was it store bought?
3.   Was it delivered?
4.   What type of pizza did you have? (Round or Square)
5.   What time did you get it/have it delivered?
6.   What topping(s) did you have?
7.   How much did it cost?

8. What location did you buy it or have it delivered from?
9. Did you give the delivery person a tip?
10. Was the delivery person male/female?
11. What race was the delivery person?
12. Was the pizzeria busy when you were there?
13. How did you get to the pizzeria?
14. How many slices did you have?
15. What was the phone number you called?
16. What did the delivery person look like?

These are sixteen questions off the top of my head and you have to consider any additional questions that may come from the answers they give. If you noticed one thing about my questions, what would it be? All the answers can be verified! You may be able to think of even more, but you see there was a lot more versatility with the "pizza" than with the "television" and your suspect won't be prepared for it. You should also note that I wouldn't ask these questions in any particular order. This way you can easily trip them up if they are lying to you. Also, an alibi like this would be a good opportunity to use the "backwards to forwards" technique of vetting an alibi. It requires the suspect to tell his/her story backwards to the beginning. Anyone who made up the story would not be able to do it.

When the investigator effectively "kills off" the alibi person or story, they are ready to move beyond the admission and into a confession or a detailed statement about who was responsible for the incident in codefendant cases.

STOP!	After obtaining an admission or a confession and before ending the interrogation, ask the suspect if he/she would like to add or change anything.

DOCUMENTED ON PAPER

Documenting the admission or confession on paper is of paramount importance. It is ideal to have the suspect write their own confession out in their own handwriting. If the individual cannot write, the police are allowed to write it for them and he/she can OK it by signing their name to it. I strongly encourage you to let them write it themselves the best they can. The defense attorney will paint them as your words and not his client's. Taking the final written statement encompasses the sequence of events that took place during the interrogation. They will include the bathroom breaks, meal and sleep breaks. Nothing can kill a defense lawyer's argument about coercion more than a statement made by the suspect on how well they were treated! But the most important reason to obtain a written, signed statement is that it locks the suspect down and provides the opportunity for the investigator to conduct Statement Analysis (see below). Often, the suspect becomes imprisoned by their own words.

At the conclusion of the interrogation, the investigator should present a lined, legal-sized pad and pen to the perpetrator and ask for their narrative or "explanation [not a statement]" in writing. Because most inter-rogations are recorded, this is also another powerful example of how the suspect was giving information freely without any coercion. Even though the investigator is at the end of the process, he/she should continue to avoid using words that enlist "consequences" for the suspect's actions. "Hi John, please write down for me how you killed Mary and how you dumped her body alongside the road. This way the jury doesn't have any qualms about sending you to the electric chair," would not be a good way to start off. If necessary, the investigator will sell the idea, "Don't you want to get your side down on the record?" or "Don't you want to explain that it was an accident and that it could have happened to anybody?"

The investigators should stay in the room during the writing of the statement and if possible have an additional witness in the room. The investigator should fight the urge to write it for them when they are totally capable of doing so themselves, especially when you are exhausted. Writing the statement for the suspect provides too much fodder for the defense attorney. It is too easily portrayed as "these are your words detective and not my client's, correct?" When the suspect is done, review their statement with them to make sure it is complete. If there are any errors or changes, ask the suspect to initial each change. The investigator should then number each page of the statement: 1 of 6, 2 of 6, etc., and ask the suspect to initial each page. All parties involved in the statement, suspect, case investigator and witness should sign the last page of the statement and put the date and time.

Once the investigator is satisfied with the results he/she will leave the room with the admission/confession and especially the pen! Investigators can never get sloppy and leave a potential weapon or escape device behind. The investigator must type a report detailing the events that transpired during the interrogation and the results, whether they were able to obtain an admission or confession and a written statement. The term negative results are never used on any police reports. There is always something to report.

Statement Analysis: Not Just the Written Word

"What we see depends mainly on what we look for."
— Sir John Lubbock

At this moment you are glad it's over. You got the suspect to confess and write a narrative statement of the events and now it's time for you to go home. Wrong. When you obtain the written statement you must read it. Written statements can provide additional information that the suspect was unwilling to say, but somehow the subconscious took over and wrote it on paper. If you look at a written statement objectively it can be considered another "crime scene." It happens more than you think. Statement Analysis is another tool for the investigator to use to find their way to the truth.

There are a few good books on the subject as well as a few good training classes with different tactics and instructor experiences. Each book/class has its own benefits, so I strongly encourage you to read them and/or take a class. Good training is something we can never have enough of. I am going to provide you with the basics necessary so that the new investigator can conduct a cursory Statement Analysis.

The words we use receive the most attention first, then the face, body and voice. It is ironic that the words and facial expressions are the least trustworthy. Why? Everyone knows that is what you will be focusing on. So they try to mask their expressions and choose their words carefully. However, when they write, most of that goes out the window because the subconscious mind takes over.

The first step in Statement Analysis has nothing to do with the actual process. The investigator is to make photocopies of the original statement. The original will then be filed with the case folder immediately so that it is not lost or destroyed. Next, in the left margin of the statement, the investigator should give each line a number starting with one. The reason behind this is to see if each part of the story, beginning, middle (actual event) and end are roughly the same size. If they are, the narrative is considered truthful in form. A statement that has a big beginning, very little about the event and a short ending would be considered deceitful in form.

Statement Analysis is something that cannot be taught or learned overnight. I am going to shorten the process by explaining to you the three (3) basic elements in a statement that screams to an investigator, "Warning!" Statement Analysis should always be done at the **PCT**:

Personal Pronouns
Change in Point-of-View
Tense changes

PERSONAL PRONOUNS

The main area to probe is the use of pronouns or lack of them. Pronouns replace specific nouns for people, places and things. The personal pronouns are: I, you, he, she, it, they and we. Investigators should hear the use of many personal pronouns when someone is telling them a story. If you don't, it shows a lack of commitment on the storyteller's part, and those areas need to be probed with follow-up questions. For instance, if somebody asked you to tell them everything you did today it would sound something like this: I woke up about 7:30 and I took a shower. After the shower I made myself coffee and got dressed. I left the house at 8:30 and met Sammy at the bus stop. We caught the 8:35 bus and made it to work by 9:00. Do you notice all the I's and We's? It shows that I took part in the day's activities. When these pronouns are absent, either in writing or orally, it should send up a flare to the investigator that something is amiss. "I" is the speaker so how can "I" not be in the story? So the next time you sign a Get Well card for the boss or someone that you are not fond off, I bet you write, "Hope you are feeling better." No use of "I." So actually, you don't care.

	Did the story start in the beginning or did it pick up in the middle of it? The very first sentence of the statement is very important and deserves a lot of attention. Are there large gaps in the story?
STOP!	

CHANGE IN POINT-OF-VIEW

When the speaker is providing their version of the story, they are doing so through their lens. If they change the point-of-view, they change everything. Writing is done in three (3) ways: First, Second and Third Person. The First Person narrative is what you should expect to hear. It is from their perspective. Anything else is a red flag and the investigator must provide follow-up questions to put the person back on track. An example of a First Person narrative is the one above—"I did this, I did that," etc. In a Second Person narrative, the speaker is removing himself from the story, which may indicate he is not using his memory. "OK, you are walking down the stairs ... (Rabon, 2003, p. 22)." A Third Person narrative is one that acts like a narrator and is more objective.

TENSE CHANGE

Because the events we investigate have already occurred, we should see and hear past tense—verbs ending in ed. Any indication of present or future tense about a personal story has to be explored as deceitful. Susan Smith was a woman that claimed her children were abducted at gunpoint. We discovered later that she drowned her own kids in the vehicle. Her statements, however, may have revealed this days before. During an active investigation, the mother refers to her children in the past tense. "My children wanted me. They needed me. And now I can't help them." Not exactly what you would say if you thought your children were alive (Adams, 1996).

Possible Statements of Deception

The following statements may provide some clues that the person is trying to deceive you and a list of possible responses that you can use to counter them:

Statement: "You know, I'm trying to be as truthful as possible."

Response #1:   "No, I don't know. Please, [insert name], explain it to me.

Response #2:   "[Insert name], when you say you are trying, that means you are not doing it. I need you to tell me what happened.

Response #3:   "As truthful as possible, [insert name]? That means to me that you are only willing to tell the truth up to a point. That's upsetting. I have been straight with you and you're omitting facts, [insert name].

Statement: "To be honest with you ..." or "To tell you the truth ..."

Response: "You are only being honest with me now, [insert name]? What about everything you said prior to this? Were you being honest back then?"

Statement: "I swear on my mother's grave!"

Response #1:   "[Insert name], tell me a little about your mother. When was her birthday? What date did she die?" When they can't answer these questions then you hit them with: "[Insert name], apparently, you were not that close to your mother, so we can leave the swearing part out and just get down to the truth of the matter."

Response #2:   "[Insert name], we just spoke to your mother; she's alive and well. Now, let's get back to the reason why we are here. This is why computer checks are so important before you start interrogating people!

Why Do People Confess?

Why in the world would a person confess and risk going to jail the rest of their lives? There is no guarantee that you are going to get the suspect to confess even after all of your hard work. There are times when you just are not going to be successful. The investigator has to understand that individuals want to get things off of their chest so they can feel better. Some religions offer penance to confess their sins and move on with their lives, and some people seek out the counsel of a psychologist to get their lives moving again by revealing what is bothering them. Some investigators are very easy to talk to especially when they have learned to effectively build rapport. It is human nature to want to talk through our problems.

There is an urban police legend that the "Guilty Always Sleep." When you have been hunting a perpetrator, especially after a long period of time, and you finally catch him/her and put them in the holding cell, something strange happens. Within a few minutes of putting them there, they curl up on a bench and go to sleep. This phenomenon, which I have personally experienced, could be explained rather easily. After being on the run, not sleeping well, nervous, paranoid, moving from place to place, constantly looking over their shoulder, the individual has no reason to do those things any longer and finally gets a chance to rest. The jig is up! Think for a moment about how you feel after you have taken a big exam or after a stressful week at work. Remember, it is only a legend and never should be interpreted as guilt.

Reasons Why People Don't Confess

In the previous paragraph I listed some reasons why people confess. Now, I'm going to cover why someone would not want to confess. There is a strong foundation to believe that people want to "confess" so they can move on. However, in a criminal investigation the stakes are much higher. The consequences of coming clean could be a lengthy prison sentence, life behind bars or even the death penalty. Sometimes, people will not give a confession out of **FEAR**:

> **F**inancial repercussions
> **E**mbarrassment
> **A**rrest and prosecution
> **R**etaliation

FINANCIAL REPERCUSSIONS

The suspect knows that if he/she goes to jail there will be an immediate financial impact on their family. There is a huge expense if they hire their own attorney or if bail must be posted. Quite often the suspect's family has to mortgage their home or spend their entire life savings. Also, the victim or the victim's family may file a lawsuit in civil court seeking damages in a wrongful death or injury suit. No money equals: cannot pay bills or rent/mortgage, no clothes and no food on the table. etc. It is a major obstacle for investigators to overcome.

EMBARRASSMENT

Arrest and possible conviction for a crime can sever the social bonds between friends and family. Can they ever earn back the trust from family, friends and coworkers? The embarrassment affects the individual's self-image; self-esteem and may cause shock and rage from the public. No one I know would want their picture posted on the front page of the news-papers.

ARREST AND PROSECUTION

The thought of going to prison is deterrence enough for most people, especially those with little or no experience with the Criminal Justice System. Prison also puts an added expense and a burden on family members. Traveling expenses, lengthy commutes for visits all take a toll on the family. Eventually, they will stop coming. The worst thought about prison an individual can have is who or what awaits them in their cell. We have all heard the jokes and stories.

RETALIATION

Imagine the following scenario: Johnny Jones is a low-level drug dealer who gets into a dispute with the drug operations best earner. During the altercation, Johnny takes out his gun and shoots him in the head. What's the first thing that is going through Johnny's mind? "I'm a dead man." Most perpetrators have a fear that someone will take revenge against them or one of their family members and in some cases they are probably right. This is what happens in cases that involve dealing in illegal narcotics or organized crime. Live by the sword, die by the sword. We have seen threats of retaliation against people that were acquitted in high-profile cases. Take for example Casey Anthony. She was the mother that was found not guilty of killing her baby daughter in Florida. She is one of the most hated people in the country and has had death threats against her.

In conclusion, the student should by now have an understanding of why interrogation is often called an art form. An investigator just isn't born with the skill of interrogation; it is a skill that is developed through experience and education. The student is encouraged to develop skills through their interactions with others and to seek out reference materials about the subject. There are many excellent books on the subject and I encourage you to explore several as you begin to develop your interview and interrogation techniques.

Here is a chart that lists the differences between Interview and Interrogation:

Interview	Interrogation
No legal requirements	Legal requirements—Miranda
Little or moderate planning before	Extensive planning and studying
Investigator does most of the listening	Investigator does most of the talking
Private or semi private location	Totally privacy
Cooperation is likely	Cooperation unlikely
Calm and pleasant	Hostile and adversarial
Seeking information	Testing that information
Victim/witness	Suspect/perpetrator
Not suspected of any wrongdoing	Suspected of wrongdoing

Internet Resources for Investigators

The Evolution of Voluntariness Standards
http://www.forensic-evidence.com/site/Police/Pol_voluntar.html

John E. Reid Interrogation Tips
http://www.reid.com/educational_info/r_tips.html

The Supreme Court of the United States Blog
http://www.scotusblog.com

Questions for Discussion and Review

1. Johnny Jones asks for a lawyer while in custody and all questioning stops. An hour later he changes his mind and calls the investigator back into the room and makes a full written and oral confession. Will this confession hold up in court? Why or why not?

2. What is proxemics? What role does it play in interrogations?

3. What is rapport building?

4. What is the most important reason to obtain a signed, written statement from the suspect?

5. Do the police always have to read Miranda to persons in custody?

6. Why is it difficult to tell a story backwards if you haven't told the truth?

7. What are the types of questions that should never be used by investigators?

8. Why does giving someone a way out of a problem work?

9. What are some of the reasons why people will not confess?

10. What are some ways that a witness can become "contaminated"?

11. What are some of the reasons people confess?

12. What are the instances where a suspect has an absolute right to counsel?

13. Why is it important for an investigator to have the "knowledge of how and why" of the case before they start an interrogation?

14. What is the reason for documenting the treatment of a suspect in custodial interrogation?

15. What is wrong with asking a leading question?

16. Why should investigators strive to keep witnesses/victims separated?

17. Why did the Supreme Court overturn Ernesto Miranda's initial conviction?

18. What is a control question? Why would an investigator use one?

19. Who should conduct the interview and why?

20. In addition to the examples given, what are other techniques that can be used to build rapport?

21. Why do you think that open-ended questions are best to use first in an interview?

22. What is the purpose of a follow-up question?

23. What is the first step of the Statement Analysis process?

24. What do personal pronouns signify in a statement?

CHAPTER 8 — INVESTIGATIVE REPORT WRITING

"The dullest pencil is better than the sharpest mind."
— Mark Twain

KEY TERMS

Investigative Report	**Active Voice**
Chronological Order	**Passive Voice**
First Person	**Past Tense**

CHAPTER OBJECTIVES

At the end of this lesson, the student will be able to:

- Define the term investigative report.
- Identify the qualities of a good report.
- Recall the elements of a good report.
- List the Six (6) Basic Investigative Questions that help gather information.
- List the times when separate reports should be written.
- Recite the strategies used to revise a report.
- Recall what to avoid when writing a report.

Whether you have been an investigator for one minute or ten years, you learned quickly how important the incident report is to your duties and responsibilities. This responsibility does not rest with the investigator alone, your supervisors play an important role in the process also. Their signature means that they approve of what's in the report. An accurately written report is a testimonial to the facts that occurred on a specific date and time and will become the primary focus in the courtroom. Remember, the final report is a reflection on you!

The investigative report is the chronological record of what happened, who it happened to, who is involved and what steps have been taken. Investigative report writing is much different than when you were a patrol officer. The patrol officer's duty is to respond to the scene, conduct a preliminary investigation, take a report and go to the next job as quickly and efficiently as possible. It obtained the minimum amount of information and punted it to the investigators or filed a copy with the clerk back at the command. Now, you are responsible to fill in all of those investigative gaps.

The defense attorney will grade your investigation on how well the case is documented. Any information that is missing (not documented) can paint you as someone who is not professional, not thorough or even worse, not truthful. These are the allegations and criticisms that you leave yourself open to when you are too lazy to write the report. Defense attorneys will argue that if it wasn't documented, then it wasn't done. It is difficult to bring something up in court that was never documented let alone testify about it. Juries won't believe you. Can you imagine leaving out the fact that the suspect was picked out of a photo array and the next report is an arrest report? That is like reading a book with a chapter missing!

Investigators must take the time to document on a report what was exactly done. Some of the best investigators I knew could crack the toughest cases with ease, but could not or would not painfully document what they did. Improper or no documentation will cost you the case. I wouldn't want to be the one that allowed a guilty person to go free because I failed to write a report. If you spent the time and effort to catch the perpetrator, just document the steps that led up to the apprehension. At least if it is documented you can locate it while sitting in the witness stand.

The report-writing doctor is here to diagnose the problem areas and provide the prescription necessary for investigative report-writing success. This chapter was designed to reduce the stress that is often created by these reports and by the bosses. Intelligence-led policing is driven by the dissemination of information. That information must be written in a report. I have broken down the investigative report-writing process into an easy-to-understand formula. Before we jump into the actual process of writing the report, I will first review the basic qualities of the investigative report. The report should not be feared. Think of it as another tool that you use to solve the case.

STOP!	Only report the facts. The investigator should never use their opinions or feelings in a report, nor should they use anyone else's point of view.

Every report has certain qualities that make it a good one. However, in my opinion, the three (3) **C's** of investigative report writing are the most important. Therefore, the report should be:

Clear
Concise
Correct

CLEAR

Whenever you write a report, act is if you are drawing a mental picture for the reader. It is important to pay close attention to details, so don't rely on your memory. Those who will read the report vary in knowledge of police work—some more, some less and some none. They can include the supervisor, district attorney, defense attorney, judge, victim, witnesses and sometimes members of the jury. Avoid using any type of jargon: police, medial or street language. Jargon can only lead to a message breakdown. Some will understand it, but some will not. Do not go out and buy a thesaurus to show everyone how intelligent you think you are either.

CONCISE

A report should be short, to the point and include the most number of facts. Its length should reflect the seriousness of the incident. There are some reports, like those that document a canvass that will be longer than others. The investigator can be concise by eliminating redundancy and wordiness. For instance, use "gang members" instead of "members of the gang," "experience" instead of "past experience," "facts" instead of "true facts" etc.

Active Voice is when the subject is doing the action. Using Active Voice in your reports will keep them concise by avoiding wordiness. For instance, "Detective Washington conducted the canvass." vs. "The canvass was conducted by Detective Washington." The first statement is an example of Active Voice and required only five (5) words. The second statement is Passive Voice and required seven (7) words. If you save two (2) words in a five-paragraph report, you eliminated forty (40) words, which is nearly half of this paragraph.

CORRECT

The most important element of the report is that it's correct. Accuracy involves detail, so ensure that the sentences are specific enough. The best written reports are absolutely useless if the facts are wrong. Pay attention to the details such as: date, time, locations and statements made. Avoid using your opinion. Commit your facts to paper ASAP because you will not recall them all later.

Investigative Report writing process has six (6) elements that must be followed in order to have a **G. O. O. D. Revised Final Report**:

Gather Information
Organize Information
Outline
Draft

Revised

Final Report

GATHER INFORMATION

Gathering information is something that you have been doing since you got on the job. It is a combination of your observations and interviews that were conducted. The same principles that were talked about in conducting interviews (Chapter 7) that gather information should be reviewed, I will not repeat them, i.e., types of questions to be used, types of questions to avoid, etc. The Six (6) Basic Investigative Questions that are used to gather information are: When, Where, Who, What, How and Why. If you are having trouble writing reports, you should write each one of these questions in the left margin of the paper and let the report write itself. This is the introductory paragraph of what took place in the investigative timeline. The six basic questions can provide you with the following information:

- **When**

When is the first question that should always be answered in your report, it creates the investigative timeline and helps prove/disprove a suspect's opportunity to commit the crime. When includes three (3) main facts: the Day, Date and Time.

"On Wednesday, March 15, 2012, at approximately 1200 hours, ..."

- **Where**

Where has to be answered from the general to the specific. For instance, when you conduct an interview, record on the investigative report where it was conducted, i.e., the victim's residence, on the street, in the Squad Room, in a prison, etc. Remember, an interview should always receive it's own report. Even when conducting a canvass of a building that has thirty (30) apartments. If two (2) people out of thirty (30) provide good information, they should receive separate reports so it is easy to locate that information later.

"On Wednesday, March 15, 2012, at approximately 1200 hours, inside of 123 ABC Street, Apartment 2A, ..."

STOP!	Never put the address of a sex crime victim on the report—it is protected by law. Instead, the address should read, "Known to the Department," or KTD for short. The same should go for registered confidential informants.

- **Who**

The "Who" are your victims, witnesses, and suspects. It is extremely important to positively identify the people with whom you are speaking by some sort of official identification. Identifying people can be difficult at times because many people still don't carry ID on them, so do your best. The important part of identifying someone is all in the timing. Do you ask for ID before or after you speak with them? I have found that asking for identification after you take a statement is the better way to go since you have built your rapport already. People may hold back information or be apprehensive about providing such information initially.

"On Wednesday, March 15, 2012, at approximately 1200 hours, inside of 123 ABC Street, Apartment 2A, Ms. Mary Jones, F/W/01/01/1958, 987-654-3210 ..."

When you mention an individual (victim, witness, patrol officer, etc.) for the first time, you should include their full name, gender, race, date of birth, address, apartment number (if applicable), cell phone number, e-mail address, etc. If you refer to them again in the same report, use his/her surname only.

I always found it easier to locate the individual's name within the report by capitalizing it. It makes it stand out, especially when trying to locate it while you are on the witness stand. For instance, here is the same opening as above only with using capitalization. Can you see the difference?

"On Wednesday, March 15, 2012, at approximately 1200 hours, inside of 123 ABC Street, Apartment 2A, Ms. MARY JONES, F/W/01/01/1958, 987-654-3210 ..."

- **What**

What describes your action or the chronological recording of the event. Whether you conducted an interview, a canvass or you responded to the scene, describe the actions with words.

"On Wednesday, March 15, 2012, at approximately 1310 hours, inside of 123 ABC Street, Apartment 2A, Ms. MARY JONES, F/W/58, was interviewed in the presence of Detective George Washington." Always include the name of your partner or other assisting investigator that was with you on your reports. This avoids the question by defense attorneys of, "Who were you with?" or "Who was present during this?"

STOP!	When referring to police officers, investigators and supervisors in reports there should be some other form of identification other than using the badge/shield number. In large departments it is impossible to locate a Detective Smith twenty years later.

- **How** and **Why**

The questions, How and Why, are sometimes not evident initially. However, you will answer the "How" question by describing the suspect's modus operandi (MO) when the situation warrants. The "Why" deals with the causes surrounding the incident. Remember, no opinions should be written in the report—just the facts. If you don't know the answer, do not answer it. A report is not the place or the time to speculate.

Organize Information

Now that you have gathered all the information, what do you do with it? The information has to be organized in a logical manner so that the story flows smoothly from beginning to end. The investigative report is no different from any other book report or term paper that you did in school. It must have an introduction, body and conclusion. The final report must tell the story, so organize the information from your notes in chronological order.

OUTLINE

An outline is something that should be created before writing the report, but it never is. The outline is a template that governs the facts of the investigation and helps maintain the flow. Creating an outline will save you time and aggravation because all you have to do is follow the outline. A minor investigative report can be completed as simply as writing a sentence for each of the Six (6) Basic Investigative Questions. However, in a major incident, the investigator is dealing with a lot of information as well as input from other sources, for example, assisting investigators. It is difficult to juggle this amount of information and then write the report. This is where the outline pays dividends.

At this stage of the process the investigator is not concerned with spelling, grammar or punctuation. These are extremely important, but will be fixed during the draft stage. This is not the final report.

DRAFT

The rough draft is just that, rough. The rough draft is written from the outline you created. The information in the outline is now put into complete sentences. A complete sentence has a noun (subject), a verb (action word) and punctuation. The noun and verb must agree. If the subject in the sentence is in the plural form, then the verb must also be in the plural form. Below is an easy chart to ensure that you have the correct noun/verb agreement. There are a couple of excellent Internet resources that will help the investigator with grammar and punctuation. I strongly recommend that you brush up on these topics. You never want to look foolish on the witness stand when the defense attorney starts pointing out your spelling, grammar and punctuation errors.

Singular (He/She)	Plural (They)
Does	Are
Has	Do
Is	Have
Knows	Know
Wants	Want
Was	Were

Examples:

- "The victim (he/she) was sent to the hospital."
- "Johnny Jones (he) is a Mops gang member."
- "The victims (they) were sent to the hospital."
- "Johnny Jones and Jimmy Jones are Mops gang members."

Whether you have been writing investigative reports for years or you are just beginning, they should always be written in the First Person and in the Past Tense. In a First Person narrative, the writer refers to himself/herself as "I" and uses the pronouns me, my and mine. The First Person makes a report easier to read and understand. The reader knows exactly who is doing the action. For example, "I conducted an interview with MARY JONES who stated ..." Police cliches such as, "the undersigned" or "the case investigator" should be avoided.

Past Tense describes an action that has already happened. Everything that we investigate has occurred, so the words on the paper should reflect that. Here are a couple of sentences from a sample Response to the Scene type investigative report: "I responded to the scene located at 123 ABC Street at approximately 2215 hours. I observed an Unknown male ..." Each verb ends in ed, which specifies Past Tense.

Punctuation is a problem for most people, including yours truly. The most glaring punctuation mistakes I often witnessed involved the lack of punctuation. When quoting a victim, witness, suspect, etc., in your report, make sure that you use the quotes when it starts and when it finishes. This alerts the reader that the statement is directly from the person. If not, it could be open to interpretation of who said what.

To show possession of something, you must use the apostrophe s ('s). For example, "the suspect's gun," "the victim's statement," "the suspect's attorney," etc.

REVISED

Any real estate buyer knows the magic phrase when it comes to houses, "Location, location, location." Well, report writing should have a similar phrase: "Revise, revise, revise again." I don't know of anyone who can write something the first time and have it come out perfect. As I revised the second edition of the text, I found a couple of errors and corrected them. It happens, but you don't want to make too many glaring mistakes, especially when they concern the facts of the case.

Near perfection only comes after hard work, practice and the discovery of hidden nuances involved in the investigative report-writing process. The report is a reflection on you, so give it your best effort. A report with spelling, grammar and punctuation errors tells a lot about you. Unfortunately, it is nothing positive.

The act of revising a report requires it to be reread and scrutinized. When revising your report remember these three (3) helpful hints:

1. ***Read the report out loud***—This is the first and least embarrassing way that people turn to when revising their reports, but it is not the best. When you read the report out loud, you can hear your errors. If you stumble when you are reading there is probably a grammatical error. Circle the statement and continue reading. After you have read the report in it's entirety, correct the errors and read it out loud again.

2. ***Ask someone else to read it***—This is the best way to get constructive criticism. I understand that your colleagues are busy, but do your best to persuade them to read it. It is easier for another person to spot your errors. You rarely find your own mistakes. An unbiased pair of eyes can dramatically improve the report's readability.

3. ***Know the difference between Spell Check and "Intent Check"***—There are no excuses for misspelled words in the age of technology. Every program has a spell check and most underline the word in red immediately. During the revision is when you correct these words. Spell check has some limitations though. It doesn't tell you if you used the right word, only if it spelled is correctly. For example, "Mary Jones stated that when she returned to her home, she noticed that there car was missing." The word "there" is spelled correctly, but it is the wrong usage. It should have been "their." There are many words in the English language that sound similar but have different meanings and spellings—also known as homonyms. Here are a few words that investigators need to watch for their "Intent":

> Effect (result) vs. Affect (change)
> Right (correct, direction) vs. Write
> There (location) vs. Their (belonging to) vs. They're (contraction of they are)
> To (toward) vs. Too (also) vs. Two (a couple)
> Threw (to propel by hand) vs. Through (end to end)
> Waive (give up) vs. Wave (motion)
> Were (past tense of to be) vs. We're (contraction of we are)

FINAL REPORT

The final report is the fruit of your labor. Each stage of the investigative report-writing process is important. No one should ever skip directly to this step. When the report is done and you are satisfied, immediately submit it to your supervisor for approval.

WHAT TO AVOID IN INVESTIGATIVE REPORT WRITING

- Do not put several days worth of work on one report. Each day should receive a separate report to avoid confusing the reader. Many times an investigator will put the date and time in the left margin and continue to write several days of investigative steps. This information won't be able to found promptly because it doesn't appear in the index.

- Do not leave out information that is detrimental to your case. If one of the witnesses failed to pick out the suspect in the line up, make sure that it is documented in a report.

- When writing reports there are some things to avoid. The writer should never use the phrase "negative results" because of its ambiguity. What does "negative results" mean? Does it mean that no one was home? or does it mean that, "The person didn't know anything?" Explain exactly what occurred so there are no mysteries.

- When quoting a victim, witness, or suspect, write down exactly what was said in quotes. Avoid using the phrase, "In sum and substance." In sum and substance means that you added your own words and therefore may have changed the meaning. This is what the defense attorney will say, so head them off at the pass and write out the entire quote no matter how long it is.

- If you must use jargon in a report, make sure that you explain what it means in plain English. Jargon is not only police language, but is medical jargon as well as street and legal jargon. Jargon causes confusion, which leads to a message breakdown. Write the report so that no matter who reads it, they will understand exactly what happened.

Figure 8.1.   Sample Investigative Report (Details Section)

Subject: Statement from John Smith

    1.   On Friday, January 13, 2012, at approximately 1430 hours, at the 7th Police District, Interview Room #1, I conducted an interview with JOHN SMITH M/A/42 DOB 01/01/1970 of 123 ABC Street, Anytown, Anycity, zip code. I read John Smith his Miranda Warnings (copy attached) and he acknowledged the questions by initialing each one and he signed the bottom of the form. Present in the room with me for the entire time was Detective George Washington.

    John Reed stated that, "I was fighting with my wife and I accidentally knocked her down the stairs. I didn't mean to do it. It just happened."

    After telling us what happened, John Smith wrote a statement which was consistent with the interview.

Interview concluded at 1555 hours.

    2.   The Miranda Warnings and the original statement were vouchered as evidence and photocopies were kept with the case folder.

SEPARATE REPORTS FOR VITAL INFORMATION

The type of crime dictates the number of reports in the case folder. A homicide investigation may have over 200 reports in it while a burglary may have ten. There are many things that you can put down in one report; however, there are certain aspects of the investigation that should receive a separate and distinct report. Most of this information deals with direct evidence.

Having separate reports for the **VIPERS** allow easy access to vital information, especially when testifying in court. The **VIPERS** are easy to find in an index and prevents the investigator from fumbling around, which is often associated with sloppiness. Trying to locate a specific statement that a key witness made under pressure is difficult. Here are the reports that must be treated like **VIPERS**, because they are dangerous if you can't find them in a courtroom setting:

Video Surveillance
Identifications
Physical Evidence
Each conferral made
Response to the Scene
Statements

Electronic Case Filing System (ECFS)

Many departments are getting away from the typewritten reports and storage boxes used for a century and have embraced more electronic automation. Electronic case management can be found not only in investigative squads but within the courts as well. The same rules apply on writing electronic reports as they would for handwritten or typed reports. However, the use of an ECFS has made it easier for the investigator to catalog, search and identify information within their cases as well as other investigators' cases. No matter what their size, police departments can now share, search and discover information from other precincts or jurisdictions.

Like any new tool in the police department the ECFS has it's Pros and Cons. The first problem will be getting the veteran detectives to embrace the new technology. For some reason cops are always reluctant to embrace change. For those departments that are thinking about going to an electronic case system or for those investigators who have been forced into it, here are some points to ponder:

PROS OF AN ECFS

- Case information is secure on the department's own servers (Intranet)
- Basic computer checks can be automatically uploaded into the case folder
- Digital crime scene photos and videos can be uploaded into the case folder
- Efficient: Victim/witness/suspect information can be carried over each time so the investigator doesn't have to type it in every time

- The electronic database of information makes it easy to search
- Excellent tool for reviewing cold cases—everything is in one place
- Easy to create patterns based on inputted information
- Replaces pin maps with computer generated ones
- Supervisors can track case progress and the workflow
- Cases can be quickly referred to the proper support units
- Case load can be distributed more evenly
- No case folders or boxes

Cons of an ECFS

- Requires extensive training in the beginning and then for any changes
- It is not a "one size fits all" type of technology
- The culture of change in policing—veterans may retire because of it
- Garbage in, garbage out—only as good as the information that is inputted
- Expensive upkeep because of vendor's fees to maintain the system
- Chance of a server failure
- Costs associated with redundant backup systems
- Increase in micromanagement
- Confidential information can be compromised
- Investigators are tied to their desks which reduces street time

Figure 8.2.   Documentation Flow Chart

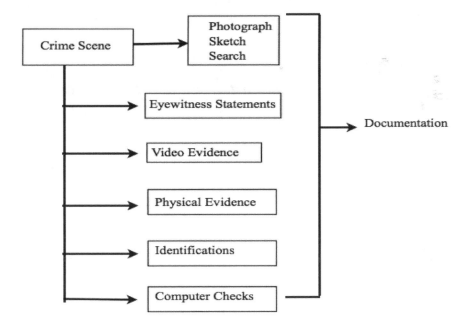

Remember, if it wasn't documented, it never happened! How would you explain on the witness stand if any of the above information was not documented in the case folder?

Internet Resources for Investigators

Purdue University Online Writing Lab (OWL) for Grammar
http://owl.english.purdue.edu/owl/section/1/5/

Purdue University Online Writing Lab (OWL) for Punctuation
http://owl.english.purdue.edu/owl/resource/566/01/

Questions for Discussion and Review

1. Why should the report be written in the First Person?

2. What are the Six (6) Basic Investigative Questions?

3. What are the situations that a separate report should be written?

4. What are the three (3) Cs to report writing discussed in this chapter?

5. How can missing information from a report paint the investigator?

6. What do quotation marks signify in a report?

7. In addition to the pros and cons associated with an ECFS, can you identify others?

8. Active Voice refers to what exactly? What does it do?

9. Why are reports written in the Past Tense?

10. What are some of the strategies that the report writer can use to check their work?

CHAPTER 9 – INTRODUCTION TO SPECIAL INVESTIGATIONS

"No, I've never thought about divorce in all these 35 years of marriage, but I did think of murder a few times."

— Ruth Graham

KEY TERMS

Uniform Crime Report   Case Assignments
8 Major Felonies   Case Management
Crimes Against the Person   Case Closings
Crimes Against Property   Exceptional Clearance

CHAPTER OBJECTIVES

At the end of this lesson, the student will be able to:

- Discuss what the Uniform Crime Report (UCR) is.
- List the Eight Major Felonies in order of severity.
- List the four Crimes Against the Person.
- List the four Crimes Against Property.
- Discuss how cases are assigned to investigators.
- Discuss the goal of case management.
- Recall the types of case closings used by investigators.

The fear of crime is a concern for every citizen in the United States. We either have been a victim of a crime ourselves or know someone who has been. Crime is a problem that has plagued societies since the beginning of time, but it has received more attention over the past fifty years or so. Crime in our towns and cities became more evident when they left the front page of the newspaper and played live in the television sets of Americans across the country. Now television has reinvented itself again by turning on an entire generation of youthful wannabe law enforcement officers. You cannot sit down and watch television without seeing a police show that revolves around the aspects of criminal investigation or a live sensational criminal trial. These shows have probably done more for recruitment for both police departments and criminal justice programs than any ad campaign ever did.

Can investigators reduce citizens fear of crime? The investigators' role is a reactive one. They respond to the scene after it has already happened. Investigators do not prevent crime initially. However, their quick thinking and actions help apprehend the individual(s) responsible for a violent crime, which prevents further victimization. This is the most important aspect of detective work.

The relationships that investigators build with the Criminal Justice System, namely the district attorney's office, helps keep the most violent offenders exactly where they belong - behind bars. This relationship is the most important. Why? Without cooperation from the district attorney's office, you'll have a hard time bringing anyone in front of a judge, especially for cold case investigators. Tension between the two sides does bubble over from time to time. Investigators want to make the arrest and close the case because that is what we are paid to do and how were are rated. Prosecutors on the other hand are rated by how many convictions they have. If they don't think they can win the case if it goes to trial or the person won't plead out, they won't take the chance. Therein lies the tension, but we have to remain professional and do our jobs. Often, investigators worry and complain about what others are not doing. The only people who we can control are ourselves. Don't worry about everyone else, we just have to do our job, which is to close cases, preferably with arrests.

The United States has seen a broad drop in crime over the last fifteen years, especially in murders. However, the number of unsolved homicides gets larger each year as the overall numbers are getting smaller. What is going on? You would expect that homicide clearance rates would be going up in an environment with less murders and computer databases coupled with the advances we have witnessed in forensic science, but they are not. This is a disturbing nationwide trend that must be addressed and reversed. So what is the problem? Have we lost too many veterans to retirement causing a substantial "investigative brain drain"? Is there no one left to teach the new guard the tricks of the trade? Is it do to a lack of training? I don't have an answer, but if we don't get a handle on the problem soon and there is a spike in violent crime, we're all in trouble.

Every law enforcement agency in the United States (totaling over 19,000) are asked to report on a voluntary basis the eight major felonies to the FBI, with a few exceptions. For example, New York City does not track the crime of Arson for statistical purposes. Each year since 1930, the FBI gathers these figures and publishes, *Crime in the United States*, which is formally known to law enforcement and Criminal Justice students as the *Uniform Crime Report*, or the UCR for short. Anytime you hear that "crime is up" or "crime is down," these are the crimes that the media and the politicians are referring to. The eight major felonies are broken down into two (2) main categories: Crimes Against the Person and Crimes Against Property.

This chapter begins the "meat and potatoes" of criminal investigation. These are the crimes that investigators will spend most of their time investigating. However as you will see, there are many subdivisions of the major felonies. These crimes are equally heinous as the eight majors but are not required to be reported for statistical purposes. However, these crimes hold valuable importance to law enforcement and investigators will give them the same attention as the others.

Note: The terms: 8 Majors, 8 Major Felonies, Index Crimes all mean the same thing.

Every good investigator seeks justice for those who can no longer do it for themselves or who are unable to do it. A closed case, especially a murder, begins the healing process for the victim's family and friends by providing closure.

I would like to introduce you to **MR Rob F. BuGGA**, the eight major felonies in order of severity (from worst to bad):

1. **M**urder
2. **R**ape

3. **R**obbery

4. **F**elony Assault

5. **B**urglary
6. **G**rand Larceny
7. **G**rand larceny Auto
8. **A**rson

If you asked someone what crimes they feared most, these would be at the top of their list. Murder, Rape, Robbery and Felony Assault are known as the Crimes Against the Person. These four (4) crimes are considered the most violent, recognizable and most reported of all the offenses. This is not to say that other crimes are not as important as these, but they are the crimes often perpetrated on society by people. Not every one of the 8 Majors has an "Attempted" charge if the perpetrator is not successful. For example, you intend to kill your friend and shoot him, but he does not die. That case will be carried as a Felony Assault and not an Attempted Murder. The perpetrator dropped down in prosecution purposes on the scale from #1 to #4. Try to explain that rationale to the victim. Could you imagine how many more murder statistics there would be if they had to include an attempted murder charge also?

Burglary, Grand Larceny, Grand Larceny Auto and Arson are known as the Crimes Against Property. This grouping of the 8 Majors tells us that the worst thing you can do is enter someone's home and take their property. As you already know, these are the hardest crimes to solve because of a lack of witnesses and physical evidence.

CI Tip Sheet

Investigators have to know the **CAP**:

Crimes Against the Person—
    Murder, Rape, Robbery and Felony Assault
Crimes Against Property—
    Burglary, Grand Larceny, GLA and Arson

A quality preliminary investigation by the first officer(s) on the scene is the key to solving any crime. A properly secured scene coupled with the proper notifications will start the investigation off on the right foot. Due to the violent nature in these crimes, the investigator should rely on Locard's

Exchange Principle (for more, see the Crime Scene Protocol) and special attention must be given to physical evidence. I'm sure you can imagine the amount of criminal incidents that occur on any given day in a large metropolitan area. This is another reason why the 8 Major Felonies have been chosen.

Case Assignments

Each investigative unit must have a way to fairly and effectively dole out case assignments. This is known as the "Catching Order." Whether it is done the old-fashioned way or through an ECFS, it has to be done. Case assignments can be done in a variety of ways. The most common is the assignment by rotation method and assumes each investigator is a generalist. Under this method, every investigator has an equal chance of "catching a case." This is the easiest method for supervisors, but it can create clearance problems. This method makes no distinction between the severity of the crime and what investigator catches it. A few investigators can be saddled with the heaviest of cases, murders, rapes, felony assaults and robberies, while others get the ground balls. It can cause tension among the group because it does not consider the complexity and length required to investigate each case.

Instead, a more effective way would be to have a separate catching order for heavy cases or use a rotation. For example, there are ten (10) investigators assigned to the squad. Every time there is a murder, the next investigator is assigned to it. If they are on vacation or out sick, they are skipped and the case goes to the next investigator. When that investigator returns from vacation/sick they automatically go to the top of the list. This way the investigator is not caught off guard, everyone knows who is "next up." The established catching order allows the investigator to arrive at work both physically and mentally prepared. The rotation keeps the investigators from being "victims of their own success." Remember, the reward for good work is more work.

Cases can also be assigned by specialty. Many of the large departments have a special investigative unit for everything: Homicide Squad, Robbery Squad, Special Victims Unit, Major Case Squad, Arson Squad, etc. These units can mitigate the number of heavy cases that the investigative unit is burden with; however, the initial response and investigative steps are taken by the investigative unit.

Pattern Case Assignments

A pattern should be created whenever there are two (2) or more similarities between crimes or the same individual(s) is/are involved in more than one incident of the same type of crime. The worst mistake you can make is not recognizing the pattern in time, whether by accident or design.

The number of incidents in a pattern can pile up quickly. Therefore, one investigator should be responsible for the entire pattern and the other investigators will act in a support role. Having one investigator assigned the entire pattern removes the problem of who has what case and how much work is being done on it. This way the pattern can be managed and supervised properly. This method is called case assignment by priority. It focuses the unit on a case/pattern and to act as a team or task force. This is reserved for those instances that there is a real risk to the community, i.e., an armed robbery suspect, a burglar that enters dwellings at night, gang war, etc.

Assigning case patterns in an Electronic Case Filing System presents the same issues as the old paper cases. The system has to be constructed so that you can electronically submit each case into a new pattern folder and close out the individual cases. If the individual cases are not closed, they will still appear as active and that no work is being done on them.

Case Management

The goal of case management in criminal investigations is twofold:

1. to keep the investigator on a schedule and
2. be used as a tool by supervisors to ensure quality cases.

Case management guidelines are set up to aide investigations so that the cases don't fall too far behind or, worse, are forgotten about all together. It is the role of the investigator supervisor to ensure that the appropriate level and coordination of work is being done. For instance, whenever you are assigned a new case, the first investigative report should be, "Receipt and Review of Case." The investigator must examine the case and determine how it should continue and this should be accomplished promptly—usually within three (3) working days of the assignment. This is a critical point of the investigation.

Investigators must act quickly on certain crimes. Waiting too long to start the case can lead to further victimization. Also, the longer it takes to interview complainants the greater likelihood that they won't cooperate or can't remember. An established set of rules helps keep the work flowing and can lead to better clearance rates.

If used correctly, case management can insure that one or two investigators are receiving all the "heavy" or pattern investigations. Supervisors have to remember that one pattern case can have ten (10) cases inside of it!

Case management is not investigation by checklist. I am not a big fan of "Checklist Investigation Sheets." There is a time and a place for checklists, but none that should govern the actual investigative process. Checklists hamper creativity and the "out of the box" type thinking that often helps solve crimes. Supervisors, should let investigators do their jobs!

Proper case management allows the opportunity for investigators to analyze the types of cases that come across their desks and establish current crime trends. Communication between investigators is vital in these situations. Case management also provides the opportunity to identify solvability factors and therefore prepare an investigative plan.

Solvability factors are those that provide the greatest chance of clearing the case, i.e., DNA, eyewitnesses, surveillance video, etc. If a case has no solvability factors then investigators must move on to the next one. Managing cases properly allows investigators to concentrate on those cases with the best chances of being cleared.

Preparing for CompStat

CompStat, short for Computer Statistics, was the brainchild of former NYPD Commissioner William Bratton and his confidant, Jack Maples. The program was designed to hold precinct commanders accountable for the crime and conditions in their area of responsibility in an open forum. CompStat was also looked to foster cooperation with specialty units within the department. This cooperation lead to the development and implementation of crime reduction strategies. Over time, the investigative squads became part of the process.

The CompStat program has been adopted and changed to meet the needs of many departments, big and small. The focus is and always has been the development of timely and actionable intelligence information.

Investigators technically don't have to worry about CompStat, their bosses do. Just remember, when your boss returns to the office holding his/her behind, yours is next. If you take care of the boss, they will take care of you. It is the job of the investigator to ensure that their cases are up-to-date with quality investigative reports. The biggest problem I have experienced in CompStat was that completed work wasn't documented in a timely fashion or not at all.

What cases are usually pulled for CompStat? If you are assigned any of the following types of cases, beware you are in the CompStat crosshairs:

- Nonfatal shootings
- Pattern cases
- Cases with identified perpetrators
- Major felonies that the were the district attorney declined to prosecute
- Robbery/Burglary/Grand Larceny cases with traceable property
- Domestic Violence cases with Orders of Protection

These are the cases that worry administrations most because of the high chance of further victimization, which in turn is not good for crime stats. For instance, in nonfatal shooting incidents, the likelihood of vengeance by either the victim or their friends, or in pattern cases, the crimes can pile up quickly, and, in decline prosecution cases, the perp is back on the street, which could all lead to more crime victimization and statistics.

All hope is not lost. There are steps that you can take to mitigate the chances of having your cases pulled:

- Make sure that your cases are up to date
- Communicate with your supervisor if any problems arise

- Enlist the help of other units to make the apprehension
- Document the hunt for known/wanted perpetrators
- Close cases in a timely fashion

Case Closings

The 8 Major felonies, as well as other investigations, can be disposed of for classification purposes in the following four (4) **REAL** ways:

Remain Open
Exceptional Clearance
Arrest
Leads exhausted

REMAIN OPEN

Depending on the investigation the case can always remain open. Homicides, rapes and crimes belonging to a pattern will remain open pending further investigation. Murder cases are never closed until an arrest is made. This is why a cold case is never "reopened" but "reexamined." When a case is left open, it is always in the back of the investigator's mind that someday he will get that lucky break. Whether a new lead is developed, or there is a change in relationships between people or there is a new discovery in DNA technologies, the investigator is always hopeful. A break in the case can come in the form of an arrest where the perpetrator wants to make a deal with a prosecutor to provide information about an open investigation or from the person who is on their death bed and makes a dying declaration. You never know when it is going to happen, so you have to be ready.

EXCEPTIONAL CLEARANCE

Exceptional clearance (EC) occurs when the police have probable cause to make an arrest but cannot do so because of an unusual circumstance beyond their control. An unusual circumstance is one where the perpetrator is dead or in a jurisdiction that does not have a treaty with the United States that allows extraditing the perpetrator for prosecution, i.e., Cuba. There are several unfriendly governments who refuse to extradite their citizens to the United States. The investigator will close the case as an EC and file the appropriate "flags" that will trip if the individual attempts to enter the United States. The EC can also be used in cold case investigations where probable cause has been established, but for some reason the district attorney refuses to prosecute it.

ARREST

An arrest occurs when the police have established sufficient probable cause (see the Criminal Investigative Process). The police take the individual into custody, charge him with an offense and deliver him to the courts for prosecution. This is always the goal set forth in each investigation.

LEADS EXHAUSTED

A case is also closed when the investigator runs out of viable leads or has encountered a fatal blow to the investigation. A fatal blow can come from a variety of things, but the most common are: when the victim cannot pick out the perpetrator in an array or lineup (see Eyewitness Identification Procedures), the loss or destruction of evidence or the lack of cooperation from the victim. Sometimes a victim cannot spend the time necessary to help the police because of family and work obligations or some victims have bad intentions and would rather "take care of it themselves."

An investigator cannot force a victim to help but must do everything he can to get the person to cooperate. One of the best strategies to persuade someone to cooperate is to remind him that others will be victims if they don't help.

Internet Resources for Investigators

FBI: Crime in the United States
http://www.fbi.gov/about-us/cjis/ucr/ucr

The Bureau of Justice Statistics
http://bjs.ojp.usdoj.gov/

Questions for Discussion and Review

1. What is a "Catching Order"?

2. What is a pattern?

3. What are some similarities, other than the ones discussed in the chapter, that can help investigators create a pattern?

4. What are the circumstances when a case can be closed as an Exceptional Clearance?

5. If someone is shot and they don't die, what crime would the perpetrator be charged with?

6. What are some of the guidelines that can be put in place to ensure better case management?

7. What can be some of the reasons for the drop in clearance rates in a lower crime environment?

8. What is meant by a "Solvability Factor"?

9. What three elements must be established to have a clearance by arrest?

10. Why was CompStat designed?

11. Why are certain cases pulled for CompStat and others are not?

CHAPTER 10 — MURDER AND DEATH INVESTIGATIONS

"Murder, though it has no tongue, will speak with most miraculous organ."
— Hamlet, Act II Scene II

KEY TERMS

Homicide	Putrefaction	Manner of Death
UCR	Postmortem Interval	Cause of Death
Algor Mortis	Vitreous Humor	Victimology
Livor Mortis	Entomology	Staged Scene
Rigor Mortis	Autopsy	Gun Shot Residue
Adipocere	Ligature	Odontology

LEARNING OBJECTIVES

At the end of this lesson, the student will be able to:

- Recall the definition of murder.
- Discuss what the "Homicide Triangle" is.
- Discuss what is involved in developing suspects in murder investigations.
- Explain what changes take place in the body postmortem.
- List and explain the classification for Manner of Death.
- Understand the investigator's role at autopsy.

Murder is the most heinous crime that one individual can perpetrate on another. Murder is defined by the Uniform Crime Report (UCR) as the willful killing of one human being by another. Simply put, you intend the death of someone and you cause death. The number one circumstance surrounding an act of homicide is that the parties involved had some sort of argument that precipitated the event. I'm sure that if we were able to know the circumstances behind each argument, the most prevalent reasons behind the crime would be love, money and drugs. These three elements make up what I call the Homicide Triangle (Figure 10.1). Love should be at the top of the triangle because it brings out the strongest emotions.

Investigators should use the Homicide Triangle when developing motives for a murder. When people in relationships are trapped within the Triangle, eventually someone is going to get hurt or killed.

There is a strange twist on how attempted murder is counted in the UCR. If someone intends to kill someone, but fails to do so, they would be charged with felony assault, the number 4 crime on the scale of the 8 Major Crimes.

Figure 10.1   The Homicide Triangle

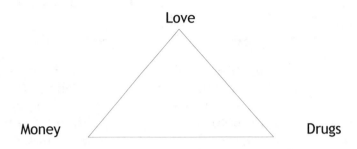

The crime of Murder has a little brother, his name is Manslaughter. Manslaughter occurs when an individual intends to cause a serious physical injury, but kills the person. For instance, in a fit of rage a wife picks up a frying pan and throws it at her husband, striking him in the head and killing him. Her intent was to hurt him, not to kill him. Unfortunately for him, she had good aim and he had terrible luck.

THE STATE OF MURDER IN THE UNITED STATES: 2010 UCR STATISTICS

According to the 2010 statistics for murder in the United States, here are some fast facts:

- There were 12,966 murder in the United States
- Over 68% of murders were committed using a firearm
- Over 48% were single offender/single victim situations
- Murders where the victim/offender relationship were known was 53%
- Almost 25% of the victims were killed by family members
- Almost 25% of the victims were under the age of 22
- 77% of victims were male and made up 90% of the offenders
- Most offenders are aged 17 – 34
- The South was the most dangerous area of the United States
- California and Texas were the deadliest states
- 64% of all murders were closed by arrest

A perpetrator does not anticipate the wheels he sets in motion when he chooses murder as the answer to solve his problem(s). Investigators take all crimes committed against innocent people seriously, but the crimes of murder and rape seem to bring out the best in investigators. An interesting dynamic takes place during a homicide investigation. Investigators that never seem to get along or talk to one another immediately agree to work together, and investigators that usually do the minimum suddenly are Sherlock Holmes. If you speak to any investigator retired or active, they can all tell you about one particular case that couldn't be solved and how it still haunts them.

Take a moment and reflect on the concept of Cold Case Homicide Squads. Police departments, with limited budgets, spend a ton of money on cases that haven't been solved, sometimes for decades. The federal government has also recognized the importance of Cold Case Squads and provides millions of dollars in grant money for departments to keep these cases active.

A cold case squad's function is twofold:

1. Protect the public from future occurrences and
2. Provide closure for the victim's family members and friends.

In the context of criminal investigation, murder is the most fascinating, intriguing and awe-inspiring of all for investigators, researchers and students. The act of taking someone's life for no apparent reason is incomprehensible to the average person. There are many questions raised during a murder investigation: Why was this person chosen? Who was responsible? How did they do it? and Why did they do it? to name a few.

Murder is the exemplar of criminal investigations. The techniques and strategies (covered in previous chapters) used to solve the ultimate crime against humanity can be used to solve all the others. Therefore, all investigators should receive training in homicide investigations. An investigator must know **TIM** to successfully develop suspects during a murder investigation:

Time of Death
Identity of the Victim
Manner of Death

TIME OF DEATH

One of the most important determinations in a death investigation is what time did the person die? Also known as the Postmortem Interval (PMI), the time of death aids the investigator in a suspicious death/murder in establishing the following: it can prove or disprove a suspect's alibi, provide a starting point for the investigative timeline and provide a marker for the 24–48 hours prior to the individual's death to establish a victimology. Unfortunately, estimating time of death is controlled by factors out of the investigator's hands. Like the old song by Chicago, "Does anyone really know what time it is?" Unless you were with the person when he/she died and was hooked up to an EKG monitor, no one will really know for sure.

It is called estimating time of death (ETD) for a reason. ETD is affected by so many factors that have nothing to do with the incident that caused the person to die. For example, was the body inside or outside? Did it happen during the cold or warm months? Was the person sick? Had a fever? Was the person engaged in some sort of physical activity prior to death? How was the person clothed? How much did they weigh?, etc. I think you get the picture. This is why it is called "estimating" or "approximating" time of death. It is not an exact science. The investigator should never take these changes in the body as the final decision, but only as a guide in establishing the ETD.

CI Tip Sheet

An investigator must **CHEW** on these factors that affect the time of death:

Clothing worn
How much did they weigh
Environmental temperature and conditions
Where the body was found

Any questions that the investigator has regarding changes in the body should be directed to the responding forensic pathologist or medicolegal investigator (MLI). The MLI can be found in both the medical examiner and coroner systems. The MLI acts as the "eyes and ears" for the pathologist and conducts an independent investigation from law enforcement, but works together as a team to solve the case.

You might ask if it is not an exact science, why bother wasting time trying to figure out the time of death? As you previously learned, the investigator needs to fulfill three (3) elements to have a suspect. These elements are known as **MOM**: The **M**eans, **O**pportunity and **M**otive. Estimating time of death has all to do with establishing the Opportunity to commit the crime and either prove or disprove an alibi. Remember, if the investigator cannot fulfill all the elements of **MOM**, he does not have a perpetrator! No matter how bad they "like" this person for the crime, the investigator must keep digging for witnesses and physical evidence, preferably, physical evidence.

The confusion about the ETD often begins with a pronunciation of death by Emergency Medical Service (EMS) workers or even doctors. The time of death is often recorded by a doctor or EMS when he walks in the door, sees a person who is obviously dead, checks his watch and says, "he/she is dead." The time on a death certificate is often indicated as "date and time of death" or "date and time found dead" (Dr. Monica Smiddy, MD, e-mail conversation, February 17, 2009). This information is only for reporting or statistical purposes and should not be used as the "real" time of death. The investigator has to use the facts of the case and drill down to a more exact time.

To help the investigator estimate the time of death, the following changes in the body should be used as a template to aid in arriving to the closest possible time. Remember, the following information and facts happen under perfect conditions. We know as law enforcement officers that nothing happens in perfect conditions. These are the changes in the body that many investigators use to estimating time of death. There are other indicators, such as stomach contents (the person's last meal), but for the everyday investigator or student, these are the changes in the body that you should concentrate on.

In many homicide investigations there is a delay from the time the incident happens until the body is discovered. The body may not be discovered for minutes, hours, days, weeks or longer and in some cases, never. The precious time lost is only one of the many obstacles that an investigator will have to overcome. For this reason, investigators must maintain **A SHARP Eye** for **Bugs** when it comes to changes in the body postmortem so an estimated time of death can be established. In addition, the interviews with the first officers on the scene are extremely important in death cases. The question, "What was the temperature (hot/cold) in the room when you entered?" and "What position was the body in when you first entered?" and "Did anyone touch the body?" must be added to your list of prospective questions.

Algor Mortis

Scene Markers
Hypostasis (Livor Mortis or Lividity)
Adipocere
Rigor Mortis
Putrefaction

Eye Fluid (Vitreous Humor)

Bugs (Entomology)

ALGOR MORTIS

Algor mortis is the cooling of the body after death and is the first stage of changes in the body. Our "normal" core body temperature is 98.6°, but is not true for 100% of the population. After death, our body will lose approximately 1.5° every hour until it reaches the ambient, or surrounding, temperature of the room. The body temperature is taken using a thermometer called a liver stick, which is sometimes not used in the liver. The investigator will count backwards to obtain an estimated time of death. For example, the pathologist obtains a body temperature reading of 95.6°. Easy math would indicate a change of 3° or 3°/1.5° or the person has been dead approximately two (2) hours. Because of the myriad of factors that can affect one's temperature, algor mortis is often considered unreliable.

CI Tip Sheet

When you think of algor mortis think of AM: Time

Scene Markers

Scene markers are items that an investigator may find at the location that may aid them in determining an approximate time of death. The last newspaper, the date stamp on unopened/opened letters or bills, television program guide opened to a specific page, credit card/ATM or cash register receipts, expiration dates on dairy products or food, DVD rentals, prescription bottles, etc. This type of information can be matched up with facts gathered during the investigative canvass, or from friends and/or family members. If you find a receipt it may prove fruitful to go to the store and ask for the surveillance footage, especially in suicide cases.

CI Tip Sheet

Scene markers can be a **PRIME** source of information used in estimating the time of death:

Papers
Receipts
Interviews
Mail
Expiration dates on food products

Figure 10.2   Scene Markers

Example of a Scene Marker:

Mail left at the door slot.
How many days' mail is there?
What are the postmark dates?
Has other mail been opened?

© 2012 Joseph L. Giacalone

Hypostasis (Livor Mortis or Lividity)

When the heart stops pumping where does the blood go? The law of gravity takes over and draws the blood from the arteries into the smaller capillaries. The blood causes a purplish/reddish color in the dependent areas of the body. Parts of the body that are in contact with a surface will appear white or "blanched." This is caused by the compression of the smaller blood vessels. For example, an individual dies on their back and is not found until fifteen (15) hours later. The investigator should expect to see the purplish/reddish color of the skin except the upper back, heels of the feet, buttocks and back of the head (Figure 10.3). Also, the same rules apply if the person hung themselves. The livor mortis will be observed in the feet and in the hands (Figure 10.3). In these scenarios they would be the dependent areas of the body. This is an important investigative tool for the investigator to identify if the body has been moved before their arrival.

Hypostasis begins immediately on death and becomes evident within 30 minutes. Lividity tends to reach maximum coloration in about eight (8) to twelve (12) hours, when it becomes "fixed" (DiMaio & DiMaio, 2001, p. 23). If the body is moved after lividity has become "fixed" the coloration will not disappear. The investigator can use lividity to determine if the body has been moved.

You can conduct a test on yourself. Take your index finger and press it against your thumb until it turns a bright red and let it go. For a split second you can see the white or blanched impression of your thumb on your index finger. This is the reason lividity can never be mistaken for bruising.

CI Tip Sheet

Here is an easy way to remember what changes in the body occur after death which are related to hypostasis (lividity): Hypostasis is really spelled with three (3) **Ps**

Pooling of blood in the dependent areas of the body
Purplish in color
Permanent or fixed in eight (8) to twelve (12) hours

Figure 10.3 Hypostatis/Livor Mortis/Lividity: Dependent Areas

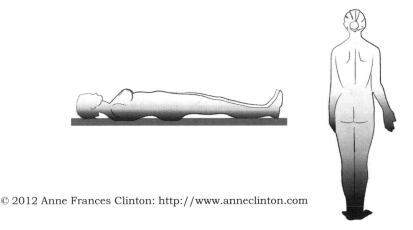

ADIPOCERE

Adipocere, also known as grave wax, is a grayish white or tan waxy-like substance that forms on the body due to the breakdown of fat during putrefaction (decomposition). It commonly occurs on bodies that are found in cool places or in water anytime between two (2) weeks to one month. Adipocere has also been discovered on bodies that have been buried (in or not in a casket) for a while. Adipocere is affected by temperature and insects (Australian Museum, 2003).

RIGOR MORTIS

Rigor Mortis, Latin for "stiffening of the joints," starts within one (1) to three (3) hours after death. Rigor Mortis sets in the body all at the same time, but it is most noticeable in the jaw first. Rigor Mortis is caused by the buildup of lactic acid in the joints causing them to "freeze" temporarily. It takes approximately ten (10) to fifteen (15) hours for the body to reach full Rigor and then will disappear within thirty-six (36) hours. Think of Rigor Mortis in the terms of a Bell Curve (Figure 10.4) at the peak would be full rigor. Of course, other factors will greatly affect the onset of Rigor Mortis, such as the heat (excels) and the cold (slows).

Rigor Mortis is an excellent way to determine if a body has been moved. Generally, people don't die with the arms frozen in the air. It will be quite apparent to the investigator when a body in the stages of rigor has been moved. If an investigator walks into the crime scene and sees the victim lying on his back and his arms are perpendicular to the ground, they know the body was moved. Only in cartoons does this happen. A question about who moved the body and why should be added to your list to ask on your arrival at the scene, "Did you touch the body?" followed by, "Why did you touch the body if rigor mortis was present?"

Figure 10.4

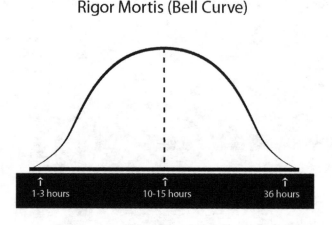

Rigor Mortis (Bell Curve)

1-3 hours   10-15 hours   36 hours

Putrefaction (Decomposition)

The last stage of death is known as putrefaction or decomposition. As rigor mortis passes, the skin in the stomach area will begin to turn green. This is due to the buildup of methane gas from bacteria and enzymes in the stomach and intestines. The general time frame for putrefaction to begin is as follows:

- One (1) week in the air
- Two (2) weeks in the water
- Eight (8) weeks in the soil

CI Tip Sheet

An easy way to remember when decomposition starts is Paul Revere's famous quote, "One if by land, and two if by sea."

Eye Fluid (Vitreous Humor)

The vitreous humor is the clear liquid found in between the lens and the retina of the eyeball. After death levels of potassium increase, which causes the cornea to become cloudy. Vitreous humor is extracted at autopsy so the level of potassium in the fluid can be determined. The level of fluid increases in opened eyes between two (2) to (3) hours and twenty-four (24) hours when the eyes are closed postmortem.

Bugs/Entomology

Depending on how long the body has been lying at the location, investigators can use insect activity to help estimate the time of death. It is a good idea for an investigator to know the basics of entomology so they can identify it and communicate what they see. Whenever, insect evidence has to be collected and/or analyzed, it should be done in coordination with the medical examiner's office, specifically a forensic entomologist. A forensic entomologist is someone that uses insects to help determine the time of death. They can also help determine if the body has been moved from one site to another, or even across a wide area and when necessary will provide expert courtroom testimony.

Within a few minutes of death, blow flies (Diptera Order) land on the corpse and lay eggs (40 – 1000) generally in an opened wound, the mouth, nose, eyes, ears or any location that gases are escaping the body. The flies will also leave eggs underneath pant legs and shirt cuffs. Besides blow flies, beetles (Coleoptera Order) are present shortly after death because they feed on the blow fly larvae. The forensic entomologist can determine the progression of developmental stages because they are predictable and take a certain amount of time. Byrd also reminds investigators that the pupa are often overlooked at a crime scene because they are often taken for vermin droppings (Byrd, J.H., 2011).

Investigators should become familiar with the types of insects that are inherent to their area by conducting research or sitting down with the forensic entomologist when the time permits.

Figure 10.5   The Lifecycle of the Blowfly

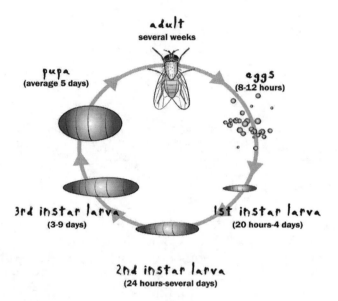

There are many things than an investigator must keep in mind when discovering or responding to a dead human body. An investigator can use the above timeframes (some with the help of forensic specialists) to help estimate the time of death. Once again, the investigator must be mindful of anything that can change the rate of decomposition by speeding it up or slowing it down. Algor, rigor, and livor mortis, decomposition, entomology and scene markers can all support the investigation community in estimating the time of death. The investigator must remain objective and constantly be aware of the factors that are out of his/her control, i.e., environment, temperature, clothing worn, etc.

IDENTITY OF THE VICTIM

The initial investigative step in a homicide case is to identify the victim. This is not as easy as it sounds. Yes, you can reach into the guy's back pocket and see if he has a wallet, but it's not always that easy. Even if he possessed a driver's license, a dead body will be listed as unidentified until a next of kin is notified and can make a positive identification. An investigator will use a license or other form of identification as only "tentative identification." To jump start the investigation, it is a common practice to take a picture of the decedent's face to show a friend or family member to obtain a tentative ID. This alone is not a positive identification. To avoid a misidentification, a family member must then ID the body at the morgue not only to the forensic pathologist but to the case investigator as well.

STOP!	Before taking a photograph for tentative identification purposes, see if the hospital staff can remove any tubes or other devices used in an attempt to resuscitate the victim.

If the victim's face is too grisly to show family members, you can employ the services of the department sketch artist to render a likeness.

If an investigator has to wait for fingerprints or DNA examinations to come back, the investigation will be delayed even longer. The longer it takes to identify the victim, the further away your perpetrator gets. If no tentative identification is available or the fingerprints are not in the system, the investigator will conduct a search of known missing person cases and attempt to match one up to the victim.

Why is the identity of the victim so important to the investigator? When we know who the victim is we learn: where he lived, who his family was, where he worked, who his friends and relatives were, who his enemies were and who would benefit the most from his death. According to the UCR, most people are murdered by someone they know, especially when the victim is a spouse. The identity of the victim provides the framework to launch the investigation.

There are two (2) tracks a murder investigation will take:

1. When we know who the perpetrator is and only have to locate them and
2. When the perpetrator is unknown or UNSUB (unknown subject).

Both tracks require a "hunt" for the perpetrator with varying degrees of investigative techniques. Of course, it is easier to track down people we know. We do this based on previous contacts, places and things that were discussed in Chapter 5: The Follow-Up Investigation.

"Why did someone want this person dead?" is always a good place to start. When you concentrate on the "why or reasons" (motive), it can sometimes lead you to the "who." Take this scenario, for example: An executive from the carting industry is gunned down in his driveway. What are some of the motives that pop into your head before your arrival at the crime scene? First, most would create the following formula in your mind: carting industry + gunned down in driveway = Mob Hit. I know I would. Other motives that should be explored in your mind about this scenario are: a possible love triangle, insurance money, revenge, a subordinate who is next in line (greed and ambition), and unpaid debts. Hypothesis formulation isn't rocket science when it comes to crime. The previous scenario doesn't sound like a random act, but a coordinated, planned murder based on information provided to the perpetrator, i.e., what time they left for work, where they would be at a particular time, etc.

Where would you start this investigation? Your first hypothesis (mob hit) would be based on background information obtained during a victimology (see Follow-Up Investigation). Does the victim have known ties to organized crime (OC)? If so, where are they in the "food chain? Were they a soldier or a boss?" If this information is either unknown or unavailable, the investigator will look into the people closest to the victim, starting with the wife. But would the investigator go straight to the wife? No. They would get to the wife in time through a circuitous path.

A smart investigator would interview only the wife after speaking to friends, coworkers and family of both the victim and the wife. This information can help an investigator validate or invalidate what the wife will tell them. For instance, a family friend tells the investigator that, "the two of them fought like cats and dogs and that he thinks the husband had a girlfriend." As an investigator, wouldn't you want to know this before interviewing the wife? How else would you know if she was lying to you? What if the investigator didn't seek out information from others and went to the wife first? She could stall the investigation enough to disappear. As an investigator, I never asked a question to a suspect that I didn't already know the answer.

CAUSE OF DEATH

There are certain medical phrases that the investigator must know when investigating homicides. These phrases have implications for investigators in both medical and legal fields. The cause of death (COD) is often confused with the phrase manner of death (MOD). They are two different things. The cause of death is an injury or disease that produces death. Cause of death examples can be heart disease, stroke, stab wounds, asphyxia, or a gunshot wound, etc.

MANNER OF DEATH

Death investigations cover what is known to a forensic pathologist as the manner of death (MOD). A forensic pathologist is someone that applies the principles and knowledge of the medical sciences to problems in the field of law. Under the title "Manner of Death" on a death certificate, the forensic pathologist will list one of the (5) five manners of death listed and explained below. The manner of death is always recorded on the death certificate and investigators should make every effort to obtain a copy of the certificate for their case folders.

A forensic pathologist attends **NASH U** when determining the manner of death:

Natural
Accidental
Suicide
Homicide**

Undetermined

** The term homicide is used only for definitional purposes—there is no criminal charge of "Homicide," it would be Murder. I am positive that police departments wouldn't want to have a unit called the "Murder Squad."

An investigator will respond to every dead person, no matter what the manner of death is. Why? Crime scenes can be staged to appear to be something else and the only way to determine what happened is with a careful inspection of the scene. Every death will be deemed suspicious until the investigation is complete and a conferral is made with the forensic pathologist. Even in obvious natural deaths, investigators will take photos and conduct a cursory investigation by interviewing family, friends and doctors. Investigators will contact the doctor directly and determine if the person was under their direct care and if they are willing to sign off on the death certificate. When the doctor signs the death certificate, the body will be released to the custody of the family.

Natural and Accidental deaths are self-explanatory and I am not going to spend a lot of time on them. Natural deaths include long battles with illness such as cancer or from old age. Accidental deaths can occur from car crashes or falling off the roof of the house while making repairs. These occurrences are not crimes and once the determination is made and foul play has been ruled out, the investigation will be closed as accidents/ naturals and no further investigation will occur.

SUICIDE

Suicide is defined as taking one's own life. The latest figures from the American Foundation for Suicide Prevention show that there were 36,909 suicides in the United States in 2009. Suicide is the tenth leading cause of death in the United States and is ranked as the fourth leading cause of death for adults aged 18–65. An investigator has more than twice the chance of investigating a suicide as they do a murder. Firearms are the preferred method of choice among males (57.6%) and poisoning is the most preferred method for females (39.1%). According to the statistics, more firearms are used in suicides than homicides.

The goal of an investigator at the scene of a suicide is to determine if it is in fact a suicide and not a homicide. He/she will accomplish this task by a careful examination of evidence at the scene and speaking with family and friends. A check of police records can determine if the person was ever brought to a hospital for a past attempt at suicide or had received medical attention for psychological issues. As noted earlier, men choose more violent methods of committing suicide then women and are more successful at it. Considering these statistics, an investigator can expect to find a weapon at the scene of a male suicide and sleeping pills if it is a woman.

In my experience with suicide investigations, it is very rare to find a suicide note, so the investigator cannot rely on any leads to identify the causes of the suicide right away. In a 2006 study conducted in Japan on suicide, only 32.5% of people left suicide notes (Japan Times Online, June 8, 2007) and a smaller study in Florida by Dr. Richard Hall (n.d.), found that only 10% of people left a suicide note. With those kinds of statistics, investigators should be leery when they encounter a suicide note. If a note is encountered, investigators can enlist the help of a forensic linguistics expert who may determine if the note is authentic. No one should handle the note unless they have gloves on. The document should be secured in a plastic security-type envelope and sent to the laboratory. The investigator should write on the security envelope before they place the note inside of it.

CI Tip Sheet

No matter what type of document you need to safeguard as evidence, write out the security envelope before placing the document inside of it.

Some killers will attempt to throw off the investigation by staging a homicide to appear as if it were a suicide. It is not far from the realm of reality that a perpetrator at one time took a criminal investigation course, read a book or watched crime shows on television all in the hopes of making themselves a better criminal. Clues of a staging can range from a bullet to the left temple, when the person was right handed, a gunshot wound to the back of the head, a gunshot wound but a gun was not recovered at the scene, a gunshot wound with a firearm at the scene but no gunshot residue (GSR) on the victim's hand or there is an obvious sign of a struggle (knocked over furniture, broken glass), or the presence of defensive wounds, or the nature and extent of the injuries sustained. An investigator develops additional information about the person from canvasses. Did anyone hear arguing, multiple gunshots, a dog barking or know about previous suicide attempts or past domestic/financial/gambling problems? Is there a "hesitation round"? A hesitation round often occurs when the individual pulls their head away at the last moment, putting a bullet in the ceiling or high up on a wall. This is not uncommon in suicide cases.

The gunshot residue test is extremely important. Gunshot residue can be found on the hands, clothes and even face of the person. Gunshot residue is composed different elements, but the three (3) main ones can be found at the **LAB**:

Lead
Antimony
Barium

Bad guys aren't the only ones to stage scenes, especially when dealing with a suicide investigation. There have been times when family members have staged a suicide to look like a homicide. You might ask, "Why would someone what to do that?" Sometimes it is a cultural embarrassment for the family and sometimes it has to do with life insurance money. Insurance companies will not pay out on a policy when the person took their own life. The family embarrassment could also stem from an Autoerotic Asphyxia Death. This occurs when an individual attempts to heighten their sexual experience by inducing partial oxygen deprivation, known as hypoxia (Criminal Profiling, 2001). Then something goes terribly wrong during the masturbatory event. The investigator must carefully examine the scene of an autoerotic death to eliminate suicide and homicide as the manner of death. Other clues at the scene may exist, which include: men wearing women's lingerie, ligatures with escape or rescue devices, semen found at the scene, sexual toys or sexually explicit material found near the incident.

In any hanging death, the investigator should see a ligature mark on the neck area that forms somewhat of a "U" from the side. The marks should be found up and around the jaw line (Figure 10.6). You will also notice in the illustration that where the knot is located on the ligature, generally there will be no marks or very slight ones.

Figure 10.6   Ligature Hanging

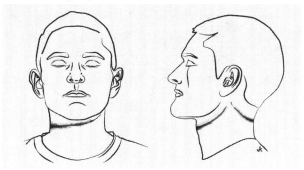

© 2012 Anne Frances Clinton: http://www.anneclinton.com

In a homicidal ligature strangulation, the investigator will see ligature marks across the neck. Due to the nature of the attack, jugular neck veins are compressed so that blood from the head cannot return to the heart, making the entire face (i.e. everything above the ligature) a reddish-purplish discoloration (Figure 10.7). This is commonly known as facial plethora in forensic terms and is only evident in homicidal ligature strangulation (Dr. M. Smiddy, MD, e-mail conversation, September 3, 2011).

In addition, other evidence of strangulation/asphyxia deaths may exist. Fingernail marks caused by the victims themselves as they attempt to get their fingers under the ligature may be visible on the skin or pinpoint hemorrhages known as petechiae (Figure 10.8) found on the eye. These provide an indication for an investigator that the cause of death was asphyxia.

Figure 10.7   Homicidal Ligature Strangulation with Plethora

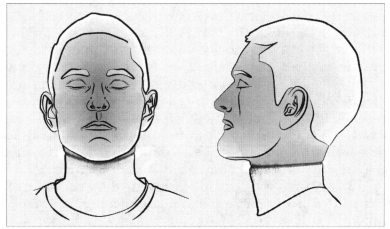

© 2012 Anne Frances Clinton: http://www.anneclinton.com

Figure 10.8   Petechial Hemorrhages

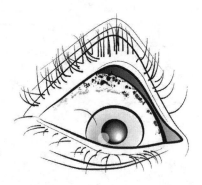

© 2012 Anne Frances Clinton: http://www.anneclinton.com

The most important interviews that are conducted in any investigation are those with friends and family members. The investigator conducts a victimology (see Follow-Up Investigation) on the person. In a suicide case, the victimology is commonly referred to as a "Psychological Autopsy." A psychological autopsy can provide insight into the deceased person's mind and what was going on, good or bad, in his/her life. The psychological autopsy is a form of behavioral profiling and investigators should seek the advice of forensic psychologists whenever possible. Financial problems, health problems, depression and relationship problems are common causes for an individual to take his/her own life. The investigator must be tactful when asking questions of the family and loved ones and this includes revealing information found in police reports, witness interviews and autopsy reports.

HOMICIDE

As discussed earlier, the term "homicide" is strictly for definitional purposes and never is used in lieu of "murder" as a charge. In a homicide investigation an investigator must fight tunnel vision and the urge to go directly to the victim's body. That is easier said than done; it is human nature to be drawn to it. The only thing that can prevent the inadvertent destruction of evidence is a slow, methodical search of the crime scene that surrounds the body. Remember, the location where the body is found is the primary crime scene because that is where most of the evidence will be found.

The goal of the investigator in a death investigation is to establish the Corpus Delicti evidence. By examining the scene, collecting evidence and conducting interviews the investigator can rule out a natural death, suicide or an accidental death. The investigator must be able to prove that the death was unlawful and that someone was responsible for it. The investigator in cooperation with the forensic pathologist will be able to come to this conclusion.

Homicide victims should have their hands "bagged" in paper by the crime scene technicians in case the victim scratched their attacker or if testing for gunshot residue will take place at the medical examiner's office. This should be a common event at every homicide where an apparent physical struggle has occurred. The scrapings for skin cells will be conducted at autopsy by the forensic pathologist and not by the crime scene technician.

One of the keys to solving any crime is proper crime scene management. We covered the main topics in Chapter 4, however, in homicide cases the question always arises who has permission to disturb the body?

There are very few people that should be allowed to disturb the body and its artifacts at the scene and they are **MC MED**:

Medical Examiner or Assistant
Case Investigator

Medicolegal Investigator
EMT
District Attorney or Assistant

UNDETERMINED

The category undetermined is also known as a C.U.P.P.I. (pronounced cup-e): Cause Undetermined Pending Police Investigation. When the medical examiner cannot determine the manner of death, they will send the case back to the investigator as a C.U.P.P.I. with a series of questions that they would like answered. You know you are in trouble at this point because the forensic pathologist is stumped. About 3% of all bodies autopsied in the United States receive this manner of death (Bryner, 2007). These equivocal death investigations, ones that are open to interpretation, are very difficult to deal with. This is why it is extremely important for the investigator to attend the autopsy. He/she may be able to answer questions or provide the evidence the medical examiner needs to make the determination on the proper manner of death classification. When a medical examiner makes a case a C.U.P.P.I, they are telling the investigator that not one manner of death is better than the other.

There is a time limit on a C.U.P.P.I. case in some jurisdictions. If the case remains undetermined for a period of time, generally within a year, it will turn into a murder statistic. This is not the ideal situation for any investigation, especially a homicide investigation. The longer the investigation goes, the less likely it will be solved.

The most common type of undetermined death that an investigator will deal with is when drugs are involved. However, the most difficult to deal with emotionally and psychologically is Sudden Infant Death Syndrome (SIDS). SIDS is the unexplained death of a healthy infant less than one (1) year of age (CJ Foundation for SIDS). The manner of death in SIDS cases is: Undetermined—SIDS.

There are over 2,300 SIDS related deaths in the United States every year, and if you are in this business long enough, you will have to investigate one. SIDS has nothing to do with choking, smothering, abuse or other signs of neglect. However, you may notice a frothy fluid in and around the nose and mouth. The investigator will consider the area a crime scene and must conduct a thorough search for any of those signs, including a complete inspection of the infant's sleeping area. Are there any objects in the crib area? Is the room temperature appropriate? The investigator should make note of these conditions and brief the medical examiner.

MAKING DEATH NOTIFICATIONS

Making a death notification is one of the worst jobs that police officers must do. This job rests solely on the shoulders of investigators in murder, suicide and equivocal death investigations. It is important that the case investigator do this because it is the first interaction with the family and the beginning of the victimology. A death notification should never be made over the telephone. Even in situations where the victim's next of kin lives out of state, the investigator should reach out to the investigating squad that covers the town so that it can be done in person. The notification is what begins the healing process. Unfortunately, I never remember receiving any formal training on how to conduct a proper death notification, so I decided to include it here.

Family members may hold key information for investigators. Because we are victimized by someone we know most of the time, the family may help generate leads for suspects and, most importantly, why they are suspected and where we can find them.

The investigator can better prepare by talking it over with his/her partner on the way over to the location. Notifications should always be done in pairs. Your partner can provide you the needed assistance to get through it, show the compassion that is necessary and obtain the information that is required.

Before making any notification, the investigator must be assured that the source and the certainty of the identification is correct. Have fingerprints come back? DNA hits? etc. The next important factor is to ensure that you are delivering the message to the right family. Before arriving at the residence, the investigator must be prepared to answer several questions: When did it happen? What happened? Who was responsible? Where did it happen? How it happened? Did they suffer? Where is the body now? What do we do now? How do I claim the body? Do you know what his/her last words were? Are they doing an autopsy? Can they visit the scene? You might think of some other important questions, but these are the ones that the family are going to demand answers for, so be prepared.

If you discover that the person who is going to be notified is alone, ask a neighbor, a member of the clergy or other relative to assist you. The investigator needs to express his sympathy in a convincing manner. "I'm sorry for your loss." The investigator must be honest with the family. Don't lie and say the victim was in an accident when they were shot to death. If necessary, ask the family if they need directions to the medical examiner's office or help with filling out the paperwork. I always had the ME's forms that were necessary for the family to complete with me. The most difficult part of the death notification is when to ask your questions. A death notification is not a ring and run. Take your time, be patient and the opening will arrive. If you have chosen the right words, expressed sincere sympathy, provided them with information, they will respond to your questions. Always respect the families position in these situations.

For those departments or investigators that need help on how to deliver the notification or what to say/not say, should reach out to the National Organization of Parents of Murdered Children (link in the Internet Resources at the end of the chapter). They are a terrific resource on how to deal with remaining family members and are available for talks and training.

ViCAP

The Violent Criminal Apprehension Program (ViCAP) was established in 1985 by the FBI to be a data warehouse for violent crimes. It is a tool for investigators so that they can determine if similarities exist for their homicide, sexual assault, missing person or other violent crime in any other jurisdiction. They attempt to link cases through modus operandi and other crime characteristics. Having one central repository maintained by one organization allows for the analyzation and dissemination of information from the host to other agencies. ViCAP is especially useful in serial crimes where the perpetrator has traveled from place to place. ViCAP is part of the FBI's Central Incident Response Group's Behavioral Analysis Unit #4.

ViCAP is now an online website and access to it has never been easier:

- The department has to appoint a liaison for ViCAP
- Investigators must obtain user credentials through LEO.gov
- More information can be obtained by calling: 1-304-625-5555
- Or via e-mail: Membership@LEO.gov

THE AUTOPSY PROTOCOL

An autopsy is the process by which a forensic pathologist, medical examiner, coroner determine the manner and cause of death. It involves the complete exterior and interior examination of a dead human body, including a full set of X-rays, determining the angle of trajectory in shooting cases and the type of knife used in a stabbing. The following exemplars will be taken from the victim at the autopsy: fingernail clippings, hair, and blood. This is why it is always a good idea to "bag" the victims hands to preserve any evidence that might exist.

A complete set of photographs will also be taken at the autopsy. If you weren't able to obtain a good photo of the victim this provides you an opportunity to get one when the victim is all cleaned up. If the victim wore glasses, put them on and take a photo. Other photographs that should be taken are of the wounds, body marks, surgery scars, and tattoos. These can help in the identification process.

There is a difference between the medical examiner and a coroner. A medical examiner is a medical doctor and coroners are not. A medical examiner is an appointed position and a coroner is an elected position who uses medical personnel to assist in determining the manner of death. According to the Center for Disease Control (CDC) in 2004, 21 states and the District of Columbia have a medical examiner system, 10 states have coroner-based systems and 19 states have both systems (Nolte, Hanzlick, Payne, Kroger, Oliver, Baker, McGowan, DeJong, Bell, Guarner, Shieh, Zaki).

The investigator must view an autopsy as an extension of a crime scene because it may provide additional information and/or evidence. How else would an investigator gain possession of bullets removed from the body? An investigator must make an **APP**ointment to see the forensic pathologist/ medical examiner/coroner the very next day. Yes, even on weekends and holidays! Death never takes a day off.

Attendance
Paperwork
Participate

ATTENDANCE

An investigator must appear at every autopsy that involves a homicide, suicide or suspicious death and be prepared to answer any questions that the pathologist may have. If the lead investigator cannot appear due to other demands of the investigation, i.e., conducting live lineups or processing the arrest, another investigator who was physically at the scene and is current with the investigation will go in his place. If necessary, the replacement will call the investigator anytime that they don't know an answer.

PAPERWORK

The investigator should take the case folder, crime scene photos, a copy of the evidence log, any sketches made of the scene or any other reports that may be necessary to the autopsy. If the pathologist is looking for information to validate their examination results, these items may provide the evidence to make a determination on manner and cause of death. These documents can help make the decision to label the manner of death something other than a C.U.P.P.I. Part of the autopsy is to take blood from the victim. It is important that the investigator conduct a follow-up conferral with the ME to determine what the toxicology report revealed, if anything.

PARTICIPATE

An investigator is not solely an observer at an autopsy. He should participate by asking questions and taking notes. The investigator should capture the following information for the investigative report: manner and cause of death, depth and general nature of wounds, whether the wounds were ante mortem (before death) or postmortem (after death), the medical examiner's opinion, and other contributing factors that were identified through the autopsy.

FORENSIC SPECIALISTS

During an autopsy, the medical examiner can seek assistance from other forensic specialists such as the forensic odontologist and forensic anthropologist. The forensic odontologist is also known as the forensic dentist. The odontologist will be asked to take teeth impressions from unidentified persons, burn victims, skeletal remains and to examine bite mark evidence. Sometimes, bite mark evidence isn't noticed for a number of hours after it has occurred. In situations where a violent struggle or a sexual attack occurred, the teeth are often used as a weapon to inflict an injury and defend against one (Forensic Dentistry Online). Whenever possible, the investigator should ask for the response of the crime scene team to come down and take photos of the bite marks/bruises for evidence and documentation purposes.

The forensic anthropologist will assist the medical examiner in cases where skeletal remains have been found. The anthropologist can determine if the bones are human or animal, the approximate age, race, weight and sex of the victim, determine if trauma was inflicted on the victim (i.e., stab wounds, blunt force trauma, gunshot wounds, etc.), how old the bones are and if the person was left- or right-handed. The forensic anthropologist also plays an important role in facial reconstruction often used for Requests for Information Posters (see Chapter 5).

Internet Resources for Investigators

FBI: Central Incident Response Group
http://www.fbi.gov/about-us/cirg/investigations-and-operations-support

The Internet Pathology Laboratory for Medical Education
http://library.med.utah.edu/WebPath/webpath.html#MENU

National Organization of Parents of Murdered Children
http://www.pomc.com/

NIJ: Death Investigation: A Guide for the Scene Investigator
https://ncjrs.gov/pdffiles1/nij/234457.pdf

Questions for Discussion and Review

1.   What is the difference between cause of death and manner of death?

2.   Why is the manner of death important to know?

3.   In addition to the examples already given, list some other causes of death.

4.   Why was the term homicide used to define the act of murder?

5.   What could be a reason for a jurisdiction not to report one of the eight major crimes?

6.   What are the three (3) main elements that compose gunshot residue?

7.   Should assisted suicide continued to be treated as a crime? Explain.

8.   Who should be allowed to disturb the body at the crime scene?

9.   What are some of the factors that affect estimating time of death? How do they affect it?

10.   Under "normal conditions" how long does it take for a body to reach full rigor?

11.   What does the term "fixed" mean when discussing lividity?

12.   The police develop probable cause to arrest an individual for murder on an old case but discover that the perpetrator is now in federal lockup for life. What case closing disposition would be used?

13. Why could a murder investigation be used as an exemplar to investigate other crimes?

14. An investigator submits fingerprints of an unknown victim. The prints come back to a match and a notification that the victim is wanted for murder. What does an investigator do about the other opened case?

15. Why is the location where the body is found become the primary crime scene?

16. What is meant by an Equivocal Death?

17. What is ViCAP? How is it used by investigators?

18. What is the job of the forensic anthropologist and forensic dentists in death investigations?

19. How long does it take for lividity to show in the dependent areas of the body?

CHAPTER 11 — RAPE AND OTHER SEX CRIMES

"Rape is the only crime in which the victim becomes the accused."
— Criminologist Fred Adler

KEY TERMS

Rape	**Date Rape Drugs**
Forcible Compulsion	**Cold Case Sexual Assaults**
John Doe Indictment	**Controlled Phone Call**
Sexual Offense Evidence Kit	**SANE/SART**

CHAPTER OBJECTIVES

At the end of this lesson, the student will be able to:

- Recall the definition of rape.
- Recall the elements of the highest degree of rape.
- List the two (2) crime scenes in rape investigations.
- Repeat the process of securing saliva as evidence.
- Discuss the different type of sexual offense evidence collection kits.
- Identify the incidents that require a John Doe Indictment.

According to the FBI's *Uniform Crime Report* (UCR) (FBI, 2010), Rape is defined as the carnal knowledge of a female forcibly and against her will. Any attempts via force or threats of force are considered rape. Any attempt at a rape will be classified as if it happened. In simple terms, rape is when someone has sexual intercourse, penis to vagina, with a female against her will by force or by a lack of consent. You will see in a few moments that state governments have defined other ways that the crime of rape can be charged in addition to forcible compulsion.

The FBI's definition of rape and statistics do not include men. Men are victims of Sodomy. Sodomy is defined as deviant sexual intercourse: mouth to penis, mouth to vagina, penis to anus and are not counted in the UCR for men or women. There is talk to finally change the 80-year-old definition of rape. The FBI is considering changing the definition to include men and other statistics as rapes (Fenton, 2011).

The crime of rape is not considered the most heinous crime (number 2) one human can do to another, but some, including myself would disagree. When someone is murdered, the pain and suffering lives on with the family and not the victim. Often rape is a crime that leaves the victim violated, their life and relationships in ruin and sometimes emotionally distraught. Sometimes the victim takes her own life because of it. Rape is a crime that often leaves the victim blaming herself and sometimes leaves the public to blame the victim too. "If she was home at a decent time, this would never have happened, if she wasn't wearing those clothes ..." and the list goes on. Unfortunately, it is too easy to blame the victim.

Rape has long been one of the most underreported crimes throughout the United States. Several factors may exist on why this is so: The victim may believe the police won't catch the perpetrator, she may be worried about unsympathetic treatment by the Criminal Justice System, embarrassment, fear of being attacked again or the fact that in 66% of all reported rapes the victim knew her attacker. To help with the decision to report the crime and preserve evidence, the U.S. Government has made it mandatory for states to conduct "Jane Doe Rape Kits," with the victim's consent, which are then kept on file in case the victim changes her mind at a later date and wishes to go forward with the investigation (Wyatt, 2008).

THE STATE OF SEXUAL ASSAULT IN THE UNITED STATES: 2010 UCR STATISTICS

The 2010 UCR reported the following statistics for the crime of rape:

- There were 84,767 forcible rapes in the United States
- 93% of all reported rapes involved force
- A forcible rape occurs every 6.2 minutes in the United States
- In 66% of all rapes that were reported, the victim knew her attacker
- 40.3% of all rapes were closed by arrest

The Rape, Abuse and Incest National Network has some interesting statistics from their website, which is found in the Internet Resources at the end of the chapter. Their statistics are from the National Crime Victim's Survey (NCVS), which is different that the FBI's UCR. Their statistics are built from anonymous victim surveys (RAINN, 2009).

According to the NCVS:

- More than 50% of all rapes occur within one mile of the victim's home
- 80% of victims are under the age of 30
- 7% of all rapes are committed by a relative
- The average age of a rapist is 31
- 52% of offenders are white males

Different jurisdictions throughout the United States have gone beyond the "forcibly against her will" stipulation and have added other ways that a perpetrator can be charged with this crime. The investigator should be familiar with the acronym **FLIP**, so they can remember the factors for the crime of rape.

The highest category of rape involves the following elements:

Forcible compulsion
Lack of consent because of the victim's age
Incapacitated mentally or mentally disabled
Physically helpless

FORCIBLE COMPULSION

The highest-degree rape charge occurs when the perpetrator uses any force, threatened or implied. It could be done with or without a weapon or through the use of physical force. The threats do not even have to be against the victim, they could be made to a child or some other person. "If you don't cooperate, I am going to burn your house down." Forcible rape would bring a higher class of felony in most, if not all, jurisdictions.

LACK OF CONSENT BECAUSE OF THE VICTIM'S AGE

State and local governments have set different age limits for when a person, generally the male, can engage in sexual activity with a female. For some of the age categories, statutory rape charges would apply, which are not counted in the FBI's UCR report. For instance, in New York State if he/she is 21 years of age or more and engages in sexual intercourse with another person that is 16, they would be charged with Rape 3°, a statutory rape. This rape would not be included in the numbers reported to the FBI for statistical purposes.

INCAPACITATED MENTALLY OR MENTALLY DISABLED

Consent cannot be given by a person who is incapacitated mentally or mentally disabled. The difference between the two categories is: if someone puts something in a drink (date rape drug) that renders her incapacitated and has sex with her, he would be charged with rape. A person who is mentally disabled or has a mental defect cannot give consent. Therefore, a person who has sex with a mentally disabled person will also be charged with rape.

Signs or statements from victims that may indicate they were drugged:

- Victim's clothes are disheveled or not buttoned properly
- Victim woke up in a strange location
- Victim was aware of the attack but couldn't move
- Victim remembers feeling dizzy prior to the event
- Victim experienced a total blackout
- Victim still feels intoxicated
- Victim's speech is incoherent or rambling
- Victim remembers events in snapshots or like a "strobe light"

PHYSICALLY HELPLESS

The victim in this category is unconscious or for some other reason cannot communicate their lack of consent.

The Sexual Assault Investigation

Sexual assault investigations should be conducted by a "specialty squad," but that depends on the size of the organization. They have garnered the necessary experience to deal with these difficult situations, especially when they involve children. However, having a specialty unit is preferred but any investigator with the proper training, supervision and determination can solve almost any case. Witnesses to sex offenses rarely exist, so the investigator must concentrate on physical evidence and victim/offender statements.

It should be the policy of the department that patrol officers should not conduct interviews with victims of sex offenses. Their role should be to provide first aid to the victim, broadcast a description if available, request the response of the patrol supervisor, an ambulance, a member of the investigative squad and to secure the crime scene. The patrol officers should wait for the investigator to arrive before asking any questions beyond what is necessary to fill out the aided report. The reason it should be done this way is that first, the investigators will be better equipped to ask the right questions; second, the victim is telling the story for the first time; and lastly, it saves the victim from telling the same horrific story three times: to the patrol officer, the investigator and at the hospital with medical personnel. The crime of rape is traumatizing enough without having to retell the story every hour.

There are always three (3) crime scenes in rape cases:

1. The location where it happened; if inside or outside it would be cordoned off and secured like any other crime scene
2. the victims themselves
3. the suspect

The investigator would treat the victim as the primary crime scene, because they are the best chance of obtaining physical evidence. Because rape is such a violent offense, the likelihood of locating transfer evidence such as hair, fibers, and fingernail scrapings (Locard's Exchange Principle) is good as well as finding body fluids such as blood, semen and saliva on bite mark evidence. Bite mark evidence is often found in rapes because of the vicious behavior exhibited by the perpetrator during the event. It is evidence that cannot be overlooked. The investigator should always consider that a tertiary scene exists—a vehicle. A vehicle used to transport the victim from point A to point B may provide additional evidence.

The investigator should be looking for any evidentiary link between the suspect and the victim that can corroborate the story. In the event that a suspect is apprehended early on in the investigation, the investigator must secure their clothes as potential evidence, including the underwear.

Saliva is a great source of DNA evidence and must be secured properly by using swabs. A swab is a wooden stick with a ball of cotton on the end of it. The location where the victim was bitten will be swabbed in a two-step process. The technique is the wet/dry method. The first swab is dipped in distilled water (water that has had all impurities removed) and the area will be swabbed; then the dry swab will be used over the same location. The swabs are then inserted in a cardboard container and submitted to the laboratory for examination. This evidence, as well as other types of biological evidence must be secured in a cool place. It shouldn't be left inside of cars or in direct sunlight. The investigator must always maintain the chain of custody.

At the Scene: Kiss Left on Rape Victim's Cheek Leads to Arrest

A New York man was identified and arrested for a rape and sodomy because of DNA. This DNA wasn't from semen or from a hair follicle left at the crime scene per se, but from a kiss he left on the victim's cheek before he left the scene. That is what got him caught. Quick thinking detectives were able to secure the evidence and within a few months got a CODIS hit. (Smith, A. *Newsday*, pg. A19). John Kluge of Holbrook, New York, was arrested, subsequently convicted and received a fifty-year sentence.

CI Tip Sheet

Two Crime Scenes in rape cases:

(1) The location where it happened
(2) The victims themselves

The investigator must be patient because the victim may still be in shock. Do not forget about your interview skills and rapport-building techniques. In rape cases, they will be tested! Because rape is a crime of power, the investigator must develop ways of returning that power to the victim. Ask if you can sit down? or ask if it is OK if I ask you a couple of questions right now? The first and most difficult task for the investigator is to ask the victim if they have showered, gone to the bathroom or cleaned themselves up in anyway. Cleaning and urinating can wash away DNA evidence as well as any drugs that may have been given to the victim. If they haven't done so, convince them of the importance of waiting a little longer so that any evidence can be collected. As always, do not use leading questions in your interviews!

An ambulance will be requested to the scene to transport the victim to the hospital for further investigation. The investigator must go with the victim because they are a crime scene!

Sex crime cases are extremely difficult to investigate because of the sensitive nature of the topic and traumatic effects it has on the victim. The investigator must ask the tough questions though. It may not be pleasant, but their initial approach, their sincerity and empathy are important factors in easing the pain of the victim. A male investigator should ask the victim if they would be more comfortable telling the story to a female investigator. Some will, but most won't. If they say they will speak to you, then you have established rapport and they trust you. Don't break that trust by using accusatory questions or statements.

It will be difficult, but ask the victim to use the exact words that the perpetrator used, the sex acts that occurred and the order that they occurred in. This information may develop or identify a specific MO. You must write the investigative report what was said and what acts occurred verbatim. One question that must be asked of the victim is if the perpetrator was circumcised. The investigator must ensure that the victim knows what it means—it may become invaluable in the case when a suspect is identified. Also, remember to ask the victim if the perpetrator took anything with them, i.e., personal object of the victim's, her driver's license, etc. Rapists often take a "trophy" or some other memento of the incident. If the suspect is apprehended, ensure that these items are on their person.

A series of photographs must be taken of any bruises, bite marks or physical evidence found on the victim's body as well as of the scene. Photos will be taken without a ruler and then with a ruler, especially evidence of bite marks. Before taking any photographs, the investigator should ask permission first.

Once at the hospital, a doctor trained in the recovery of sexual assault evidence or a Sexual Assault Nurse Examiner (SANE) will give the victim an examination and determine if she requires immediate medical attention. A SANE is a registered nurse who has completed training in the forensic sciences and provides trauma counseling as well. She is part of the hospital Sexual Assault Response Team (SART) and if she is not currently on staff, she is paged to respond to the hospital. When the medical examination begins, there is no reason for the investigator to be in the room. Investigators must provide privacy and avoid causing additional embarrassment to the victim by being present in the room. Generally, a clean sheet of white paper will be laid out on the floor and the victim will be asked to disrobe over it. If there were any hairs or other fibers on the victim they will fall onto the paper. That paper must be collected and properly secured.

Depending on the preliminary investigation, the doctor/SANE will prepare a sexual offense evidence kit and/or a drug-facilitated sexual offense evidence kit with the permission of the victim. The victim will be asked to sign a consent form for either kit to be performed. Both kits are designed to collect and preserve evidence for prosecution, including the victim's clothing. In cases where the rape occurred after 96 hours, the doctor/SANE will determine if the kit should be done. After 96 hours the chances of recovering evidence is very slight. The sex offense evidence kit contains slides, swabs and containers to collect evidence. The drug-facilitated sexual offense kit requires a blood sample for toxicology testing. Date rape drugs such as Ecstasy, Rohyponol and GHB are fast-acting depressants that target the central nervous system, often incapacitating the victim both physically and mentally (Office for Victims of Crime, 2008, p. 44).

After the doctor/SANE completes the exam and the sexual offense kit(s), he/she will seal the kit and sign his/her name on the front of the kit, starting the chain of custody. When the investigator receives the kit, he/she will sign underneath the doctor's signature. The kit will be kept in a cool dry place until the interview and testing is completed. The kit will then be vouchered and delivered immediately to the laboratory for testing.

Investigators will put together a complete victimology on the victim (see Chapter 5). Results from the background checks may provide information about who the perpetrator is. Investigators should also check modus operandi files and other reports to make sure that it doesn't fit a rape pattern. After the examinations are completed the investigator must sit down with the victim and chronicle the timeline of events, before, during and after the incident. Does the victim know the perpetrator? If not, how would she describe him. Where did she meet him? What did he say during the event? If known, where did the attack take place? The police will not wait for the DNA testing to come back before launching the investigation. If the victim does not know the perpetrator, the investigator will ask the victim to view police photo mug books. This may take more convincing. If the victim cannot identify anyone through photos a police sketch artist should be called in.

The location of the rape will be treated just like any other crime scene, but special attention will be given to the room where the act occurred, generally the bedroom. Are there any drinking glasses present or cigarette butts? Drinking glasses may contain remnants of date rape drugs and should be collected and packaged properly to avoid breakage. The investigator will ensure that the bed sheets and any clothing that was worn are secured and packaged in paper.

Remember, all evidence that can contain body fluids will always be secured in paper and never in plastic. The crime scene tech will make an intensive search for hair follicles and other trace evidence. However, the investigator may have some Fourth Amendment issues to be concerned with. For instance, if the crime happened inside of a location where the suspect has an expectation of privacy, then the police will need to obtain a search warrant. If you consider the fact that most victims of rape know their attackers, there is a good possibility that they live together. Also, if investigators develop probable cause that the suspect has stored, has the ingredients for or has made a date rape drug, then a warrant must be obtained. It is always better to err on the side of caution and obtain the warrant.

When searching for evidence in the bedding, it is important to strip the entire bed. Semen and saliva may permeate the sheets and stain the mattress. Also depending on how old the sheets are, hair follicles can slip through the threads of the top sheet and be found on the mattress cover or the mattress itself (Figure 11.1). The same should be done for pillows and pillow cases.

Figure 11.1   Hair Follicle Found Under the Sheet

The bathroom can be a treasure trove of forensic evidence. When we are soiled where do we go? The perpetrator often uses the bathroom to wash after the event. Many times the perpetrator will remove the condom (if used) and throw it in the pail or flush it down the toilet. They then proceed to wash their hands and genitals and towel dry before getting dressed. I have seen rapists who used a condom to prevent leaving semen in the victim, only to throw it out in the garbage pail! In addition, the towel often contains male DNA after washing. The condom wrapper may provide a latent print or Touch DNA, so let crime scene personnel collect. The investigator has to make a conscious effort to have these items retrieved by crime scene unit personnel and submit them for proper testing.

If the suspect takes the condom with him from the crime scene that says a lot about them behaviorally. It tells us that this was not a consensual act. Sexual assault investigations have seen the results of the "CSI Effect." Perpetrators are more aware of the physical evidence that they leave behind in sexual assaults. The police community has seen cases where the perpetrator forced the victim to shower after the attack or doused them and the crime scene with bleach.

Investigators can run into a roadblock at any crime scene, but especially where a sexual assault occurred. Because the victim and perpetrator often know each other, the question will arise, "Did he live or frequently stay at the location?" If so, most evidence you find in the bed or on clothes can easily be explained away by a defense attorney. "Of course you found pubic hairs in the bed. My client has been living there for over a year and a half!" This should never be a reason not to collect the evidence! Investigators must apply inclusiveness when processing a crime scene. You never know what may prove to be more important down the road.

DNA tests results can provide the following information for investigators:

1. No DNA evidence was recovered (or only from the victim)
2. DNA evidence revealed a male (or several) donor(s) that is/are *not* in CODIS
3. DNA evidence revealed a male (or several) donor(s) that is/are in CODIS

The first result is an investigator's worst nightmare, but there is nothing they can do but continue the investigation. Even though DNA was not recovered does not mean a rape did not occur. The suspect could have used a condom or did not ejaculate inside of the victim. This is why getting the victim to the hospital is extremely important. The sexual-offense collection kit not only takes DNA swabs, but also the following: fingernail scrapings, pubic hair combings and the victim's clothing.

A DNA hit, whether it is or isn't in CODIS, provides probable cause to arrest. However, the investigator will employ several investigative steps before arresting the suspect in hopes of getting a confession. Let's test what you learned so far. Take a piece of paper and write down some investigative steps. If possible, do not look at the steps that I would take below. The question is, "What would you do if you were the case investigator?" Here is a sampling of investigative steps that need to be taken:

- Conduct a thorough search for surveillance camera footage
- Make the victim feel safe and secure
- If you are male, ask if they prefer to speak to a female investigator
- Secure bedding and victim's clothing
- Ask the tough questions with empathy
- Establish a timeline of events of the victim for the past 24 – 48 hours
- Does the attack have any similarities to others?
- Complete a victimology on the victim
- Conduct a thorough background check on the suspect paying special attention to previous brushes with the law
  - o Active warrants?
  - o Domestic violence complaints
  - o Registered sex offender?
  - o Ex-wives or girlfriends can be interviewed on his past behavior?
- Place a photo of the suspect in an array to show the victim(s) (if a stranger)
  - o A single confirmatory photo can be shown to the victim in cases where the perpetrator is known to the victim
- Establish a record of the suspect's whereabouts on the date in question
- Surreptitiously obtain a DNA exemplar on suspect(s)
- Can the person be matched to fingerprints left at the scene
- Swab areas at the scene for Touch DNA

Controlled Phone Calls in Sexual Assault Cases

When investigators have a suspect, but cannot establish the link to the victim or to the scene, they may have luck with conducting a controlled phone call. Before conducting a controlled phone call, the investigator should confer with his supervisor and the district attorney. The district attorney may have some specific questions answered or asked in a certain way. A controlled phone call is not an invasion of privacy nor is it a violation of the Fourth Amendment (*United States v. White* 401 U.S. 745

(1971)). In addition, make sure you know the rules of recording conversations in your home state or if the call is going to be made from state-to-state. Controlled phone calls work especially well in acquaintance/relative rape cases. Because rape is a crime of power, the perpetrator is often arrogant, which could lead him to make incriminating statements over the phone.

A controlled phone call can be empowering to the victim because she is provided the opportunity to help in their case. Ask your victim if she would be willing to confront the suspect over the phone about the incident in an attempt to get him to make an admission. The victim must be willing and should never be pressured to do so. Here are some questions/statements that may get the suspect talking: "Why did you do this to me?" "Do you know that you really hurt me?" "I thought you were a nice guy and that I could trust you." "Did you use a condom at least?" "Is there anything I should be worried about?" "Do you have any diseases?" "When was the last time you were checked out?"

The investigator should inform the victim not to use the word rape initially. The same thinking applies here as when we discussed not to use words such as murder, killed, etc., in the interrogation room. It conjures up too many bad thoughts and may shut the person down. The idea is to get them talking.

Dealing with the Media in Sexual Assaults

Dealing with the media in sexual assault cases is much different from any other type of case. As an investigator, you must make sure that you never release the name of a sex crime victim or her address, or the suspect's address if that is where the crime was committed. Not even by accident. The identity of the victim is protected by law so you must be careful what is released. The victim is the only one who can agree to go public with her identity.

Here are some points to use when dealing with the media in sexually related offenses:

- Do not put the victim's name on any reports—refer to them as "The victim known to the Department"
- When referring to the place of occurrence (if it is the victim's dwelling) use "Confines of" or "vicinity of"
- The same rules apply to Crime Stoppers Posters or other Requests for Information (RIPs)
- Prevent the victim from being seen by the media at the police station

Cold Case Sexual Assaults

Old sexual assault cases make for good cold case investigations as long as the evidence can be located and tested. Finding the evidence from the case isn't the only problem. How they were packaged is another problem altogether. Before the law enforcement community learned about DNA, just about everything was vouchered and secured in plastic security envelopes. We now know that plastic degrades and destroys DNA evidence because of moisture build-up inside of the packaging. Now, all evidence that can possibly contain DNA evidence is stored in brown paper bags, which allows it to "breathe."

Many states have a statute of limitations for the prosecution of most crimes, except for murder, so investigators must act quickly. Because there may be a statute of limitations, investigators should team up with the district attorney's office and make an effort in the prosecution of old sexual assaults.

Investigating cold sexual assaults should be a four-step process:

1. Find and review the case
2. Submit evidence for DNA testing
3. Sit down with the ADA with the results
4. Contact the victim after conferring with the ADA

CI Tip Sheet

Contact the victim only after conferring with the ADA on how to continue with the investigation. There is no reason to drag up all the unpleasant memories, only to disappoint them again.

If the investigator obtains a DNA profile, but a male donor cannot be identified in CODIS, the investigator will bring the "profile" to the district attorney's office. The ADA will determine if the case will be presented to a Grand Jury for a "John Doe" indictment. This is good and bad for investigators. A "John Doe" indictment stops the clock on the statute of limitations. This is good because a profile can be entered into CODIS years later and get a hit on the profile. A statute of limitations places a time frame on when a crime can be prosecuted. A "John Doe" indictment stops that statute. The flip side of obtaining an indictment on the UNSUB, unknown subject, is that an indictment is an accusatory instrument. If you remember from Chapter 7: Interview and Interrogation, once an accusatory instrument has been filed, the subject, whoever it may be, will have an absolute right to counsel. That means the police cannot talk to him without the lawyer present. Good luck getting a confession.

Sexual Offender Databases

Over the past few years, online databases for each state began appearing all over the Internet, including some private ones. The FBI now has a webpage that contains links to all of these official sites. The link can be found in the Internet Resources for Investigators at the end of this chapter and will be extremely useful if your department does not have a sexual offender monitoring unit.

Sexual offender databases can prove to be a gold mine of information for investigating any type of sexual offense, but most importantly in stranger rape cases and sexual offenses against children. Some sites provide a photo of the suspect and other identifying features, tattoos, scars, birthmarks, etc. According to statistics discussed earlier in the chapter, sexual offense by strangers is around 25% of all cases. A specific geographic area or modus operandi may be the lead you need to launch the investigation. Sexual Offender databases are a good tool for the investigator, but I would not allow a victim to view it like some sort of electronic mug book. It would be too suggestive and you'll be providing fodder for the defense attorney.

Remember, whenever a suspect is identified, the investigator must conduct the proper computer checks to make sure that the person even had the opportunity to commit the crime, i.e., he was in prison, dead, etc.

Referrals for Victims of Sexual Offenses

The job of the investigator is not done in a sexual assault investigation until they provide a list of counseling centers and other referrals for the victim. Sexual assaults are such violent crimes that many victims suffer from post-traumatic stress disorder (PTSD). These signs may not be evidence right away, so the list of referrals is important. Many hospitals, if not all, have some information regarding rape crisis centers, but a link was added to a nationwide database of counseling centers that may assist you in pointing the victim in the right direction.

Internet Resources for Investigators

FBI: Sexual Offender Website Database
http://www.fbi.gov/scams-safety/registry

Rape, Abuse and Incest National Network: State Resources
http://www.rainn.org/get-help/local-counseling-centers/state-sexual-assault-resources

Questions for Discussion and Review

1. What type of packaging should be used for items with body fluids on them? Why?

2. In 66% of all rapes the victim knew their attacker. Explain why there is only a 40% arrest clearance rate?

3. Why does the public often place blame on the victim and not the perpetrator?

4. What role can a victimology play in a rape investigation?

5. Why would an active warrant on an unrelated matter be a possible "gift" for investigators? Explain your answer.

6. What are the two (2) crime scenes in sexual assaults?

7. What type of information could an investigator obtain from an old girlfriend(s) or wife?

8. What is the purpose of a controlled phone call? How and why is it used?

9. Explain the purpose of the SANE/SART.

10. Do rapists participate in lesser crimes before "graduating" to rape? If so, what types of crimes?

11. What kind of water is used with swabs?

12. What role can bite mark evidence play in rape cases?

13. How many hours should a sexual-offense evidence kit be prepared within?

14. What is the name given to the indictments that "Stop the clock" on the statute of limitations?

CHAPTER 12 - ROBBERY

"You get much further with a kind word and a gun, than you can with a kind word alone."

— Alphonse Capone

KEY TERMS

Robbery
Firearms
Traceable Property
Confidential Informants

Pawnshops
Subpoena Duces Tecum
Debriefing

CHAPTER OBJECTIVES

At the end of this lesson, the student will be able to:

- Recall the definition of Robbery.
- Define traceable property and how it can be used to solve robberies.
- Discuss the property most often stolen in robberies.
- Distinguish between the types of records that can be subpoenaed.
- Recall the proper use of confidential informants.

The FBI Uniform Crime Report (UCR) (2010) defines robbery as the taking or attempting to take anything of value from a person by force or threat of force. In simple terms, robbery is the forcible taking of property from another—with or without a weapon. The use of force must be imminent and it can be used, simulated, implied or threatened. The victim must feel compelled to hand over their property or risk being hurt by the **FIST**:

Forcibly take property
Imminent
Simulated, implied, used or
Threatened use of force

THE STATE OF ROBBERY IN THE UNITED STATES: 2010 UCR STATISTICS

According to the most recent FBI UCR (2010) Robbery statistics:

- There were 367,832 reported robberies in the United States in 2010
- Firearms were the choice of weapon 41% of the time
- Strong arm robberies accounted for 42%
- The average dollar amount stolen was $1,239 per robbery
- The average bank robbery yielded $4,410 per robbery
- 43.2% of all robberies occurred on the street
- 28.2% of all robberies are cleared by arrest—therefore 71.8% of all robbers are still out there
- Every 1.4 minutes a person is robbed in the United States

Robberies occur so often that most investigative units have individuals assigned to do only robbery investigations. Robberies can quickly turn into pattern cases and because of the nature of the crime, someone is going to get hurt. The key to solving robberies is to arrive at the scene quickly and persuade the victim to canvass for the perpetrator(s). Robbery investigations are usually "hot," meaning they just occurred. The investigator's skill in communication must persuade the victim to cooperate and follow through with the investigation. The victim's memory clock is ticking. The longer the investigator waits or has to convince the person, the greater the chance the victim will not be able to identify the perpetrator. Many people, "Don't have the time," "Glad they weren't hurt," "Have to go to work" or they "Have to run to pick up the children." The ten dollars that was stolen is "No big deal." If necessary ask the victim if you can help them out so that they can cooperate fully with the investigation.

If the victim does not see anyone on the canvass, the investigator should immediately take them to the station house to look at mug books. This can be time consuming. So investigators will try to make it as easy for the victim as possible. Investigators can arrange to have the victim's children picked up at school or buy pizza so they don't have to worry about dinner—all in an effort to secure their cooperation. I bought a number of pizzas in my time and they all paid me back.

The Robbery Investigation

Two key factors that will determine if a robbery case is solvable are:

1. If the victim is able to pick out the suspect from photos.
2. If the property stolen is traceable.

Most robberies are a blitz-style attack, usually from behind, on some unsuspecting person. In those instances, eyewitness identification will be impossible. Even if the victim had an opportunity to see the perpetrator, he/she still may not be unable to identify the perpetrator because of fear. In those instances, the investigator will ask, "Tell me about the person who robbed you," and the response will be, "He had a silver gun." "Was he White? Black? Or Hispanic?" "He had a silver gun." Tunnel vision is quite evident in victims of robbery. If the victim did not get a good look at the perpetrator, then ask them about their voice, clothing, how they were approached, what they immediately said, their mannerism and direction of flight. This information can then be checked with other cases that may be part of a pattern. Before closing out a case because no description or information is immediately available, put the case off to the side and reach out to the victim in a couple of days when they may have recovered from the shock. Remember, quality interviews are always done in person.

Robbery perpetrators sometimes use a mask or other device (stocking, bandana, etc.) to change their appearance to avoid identification. Investigators must ask the victim if the suspect was wearing any of these types of items and pass that information along to the evidence collection team. These items may contain DNA from the suspect(s).

Eyewitness identification procedures were covered at length in Chapter 6, so I will concentrate on traceable property in this section. If the suspect is unable to identify the perpetrator, investigators must track down the property. However, two problems exist for investigators:

1. If the perpetrator took cash during the robbery, with the exception of a bank robbery, it will not be traceable.
2. When investigators locate the property and it is in the possession of an individual, does it mean that it is the person who robbed (took) it? No. In this scenario you would have at best a criminal possession of stolen property charge. But, that individual will be a possible link to the person who originally stole the property.

Traceable property is any property that can be tracked via the nature of the item: i.e., cell phone, credit card, debit card, ATM card, bus pass, or subway/train pass. The items most likely to be stolen fall under Ronald Clarke's **CRAVED** model (Clarke, 1999, p. 28).

Concealable
Removable
Available
Valuable
Enjoyable
Disposable

The items most likely to fall under just about every category in Clarke's model are small electronic devices. These items are often the target of the youthful robbery offender. Yesterday it was MP3 players, today it is the smart phone and tablet—small, expensive, but useful devices that everyone wants. Eventually, the property is going to end up somewhere when the person needs money or is tired of using it, or they get one of their own. The trend I noticed in robberies is that once the market becomes flooded or the product becomes cheap enough, no one wants to steal it anymore.

Where an investigator looks depends on the type of property that was stolen. Investigators attempt to investigate backwards: Find the property to find the perpetrator. Here is a sampling of where stolen property can show up:

Jewelry = pawnshop
Small electronic devices = online auction and social networking sites

Jewelry, such as watches, necklaces and rings can be turned into immediate cash through local pawnshops. However, over the past decade or so, local governments have exerted pressure on these types of businesses and have established administrative rules for secondhand dealers, AKA pawnshops.

Many states now require secondhand dealers to photocopy identification of individuals selling items as well as keep a log. Investigators will peruse these logs in the hopes of identify suspects from past robberies. A new trend for dealing with pawnshops is the requirement of secondhand dealers to take digital photographs of the property and upload them to an online site for law enforcement to use. This aids law enforcement in not only identifying suspects but recovering stolen property as well.

Obtaining an accurate description of the jewelry is important. Victims may have it insured and therefore have pictures of it or in cases with unique jewelry; an investigator can use the services of a sketch artist. The sketches can be made into Request for Information Posters (RIPs) and given to the pawnshop owners so they can be on the look out for it. If your department doesn't have a "Jewelry Chart" that has photos of all the different types of designs and names, obtain a jewelry catalog for victims to look through. The more accurate a description is of the property, the better your chances are of finding it. Don't forget the value of surveillance cameras in pawnshops. Many of them have state-of-the-art technology deployed. Ask them to pull the footage.

The Internet has created other opportunities for perpetrators to cash in on their ill-gotten goods, by listing and selling the items on the World Wide Web on websites that I refer to as the electronic pawnshop. Victims also know this and often find their own items for sale on the Web and notify the police. Investigators must obtain a subpoena for seller/buyer information and are probably better off contacting the department's computer crime squad to help them with Internet related matters.

Investigators have seen a new trend with the Internet: social networking and video sites. More and more investigators are finding themselves trolling the Net for information about crime and criminals. Whether it is a "how-to video" or the video recording of the actual robbery, both can be obtained without a warrant. No one has a right to privacy about anything they put on the Net.

In cases that involve credit cards, cell phones, transportation cards, etc., the investigator must convince the victim not to cancel their service. This way the case can be investigated in "real" time. The investigator must contact the company/bank and tell them what is going on so that the victim isn't charged for any usage. Some police departments have funds that are used to keep the account active.

Once a bank or cell phone company is on board with the investigation, they can notify the police of when and where the item is being used. If investigators are lucky enough to arrive at the scene when the perpetrator is still there, great, but if they can't, an immediate request for video surveillance footage will be made. Investigators must get into the habit of requesting two copies of the surveillance tape whenever possible. One will be vouchered and kept with the case folder and the other will be used for viewing purposes. This prevents the destruction and/or inadvertent loss of the video evidence. Investigators must act quickly to secure surveillance evidence. Some recording devices will re-record over old footage after a certain number of hours.

Cell phones offer a unique way to track individuals wanted for serious crimes. Each cellular device is connected to a satellite through cell towers. When the devices are used, they connect to the nearest cell tower. These towers can track down the actual location of the phone to within a few feet. Investigators must be on standby and be able to respond to a location at any given notice. This electronic surveillance measure is called a Pen Register Trap and Trace. Law enforcement officials need to obtain a warrant from a judge, by establishing probable cause and filing an affidavit. This technique is usually reserved for homicide and robbery pattern cases.

Cell phones offer additional information about the robber. Investigators will prepare what is called a Subpoena Duces Tecum for the phone records from the time of the robbery forward. You wouldn't believe how many thieves call someone they know after stealing the device! A Subpoena Duces Tecum orders the production of documents that may be used in a criminal proceeding. The investigator should check with the department's legal division on the proper procedure and wording for the subpoena. Also, many of the hot trendy smart phones that thieves like to steal are equipped with all kinds of *apps* that can aid in your investigation. There are many requests that you can ask for:

- Subscriber and Billing information
- Line Usage Dial outs (LUDS) and Tolls (long distance)
- Special Computer Runs—"Dump"
- Text messages (SMS)

There are fees involved in these requests, so ensure that you follow the department's legal unit, because if not they will be sending the bills to your squad in your name! Remember, when securing a subpoena for cell phone records you also need to ask for the text messages as well. Many phone companies require that request to appear on the subpoena.

The subpoena must be written in four (4) parts:

1. The type of request you are asking for (or combination) and the phone number(s) you want the information on; check with the company, some allow up to ten (10) phone numbers on one request.
2. The reason the request is being made—in connection with a homicide, robbery patterns, etc.
3. The period that must be covered (some companies keep records for only eighteen (18) months
4. Contact information—investigator's rank, name, address, phone number, e-mail address and case number

The subpoena must be sent to the right legal department or law enforcement line. For a complete list of providers and their addresses for subpoenas, check out Search.org in the Internet Resources at the end of this chapter.

At the Crime Scene: iGotya App

A twenty-year-old man was arrested after he swiped a cell phone from an unsuspecting woman. However, what the thief didn't know was that the owner was more tech savvy than him. The iPhone he took had an App called, iGotYa, which takes a photograph anytime an incorrect password is entered into the phone. That wasn't the best part. The App then e-mailed a photo of the thief, who was subsequently identified and arrested when his photo was posted all over the news and the Internet (CBS News, October 8, 2011).

Robberies occur on the street more than any place else. So an investigator must reach out to the street for answers. Anyone that has their eyes and ears on the street may prove helpful. A canvass for surveillance cameras can be fruitful, but investigators place a greater value on human intelligence or HUMINT, in the form of confidential informants (CI). The rules about using CIs were discussed in Chapter 5, so I am going to discuss the pros and cons of using CIs in this section. Remember, the investigator must conduct background checks on potential informants and always identify the motive of the person before they sign him/her up as a confidential informant! CIs can play a pivotal role in solving many of the 8 Major Felonies, as well as provide information on narcotics and gang activities. The investigator will always keep in mind the value of obtaining an informant when investigating any case, but managing them correctly is always a test of your time and patience.

The use of confidential informants (CIs) has both pros and cons for an investigator.

The pros of using a CI are to **SEW** the pieces of the puzzle together:

Street knowledge
Exactly where to find your suspect
Wear a wire or introduce a police undercover

STREET KNOWLEDGE

Many perpetrators use robberies to support their drug habit. So much of what the investigator needs to know comes from the street. CIs live on the street and many times are drug users themselves. They know who is doing it, where they operate and what they like to do. Investigators call this the Modus Operandi (MO) or method of operation. A unique MO in robbery cases can help in establishing a pattern. A pattern is two (2) or more crimes with similar MOs or likenesses.

The crime analyst or crime analysis unit is an important part of developing intelligence for a robbery investigation. These members of the department can help you narrow down time frames, descriptions, provide maps and MOs. They are also in contact with surrounding precincts or jurisdictions for those incidents that occur near borders.

EXACTLY WHERE TO FIND YOUR SUSPECT

Investigators spend a lot of time tracking the whereabouts of their suspect. These efforts can be exhausting when challenged by an experienced perpetrator who is on the run. CIs know where they hang out, what apartment they live in or where their girlfriend lives. Investigators are often faced with information that a suspect is hiding out in a certain building, only to find that there are over 500 apartments! Good CIs know how to find out this type of information. Accurate and timely information is worth the money. CIs can be in constant contact with new technology with the use of cell phones and text messages by providing an accurate description of what the suspect is wearing and exactly where they are standing.

WEAR A WIRE OR INTRODUCE A POLICE UNDERCOVER

A wire worn by a CI can provide evidence that is invaluable. An admission or even a confession on tape will be the words that seal a suspect's fate. A wire can be used to dismantle robbery, auto theft and burglary rings as well as narcotic operations. If the informant does not want to wear a wire or wearing one would be too dangerous, the informant can try to introduce a police undercover into the operation. This technique has been successful investigating organized crime cases in the past, but it is fraught with danger. For that reason, departments have strict rules on who can do these types of investigations and must provide specific training for it.

The cons of using a CI are sometimes a **LAST** resort:

> **Li**e to keep the money coming in
> **A**ddicts
> **S**ometimes not reliable
> **T**rouble

LIE TO KEEP THE MONEY COMING IN

An informant knows that if he/she provides information, he/she gets paid. Some will play the system, "I keep talking and they'll keep paying." Investigators must corroborate the information that is received so the police department doesn't get ripped off. Remember who you are dealing with.

ADDICTS

When a CI is or was a drug user, their credibility is tainted. Some jurisdictions/agencies may use this reason to disqualify someone from being a CI.

SOMETIMES NOT RELIABLE

CIs live and operate on the street, which makes it difficult to find them. Couple this with drug use and the investigator has the makings of a disaster. CIs have also been known to play the role of double agent, so investigators must not reveal pertinent information about themselves or the case. You should never meet with an informant alone. If that area happens to be the station house, avoid leaving any reports out and ensure that all weapons are properly secured.

TROUBLE

The next time a CI gets into trouble with the law, who do you think he/she is going to call? Yes, the investigator that is using them as a CI. Many informants think that providing information for money to the police is a get-out-of-jail-free card. Many will sign up with this exact thought in mind and will think nothing of calling you from central booking at 0300 hours!

Computer checks can also provide the information that an investigator can use to solve robbery cases and establish patterns. Sometimes suspects are arrested in other jurisdictions for similar crimes. This may present itself as the needed break in the case. Searching through Stop, Question and Frisk reports to match descriptions against your perpetrator or to identify persons who where stopped in the vicinity of reported robbery occurrences are also good starting points. The same checks can be done for criminal court summonses and bench warrants. At the very least, this information can pinpoint where the suspect likes to hang out or lay their head.

Robberies are crimes that plague all societies today. As investigators we are not out on the beat preventing that initial act anymore; however, our job is to prevent it from happening again. Because of the blitz-style attack and violence that ensues, many of the perpetrators are never caught, so investigators have to deal with what they have. Conducting the proper canvasses, computer checks, subpoenas and tracking-down property are the best methods to identify and apprehend robbery perpetrators.

Debriefing of Prisoners

Another way to develop information about street robberies and who is doing them is a special questioning technique called a prisoner debriefing. A debriefing is a short interview with a prisoner regarding his/her knowledge about other crimes. It consists of a series of pointed questions regarding various crimes. Because the investigator is not asking them about their charge, no Miranda Warnings are necessary. Investigators should make a habit of when they arrive at work to peek inside of the holding cells to see if any prisoners are present awaiting transport to central booking.

The debriefing process is rather simple, but often overlooked. When trying to solve robberies and other property related crime, investigators must pull out all the tricks. First, obtain a list of the prisoners and their rap sheets. Look to interview the prisoner that has the most to lose first or the prisoner that lives/works in the area where the crimes are occurring. He/she maybe willing to provide information for court consideration. Each prisoner should be removed from the cell area by a uniform officer and brought to the squad for a debriefing. This way other prisoners aren't concerned about why the "suits" are pulling them from the pen. You have to protect them from the others or you can forget about ever getting a word out of them.

An investigator uses all the techniques required to obtain information from people, i.e., introduction, rapport building, etc. Explain to the prisoner why they are in the squad room to allay any fears. Debriefings work best when there is a preprinted form so that you don't forget any of the topical questions. For instance, prisoners should be asked about the following crimes and/or the people responsible for them:

- Terrorism
- Homicides
- Robberies
- Shootings
- Burglaries
- Sexual Assaults
- Selling of illegal narcotics
- Selling of weapons
- Where stolen property is sold
- Gang members/affiliation
- Where bodies are buried
- Fake identification

If the investigator obtains information during a debriefing that does not fall under their purview, i.e., narcotics, vice, etc., they must make a notification to that unit and provide the prisoner's information so that they can be interviewed again by the specialists. After completing the debriefing, whether it was positive or negative, the investigator should record the information in a log for future reference.

STOP!	Investigators cannot not "make a deal" regarding court consideration. Only the District Attorney or an ADA can do that!

Internet Resources for Investigators

FBI Bank Robbery Page
http://www.fbi.gov/about-us/investigate/vc_majorthefts/bankrobbery

Search.org - Subpoena Request List
http://www.search.org/programs/hightech/isp/

Questions for Discussion and Review

1. Johnny Jones walks up to Sammy Smith and states, "If you don't give me that MP3 player I am going to burn down your house next week." If caught, would Johnny be charged with robbery? Why or why not?

2. In your opinion, what crime do you think the general public fears the most and why?

3. What eyewitness identification method(s) would be used to identify robbery perpetrators?

4. What is the purpose of a subpoena duces tecum?

5. Why are robbery cases so difficult to solve? Explain your answer.

6. List some similarities in robbery cases that can lead to the development of a robbery pattern.

7. What are the pros of using confidential informants?

8. What are the cons of using confidential informants?

9. How can crime analysts help investigators solve robberies?

10. What is a prisoner debriefing? What is the purpose of one?

CHAPTER 13 — AGGRAVATED ASSAULT

KEY TERMS

Felony Assault	**Serious Physical Injury**	**Stippling**
Deadly Weapon	**Nonfatal shooting**	**Range of Fire**
Dangerous Instrument	**Entrance/Exit Wound**	**Domestic Violence**

CHAPTER OBJECTIVES

At the end of this lesson, the student will be able to:

- Recall the definition of Aggravated (Felony) Assault.
- Discuss the difference between a simple assault and a felony assault.
- Discuss the difference between a deadly weapon and a dangerous instrument.
- Recall steps taken in nonfatal shootings and stabbing investigations.
- Recall the difference between a gunshot entrance and exit wound.
- Discuss the range of fire and the different types of gunshot wounds.

The FBI's 2010 *Uniform Crime Report* (UCR) defines Aggravated Assault as an unlawful attack by one person on another with the purpose of inflicting severe or aggravated bodily injury. In simpler terms, you intend to cause a serious physical injury to another person and you do so or you cause any injury (however slight) with a deadly weapon or dangerous instrument. A serious physical injury (SPI) can cause protracted health issues and/or death of the victim. Examples of serious physical injuries are stab wounds, gunshot wounds, blunt force trauma and broken bones. Remember, only people can be assaulted. Aggravated assault is always a felony, but it must be distinguished from a simple assault. This is why it is commonly referred to as Felony Assault and will be throughout the rest of this chapter.

Felony assault has a little brother, his name is simple Assault. Simple Assault is always a misdemeanor and occurs when one individual causes a physical injury (PI) to another. Examples of physical injuries are: a black eye, bloody lip, broken nose and various other types of bruising. If no physical injury occurs, or a physical injury is not visible, it is a violation known as Harassment. Violations are not enforceable by the police unless it happens in their presence (exceptions are made in domestic violence cases by statute).

THE STATE OF AGGRAVATED (FELONY) ASSAULT IN THE UNITED STATES: 2010 UCR STATISTICS

Fast facts about Felony Assault from the 2010 UCR:

- There were 778,901 aggravated assaults reported in the United States
- 56.4% of aggravated assaults were closed by arrest
- There is an aggravated assault in the United States every 40.5 seconds

- A weapon of opportunity is the most used during felony assaults (33.1%)
- 20.6% of all aggravated assaults were committed with firearms
- 19% were committed with knives

Most jurisdictions recognize nine (9) deadly weapons (DW). The mere possession of these weapons is an automatic felony charge and no intent to use the weapon must be proved. The nature of these weapons is to assault, kill or maim. They serve no other useful or lawful purpose and it doesn't matter how big/small they are. "This switchblade is less than four inches." It doesn't matter, it's a felony. If they are used in a felonious assault, the perpetrator will also be charged with a felony criminal possession of a weapon in addition to the felony assault charge.

The most common nine (9) deadly weapons are:

1. Loaded, operable firearm
2. Ballistic Knife
3. Dagger
4. Switchblade
5. Gravity Knife
6. Metal Knuckle Knife
7. Metal Knuckles
8. Billy Club
9. Blackjack

Any item that does not fit in the above categories is classified as a dangerous instrument (DI). Dangerous instruments have a useful or lawful purpose and the police and prosecution have to show intent in order to charge someone with criminal possession of a weapon. For example, carrying a pencil in your pocket is not a crime, but if it is used to stick someone in the eye, then it becomes a dangerous instrument. It doesn't matter how slight the injury is if a deadly weapon or a dangerous instrument is used. It is still a felony charge.

CI Tip Sheet

Here is a quick reminder on when someone would be charged with Felony Assault (varying degrees):

PI + DW/DI = Felony Assault
SPI = Felony Assault
SPI + DW/DI = Felony Assault

Felony Assault Investigations

The most likely felony assault an investigator will "catch" is a nonfatal shooting/stabbing. Remember, the charge is not attempted murder but felony assault—even though the perpetrator's intent was to kill them. Nonfatal shootings/stabbings are also the most likely to cause the investigator a headache. Some of your victims will not be cooperative in the investigation. This spells trouble. Instead, your victim will be thinking about taking care of it through an act of revenge or "street justice." The famous, "Heard the ping, felt the sting and didn't see a thing!" This revenge can be extracted against the perpetrator or one of their "crew." Investigators have to work quickly to identify and arrest the perpetrator or there will be a murder or an additional nonfatal shooting/stabbing. The role of investigators here is to stop the violence from spreading.

Here are some investigative techniques that may be used in a Felony Assault investigation:

The hardest parts of a felony assault investigation are to prove the element of intent, establish the extent of the victim's injury and identify the type of weapon used in the attack. Because many shootings and stabbings occur inside/outside of licensed premises (bar, nightclub, pool hall, etc.), the investigator could do the following:

- Ask for Surveillance camera footage
  - o Also think ATM machines, gas stations and red light traps at or near the location
- A list of patrons (many bars scan drivers' licenses at the front door)
- Conduct a hospital canvass for additional victims and potential witnesses
- Prompt on the scene interviews with witnesses
  - o Including the entire bar staff
    - Wait staff, bartenders, cooks, bar backs, etc.
- Request a license plate reader to "collect" the plate numbers of vehicles parked in proximity of the location

If video surveillance does not exist, investigators must rely on victim and witness statements. This can become a problem when assaults happen in nightclubs or bars. Many of your witnesses, including your witness have more than likely been drinking. This presents another obstacle that investigators must overcome.

Gunshot Wounds and Range of Fire

To add to the investigator's level of professionalism, it is always important to know the nomenclature that comes with the territory. When recreating the crime scene, investigators often have a difficult time of establishing who was standing where and doing what. Sometimes the investigator has to go by the number of gunshot wounds and the location of entrance wounds on the body and the type of wounds that the victim received so that they can determine the events that occurred. This is all done by the investigator so that stories put forth by victims, suspects and witnesses can be corroborated. This section will cover wounds made by handguns. Rifle and shotgun wounds will have different entrance wound appearances. First, the investigator must be able to tell the difference between gunshot entrance and exit wounds. It sounds easier than it is. The exit wound tends to be larger than the entrance wound and irregular in shape, but not all the time. Ultimately, the forensic pathologist will tell you which wound is which, but that doesn't help you at the scene.

A gunshot entrance wound tends to be round (circular) with a rim of abrasion—or abrasion collar. This is caused by the bullet turning and scraping (or abrading) the skin as it enters the body. Depending on how close the muzzle of the gun is to the victim, the more searing or burning of the entrance wound you will find. Most cases involve a penetrating wound—one that only has an entrance wound. The bullet will enter the body, hit bone or some other organ, lose momentum and become lodged within the body. The medical examiner will use X-rays to identify the location of the bullet in the body.

Some bullets may exit the body. These wounds are referred to as perforating gunshot wounds. Gunshot exit wounds tend to be irregular, torn or lacerated because of the angle from which the bullet leaves the body and because the skin is forced outwards. Exit wounds do not have soot or burn marks either.

At the Crime Scene: JFK: Entrance or Exit Wounds?

If you are a fan of history, then you know how important it is to distinguish between what is an entrance wound and what is not. The John F. Kennedy assassination, investigation and autopsy has caused arguments and talks of coverup for over 50 years because of the wounds that the President sustained. Were the two shots from the same perpetrator?

The Zapruder film of the assassination has left even more questions about the direction of the bullet(s) and how many shooters were responsible. If this much doubt about entrance and exit wounds can be created with the assassination of a U.S. president, then what could happen with your case? A defense attorney can easily create reasonable doubt when you don't know who was standing where and what they did.

The next phase of the gunshot wound investigation is the range of fire or the distance between the muzzle of the gun to the target, i.e., the victim. The distance the shot was fired can prove/disprove a suspect's alibi of self-defense or refute their statement as to where they were positioned. The range of fire distance of gunshot entrance wounds can be broken down into four (4) categories:

1. Contact (Tight or Loose)
2. Close Range
3. Intermediate Range
4. Distant Range

A contact wound is exactly what it sounds like. The muzzle of the gun is placed directly against the victim before the trigger is pulled. A contact wound often leaves a burned, seared or blackened edge. A tight contact wound may leave an impression or muzzle imprint on the victim's skin. Soot or fouling may be seen in or around the entrance wound. It may leave dark soot on the skin surface. An intermediate gunshot wound may/will cause small marks on the skin surface referred to as stippling or powder tattooing from burnt and unburnt powder residues ejected from the barrel of the gun. Stippling, unlike soot cannot be rubbed or washed off. Anything beyond three (3) feet the investigator will not see stippling—even three (3) feet is pushing it. A distant range wound is usually more than three (3) feet. There will be a "clean" entry wound with an abrasion collar, meaning no signs of powder burns or stippling (e-mail conversation, Dr. Smiddy, February 9, 2012).

The investigator must recover any bullet or bullet fragments whether they are from the hospital or from the medical examiner. These bullets should be put in a container or similar type device as well as affixed with a biohazard label. The investigator must ensure that they are vouchered and sent to the police laboratory for ballistic testing and entry into IBIS.

Domestic Violence

Unfortunately, domestic violence is a problem that has plagued our society since its inception. According to the website Domestic Violence Statistics, in 2011 a woman was assaulted in the United States every nine (9) seconds and everyday three (3) women were murdered by their husband or boyfriend. These are alarming statistics. The squad must follow up on all domestic violence cases that were left open by patrol for one reason or another whether they are misdemeanors of felonies. Domestic violence is one of those crimes that can lead to further victimization and escalate quickly to murder. Depending on your jurisdiction's definition of who or what is considered a domestic relationship, investigators often have to act quickly. Domestic violence investigations don't involve just spousal abuse but child abuse and sexual abuse as well. Investigators may have to reach out to specialty units for assistance.

In cases where the suspect has caused a physical injury or committed a felony (used a dangerous instrument) and fled the scene, the investigator must deploy all the necessary techniques described in this book when searching for a known perpetrator. Tracking a suspect by his hangouts, past friends, girlfriends, place of employment and, of course, mom, are always the first steps investigators should take. Due to the nature of intimate violence, investigators must show a sense of urgency when assigned an open domestic violence case especially ones with an order of protection (restraining order).

Investigators should re-interview the complainant and attempt to develop leads on the suspect's whereabouts. If there is a real danger of the suspect coming back to the residence, the investigator can encourage the victim to stay with a friend or family member until the perpetrator is apprehended. Take photographs of injuries if it wasn't done during the preliminary investigation by patrol. Sometimes bruises aren't visible until a few hours later. In addition, the investigator should take photos of any broken items or anything else that may help the case.

Internet Resources for Investigators

NIJ Firearms Training
http://nij.gov/training/firearms-training/glossary.htm

National Integrated Ballistic Information Network
http://www.nibin.gov/

Safe Horizon: Domestic Violence Advocates
http://www.safehorizon.org/index.php

Question for Discussion and Review

1. In order to have a felony assault, what must there be?

2. After a "Weapon of Opportunity," what is the most likely used weapon in a felony assault?

3. What is the difference between an entrance wound and an exit wound?

4. Why should investigators take pictures of victims after the fact in domestic violence cases?

5. What is tattooing? What causes it?

6. What is the difference between a penetrating wound and a perforating wound?

7. What are the four (4) type of gunshot wounds discussed in this chapter?

8. What is stippling? What causes it?

9. After handguns, which weapon is used most to kill people in the United States. Rifles or shotguns?

CHAPTER 14 — BURGLARY

"We've basically built doors for 4,000 years and still have burglaries."
— Johannes Ullrich

KEY TERMS

Burglary   **Modus Operandi (MO)**
Building   **Tool Mark Evidence**
Dwelling

CHAPTER OBJECTIVES

At the end of this lesson, the student will be able to:

- Recall the definition of Burglary.
- Recall the main element of the crime of Burglary.
- Discuss strategies for solving Burglaries.
- Discuss the post-burglary arrest investigation.

When laws were first put into place throughout history, the idea was to protect your own property from someone or something. A person's home was always considered the "Castle" and therefore every effort was made to protect it by establishing laws and punishments designed to deter crime.

The crime of Burglary is the first crime in the Crimes Against Property section of the Eight (8) Major Felonies. In ranking of all property crimes, this is by far the worst. If you have ever had your home burglarized, you know that sick empty feeling it engenders. Law enforcement officers must understand the violation that people feel after their homes have been burglarized and employ empathy when investigating these cases. Think of it in these terms: by the time you finish reading this chapter there will be nearly 100 burglaries committed in the United States.

When mentioned on the news or in passing, the crime of burglary is often confused with robbery. It has been noted earlier that the definition of robbery is the forcible stealing of property. How many times have you heard the following, "My house was robbed!" A quick reminder: people get robbed, houses get burglarized.

In order to commit the crime of burglary, certain elements must be present: The perpetrator must be a **BIKER**:

Building
Intent to commit a crime therein
Knowingly
Enter or
Remain unlawfully

Building

A building is defined as any walled-and-roofed structure that is used for overnight lodging or to conduct business out of. The definition of a building would include dwellings, vessels, trailers, hotels, motels, RVs and stores to name a few. These locations can either be locked, unlocked or abandoned. If the suspect breaks into an ice cream truck, telephone company truck or a mausoleum, they will be charged with burglary as well. If you think about it, a mausoleum is used for forever overnight lodging! A dwelling, a private location where people sleep and live, is considered a higher degree of burglary in most jurisdictions.

Intent to Commit a Crime Therein

The individual who enters the building must have the intent to commit a crime therein—it doesn't have to be a felony. This is the essential element of the crime of Burglary. A burglar enters a home/commercial establishment for a reason: cash, jewelry, electronics or any item that can be turned into cash. The rationale behind almost all burglaries is to commit some sort of larceny. Ironically, the perpetrator does not actually have to remove any property.

Knowingly

This is a self-explanatory culpable mental state. The individual knows he doesn't live or work at the location and shouldn't be there.

Enter

The individual actually has to gain access to the building; if not, he could be charged with attempted burglary. He doesn't have to break in; walking into an open door is good enough.

Remain Unlawfully

The individual inside of the house was not invited in by the owner. For instance, you are invited to a friend's house for a Christmas party. You go to the room where everyone puts their coats and you see a pocketbook on the nightstand. You look around, reach in and remove $100 in cash from the purse and stuff it in your pocket. If caught, you would not be charged with burglary because you were there lawfully and you did not have the initial intent to commit a crime therein, it was an afterthought.

The State of Burglary in the United States: UCR 2010 Statistics

According to the 2010 report by the FBI, *Crime in the United States*, a burglary occurs in the United States every 14.6 seconds to the tune of over

2 million a year. It also has the lowest clearance rate, 12.4%, of the 8 Major Felonies. That means 87.6% of all burglars are walking around and living in our neighborhoods! The statistics are not that much better overseas either. For instance, in Britain, 24% of all burglaries are cleared by arrest. However, law enforcement in the United States must look at the way the police in the United Kingdom investigate burglaries because obviously they have a 10% lead in arrest clearances. Of the 2 million burglaries that occur every year, nearly 74% of them are committed against homeowners. This is a dramatic increase of residential burglaries over 2009 (68%) and may be an indicator of the economic conditions in the United States.

This is why many police departments across the country have turned to crime prevention techniques to help stem the tide of burglaries. One reason burglaries go unsolved is because there are so many burglaries, police departments cannot afford to send a crime scene unit out to every reported burglary. It is either left up to the patrol officer to conduct a preliminary investigation or send in the evidence collection team. Unless someone is caught in the act, leaves prints and/or DNA behind, it is extremely difficult to identify and arrest the perpetrator(s).

Burglary Fast Facts:

- Burglary is always a felony
- The #1 burglar method to get into a home is by forcing their way through the front door
- The #1 burglar method to get into a commercial establishment is through a back door at night
- 74% of all burglaries occur in residential properties
- A forcible entry into the location is not necessary in order to be charged with burglary—walking through an opened door will do it
- Most burglaries occur during the daytime when people are at work
- Busiest months for burglary are during the summer—when people are on vacation
- $4.6 billion worth of cash/goods are stolen in burglaries every year
- Depending on what jurisdiction you live in, the classification of felony may differ
- If the burglar is armed with a deadly weapon and enters a dwelling, a higher class of felony would be charged
- Burglary does have a younger brother, his name is Criminal Trespass
  - You commit the crime of criminal trespass when you enter fenced land or in a building (no intent to commit a crime)—it is the acronym BIKER without the I

Investigating Burglaries

Entry points into the location must be given the most attention in burglary investigations. Burglars are in such a hurry to get into the place that they may leave behind physical evidence, fingerprints or DNA. Because of the low clearance rate, we see that burglars often come prepared to mitigate their chances of being caught. Here are some other investigative techniques that might be used during a burglary investigation:

- Check the location for past calls for police services
    o Suspicious person(s)?
    o Previous sexual assaults
- Was anyone stopped at or near the scene?
    o Check Stop and Frisk records
- Canvass of the neighborhood should be made for information
    o Any unexpected utility company personnel going door-to-door?
    o Any unusual persons/vehicles noticed?
- Check police computer databases for recently released burglars residing in your jurisdiction
    o Does the burglary fit a particular MO?
- Check for possible surveillance video—even in residential neighborhoods
- Interview the homeowner
    o Ask owner if anything has been obviously moved or touched
- Have location or item dusted/swabbed for DNA?
    o Any victimization of burglary in the past?
    o What do they do for a living?
- Was any property taken that is traceable?
- Obtain a complete list of property taken
    o Coin/stamp collections
    o Unique jewelry
        - Think of using a sketch artist to draw unique jewelry
    o Credit cards
    o Cell phones
    o Follow up on the property with local pawn shops and Internet sites
    o Ask victim if they notice anything else that is missing to contact you
- Attempt to drill down to the exact time of the occurrence
- Identify patterns by time, place and Modus Operandi
- Entry and exit points should be "dusted" for fingerprints and/or swabbed for Touch DNA—especially walls by a window. Since force is used to gain access it shouldn't be to difficult to find entry points
    o Take elimination prints/swabs from residents
- Tool marks may exist at entry/exit points—try to take the entire mark as evidence after photographing it

Investigating burglaries often requires the help of units outside of the investigation squad. They have the necessary expertise, know-how and equipment to do their jobs. Outside units are additional resources that allow investigators to close cases. Teamwork is what makes law enforcement more efficient. If you have been in law enforcement for any amount of time, you know that drug abusers are often the burglars in the neighborhood. Investigators must coordinate efforts with their narcotics teams and conduct sweeps in and around the area where burglaries are occurring. The best times to conduct narcotics operations (buy and bust or observation points (OPs)) is in the early morning when users are feeling the need for their "fix." Investigators must be ready to debrief the prisoners when they come in, especially those who may experience the downside of missing their drugs.

Post-Burglary Arrest Investigations

If the suspect has any property on them from what may be a potential burglary, consider pulling previous burglary complaints to match descriptions. In addition, can the usage of the stolen property be traced (cell phones, credit, ATM, debit cards)? Investigators at this stage should determine if they have probable cause to obtain a search warrant for the perpetrator's residence, especially in pattern-burglary cases.

The clearing of one (1) burglary may lead to information that leads to the clearing of others. Often the burglar is responsible for many of them in the area, or a pattern. If suspect has waived his/her Miranda Rights and has supplied an admission or confession, why stop there? Investigators should get into the habit of asking burglars about their specific type of MO—you or another investigator down the road may be faced with a similar pattern. For instance, how did they get to the scene (walk, taxi, drive, etc.)? What did they do once they were inside of the location? Why not start the next investigation with who did them that way before?

Other things to consider asking during the post burglary arrest debriefing:

- Were these burglaries committed with anyone else?
- Do they use lookouts?
- Do they know of any other individuals involved in residential/commercial burglaries?
- Did they use tools or other devices to gain access
- How did they circumvent alarms (if applicable)
- Where do they commonly sell stolen goods—may be an idea to bring up with the district attorney to acquire more information for a deal
- Where is the "stash"? Residence? Backyard? Storage facility?
- Where do they buy their drugs? (If applicable)

Internet Resources for Investigators

Property Room
http://www.propertyroom.com/

Center for Problem Oriented Policing
http://www.popcenter.org

Questions for Discussion and Review

1. If Johnny Jones enters an opened mausoleum with the intent to steal something from inside and is caught, what crime will the police charge him with?

2. Johnny Jones is out the next day and sees a parked, unattended ice cream truck on the side of the road. He breaks the window and takes a fudge pop. If caught what crime would Johnny be charged with?

3. Mary Smith is homeless and breaks into the backdoor of a factory to get warm and shelter from the cold. The police are called and they arrest her. What is the charge?

4. A car belonging to the phone company is parked in front of a building during a maintenance call at a residence. Johnny Jones reaches through a slightly opened window and removes a telephone handset. He is apprehended on the spot. With what crime would he be charged?

5. Why do burglars choose rear doors in commercial establishments at night?

6. Johnny Jones knocks on the door of someone's home. Mary Smith opens the door and Johnny forces his way in. He punches and ties Mary up to a chair. He then proceeds to ransack the house, taking money and jewelry. If Johnny is caught, what crime(s) would he be charged with?

7. Why does the crime of Burglary have such a low rate of clearance by arrest?

CHAPTER 15 – GRAND LARCENY &
GRAND LARCENY AUTO

"I don't need to worry about identity theft because no one wants to be me."
— Jay London—comedian

KEY TERMS

Larceny	Identifiers	Chop Shop
Fence	FTC	Insurance Fraud
Identity Theft	Credit Bureaus	NICB

CHAPTER OBJECTIVES

At the end of this lesson, the student will be able to:

- Recall the definition of Grand Larceny.
- Recall some of the ways that Grand Larceny can be committed.
- Discuss the problem that exists in investigating Identity Theft cases.
- Discuss the steps taken to solve Grand Larceny and Identity Theft related cases.
- Recall the definition of Grand Larceny Auto.
- Recall the reasons why vehicles are stolen.

The FBI's Uniform Crime Report (UCR) defines larceny as the taking, obtaining or withholding the property from another, without force. Remember, if any force is used or threatened the crime would be a Robbery. Because larcenies occur at such a high rate, cities across the United States report a category of Grand Larceny for UCR reporting purposes that sets a dollar amount or action surrounding the crime. For example, in New York State* there are many ways to commit Grand Larceny, but the three most likely are:

1. Take property valued over $1,000—i.e., $1,000.01
2. Take someone's credit card/debit card—possession alone
   a. Having the numbers is good enough
3. Theft from the person, i.e., chain or purse snatch, pickpocket
   a. No force: Force = Robbery

For example, Johnny Jones is walking down the street with a knife in his pocket. He sees an older woman walking down the street with a pocketbook dangling from her forearm. He runs up behind her and cuts the straps of her pocketbook, grabs it and runs in the opposite direction. The crime in this scenario is a Grand Larceny.

*Each jurisdiction may be different

> **CI Cheat Sheet**
>
> Force = Robbery

THE STATE OF GRAND LARCENY IN THE UNITED STATES: UCR STATISTICS

- Larceny is the most popular type of property crime
- There were over 6.6 million larcenies in the United States in 2007
- 18.6% of all larcenies are cleared by arrest
- There is a larceny every 4.8 seconds in the United States

Most Grand Larcenies have to deal with some type of physical property, so investigators must first look at the locations where stolen items can be "fenced." Crime analysis, the collection of data and crime statistics, may help put together patterns of larcenies in a specific geographic area. The location and times when these crimes are committed may provide the lead necessary to solve the case. However, without a good description, investigators face the same problems as they do in robbery investigations.

- Pawnshops, secondhand jewelers and online auction sites provide the perpetrators an avenue to sell their stolen goods. To learn more about how an investigator can use these avenues, see Chapter 12.

- Identify any "Traceable Property," cell phones, credit cards, etc., and try to investigate them in real time—especially in cases with credit cards. Banks and credit card companies can keep the account open and report where and when the card was last used. If the event is in the past, the investigator must respond to the location as fast as he can in order to obtain video surveillance footage.

- Decoy operations are also an option for investigators, but do pose a threat to the safety of the decoy officer and to the general public. A decoy operation should never be employed unless the individual at the very top of the organization has authorized it and everyone involved is properly trained.

Identity Theft Investigations

The toughest challenge that investigators face in grand larceny investigations is the crime tie-in with Identity Theft. Identity theft is a crime that involves one person assuming the identity of another and opening credit cards, bank accounts and other financial services with the intent to defraud. The suspects in these cases obtain cash, property, goods and services before the victim has even realized what has occurred. The major problem is that these types of crimes often cross state and international borders and electronic frontiers. This is what makes identity theft difficult to investigate—no active viable leads with jurisdictional issues. However, the investigator can make their life easier by collecting financial institutions and Internet providers contact information on their down time. A good contact can save time, aggravation and eliminates the confusion on what subpoena gets sent where.

The crime of identity theft begins when some or several personal identifiers (Full name, Address, DOB, Social Security Number, Credit Card numbers, PIN numbers, etc.) are compromised and used to defraud another. The first step in addressing these cases is to determine if the person is a victim of identity theft, attempt to locate the jurisdiction where the crime has occurred and help the victim to triage their situation. The investigator determines if the person is a victim when presented with the documentation that shows unusual account activity, obviously forged signatures and other documents that the victim is not responsible for the actions. This information and the determination must be included in the initial police complaint report. Therefore, the investigator should ask the complainant for several writing and signature exemplars for handwriting analysis.

When interviewing the complainant, the investigator must pose certain questions. Here are some suggestions that should be asked in the initial interview with the victim in an identity theft case:

- Have you been burglarized recently?
- Has this ever happened to you before? If so, when and where?
- Have you opened a bank account recently and not received the ATM card?
- Who has access to your accounts?
- Where do you keep your financial information in the residence?
- Who has access to the location?
- Do you go to the same restaurant/bar often?
- How do you think the perpetrator obtained the PIN?
- Have you been receiving all of your mail recently?

When you discover that the crime has happened in another jurisdiction, you must enlist the help of that department in solving this case. The investigator will also conduct background checks on the complainant. Often, the individual becomes a victim of identity theft from someone in their own family.

The investigator must provide the victim with the information to stop further criminal activity and to recover from what has already occurred. The credit card companies/banks are going to require certain information from the victim to start their own investigation. This information includes a copy of the police complaint, an investigation number and the name and contact information for the investigator assigned. The victim will also need this information for the three (3) credit bureaus:

Experian	Trans Union	Equifax
www.EXPERIAN.com	www.transunion.com	www.equifax.com
1-888-397-3742	1-800-680-7298	1-800-525-6285

If the victim hasn't done so already, tell them to contact the Credit Bureaus and report the situation and ask for an "Alert" to be placed on the accounts. Alerts do not last forever (usually 90 days), so remind them to ask the company how long it will last and if it needs to be renewed. When the victim files an official police report, explain that they are entitled to a credit report. The victim should also fill out the FTC's Identity Theft Affidavit form (Found in the Internet Resources) to send to the Credit Bureaus. If they have already completed this, the investigator should obtain a copy of the Affidavit for their files. In addition, explain to the victim about the ability to file a complaint of identity theft directly to the Federal Trade Commission (FTC). A link to the online form can be found at the end of this chapter.

The FTC's site also provides other information for victims including sample letters that they can use for filing complaints with financial institutions. The FTC complaint does not replace the need for a police report. It is helpful in filing the complaint with the federal government because of the jurisdictional boundaries that often exist in these cases.

At this stage of the investigation, determine if the victim has closed down the accounts. If so, the investigator must contact the financial institution's law enforcement department who will provide the information required to launch the investigation. If the accounts haven't been closed down, they can be bait. Investigating an "open" account can be dangerous financially for the victim if not done properly. The investigator must reach the financial institution to determine if this avenue is available and often it requires a request on department letterhead. There is no guarantee that the financial institution will keep the account open—it is their decision to do so, not ours. The investigator should consult with his/her supervisor or legal department before starting an "open" account investigation to ensure they are following protocol.

Advise the complainant to keep a diary of the persons and institutions that he/she conferred with as well as a folder containing all the documents.

Grand Larceny Auto (GLA)

The crime of Grand Larceny Auto is actually listed under the statute of Grand Larceny in most jurisdictions, but for reporting purposes it is easier to track as two "separate" crimes. The FBI's UCR defines Motor Vehicle Theft as the theft or attempted theft of an automobile without the owner's consent. An automobile is something that is used on land, is not on rails and is self-propelled. Anything that uses human power to move, i.e., bicycle, is not considered a motor vehicle.

Generally, the investigative unit is not responsible for investigation auto theft unless it is part of a pattern or a link to organized crime. Most often the patrol officers will close a single auto theft case and file it. Most departments have specialty units and investigators that are solely dedicated to this task. However, when someone is arrested for a vehicle related theft, investigators should take the opportunity to debrief him/her in an attempt to identify a car theft ring or a chop shop.

THE STATE OF GRAND LARCENY AUTO IN THE UNITED STATES: 2010 UCR STATISTICS

- There were 737,142 vehicles stolen in the United States
- 73% are automobiles
- $4.5 billion dollars worth of vehicles are stolen every year
- A motor vehicle is stolen every 42.8 seconds in the United States
- Only 11.8% of all GLAs are closed through arrest
  - o Lowest clearance rate of the 8 Majors

Motor vehicles are stolen for a variety of reasons and motivations. However, they are stolen most of the time for the Pure JOY of IT.

Parts

The main reason why a vehicle is stolen is for the parts. The parts are more valuable then the "whole" motor vehicle. The thief often is provided a shopping list of vehicles that are "requested" by a buyer. After stealing the vehicle, the thief takes it to a chop shop. Chop shops are locations where stolen cars are brought so that parts can be "surgically" removed to be resold to unsuspecting customers at full price either at the point of sale or through an insurance claim. These parts end up for sale through several routes including classified ads, trade shows and online auctions.

Investigating chop shops is a long process, but it can be made easier with the use of confidential informants and static surveillance.

JOYriding

Joyriding is generally done by juveniles for fun and excitement. Joy-riding juveniles target fancy cars that would be fun to drive. These autos are generally left within the vicinity after the kids got bored (or scared) of driving it. In these cases there is little damage done to the car and they are often left parked legally so that they can distance themselves from it.

Insurance Fraud

Insurance fraud is another problem for investigators as the owner stages the crime to look like a GLA. Many times the owner does not do a good job and the amateurish of the crime is evident. Many police departments have initiated a preliminary theft report that requires the owner to make a full written statement of the event with the intent on charging them with Filing a False Report if it is determined that they lied. In an economic downturn like we are experiencing now, the investigator will see a rise in "auto thefts." Many of them will turn out to be insurance fraud. Investigators will also see fraud cases when the suspect has leased the car and is way over the mileage.

The investigator has a tool at his disposable when insurance fraud is suspected. The National Insurance Crime Bureau (NICB) is a not-for-profit organization that is partnered with insurance companies and law enforcement agencies to help combat insurance fraud in many categories, but it is heavily vested in vehicle theft. When an insurance company suspects fraud, its special investigations unit contacts NICB. NICB acts as the liaison between the insurance company, law enforcement and the prosecutor's office. NICB is also the organization that produces the valuable Vehicle Identification Number (VIN) books.

When an investigator suspects fraud, he should do what he always does, ask lots of questions! Where do you usually park the car? Was it left in front of the house when they have an empty driveway or garage? How bad is the condition of the vehicle? I purposely posed the question this way to see if the complainant responds in the present or the past tense. I would look to see if they were being truthful by stating, "It was in good condition." "Do you have the keys to the car?" "Can I see them?" If the car was stolen and they reported that it wasn't left running at the coffee shop or something, then they should have them, right? There are several ways that an investigator can go at this and each situation is dynamic, so different questions need to be asked.

Transportation

People steal cars just to go home or work. My experience has told me that Friday and Saturday nights are popular for these types of incidents. Why take a train or a cab home when I can grab a car?

Internet Resources for Investigators

The Federal Trace Commission (FTC) ID Theft Information Site
http://www.ftc.gov/bcp/edu/microsites/idtheft/

The FTC's Identity Theft Affidavit
http://www.ftc.gov/bcp/edu/resources/forms/affidavit.pdf

The FTC Online ID Theft Complaint Form
https://www.ftccomplaintassistant.gov/

The National Crime Insurance Bureau
http://www.nicb.org

Questions for Discussion and Review

1. What are the three (3) ways a person can commit grand larceny that were discussed in this chapter?

2. Why are Identity Theft Cases so difficult to investigate?

3. What is the reason to ask someone if they have ever been a victim of fraud before when reporting it?

4. When taking a report for identity theft, why are the details so important?

5. What are the reasons and motivations for stealing vehicles?

6. What is the main reason to steal a vehicle?

CHAPTER 16 — ARSON

"It's arson. There's no lights, no electricity and no gas. What else is going to start it?"

— Jay Lewis

KEY TERMS

Arson
Accelerant
Point of Origin

CHAPTER OBJECTIVES

At the end of this lesson, the student will be able to:

- Recall the definition of Arson.
- List the elements of the fire tetrahedron.
- Recall some of the steps in investigating Arson.
- Discuss some of the reasons why people resort to Arson.

We have come a long way from ancient times when people worshiped fire as if it were one of their gods. The crime of arson is defined by the FBI's Uniform Crime Report (UCR) as the willful burning of a house, public building, vehicle, aircraft or other personal property of another. In order to have a fire there must be some ignition. The ignition starts when fuel, oxygen and heat come together causing a chemical reaction. When these four (4) elements come together it is known as the Fire Tetrahedron. If any one of the elements are removed, the fire dies out.

For investigation purposes, not every police department is required to report the crime of Arson to the FBI for UCR statistics. According to the UCR, 15,475 agencies of the over 19,000 law enforcement agencies reported arson figures in 2010. Nearly one-third of police agencies do not report Arson, probably because the number of reported incidents is quite small compared to the other major crimes.

THE STATE OF ARSON IN THE UNITED STATES: 2010 UCR STATISTICS

- There were 56,825 cases of arson reported in the United States
- 19.5% were cleared by arrest
- 11,296 people were arrested for Arson in 2010
- More than half of the individuals arrested (5,683) were 18 years of age or younger
- California had the most arrests for Arson (1,133), followed by Pennsylvania (644)
- 18% of arson incidents were in abandoned buildings

Fires start for many reasons but are generally classified into four (4) types: Natural (lightning), Accidental (kitchen, candles, etc.), Intentional (arson) and Undetermined. The investigation starts with the patrol officer protecting the scene and ensuring that no one gains access after the fire has been put out. Investigators should check with fire personnel or the buildings department before entering any structure that had a fire to ensure that it is sound.

Due to the nature of the crime, arson investigations are extremely difficult. Whatever physical evidence of the crime was not destroyed by the fire is often destroyed inadvertently by the fire personnel while putting it out. Water, foam, axes and other equipment used to suppress the fire also has a harmful effect on evidence. Arson investigations are conducted by investigators in both the police and fire departments. In most cases, because it is a crime scene, police personnel generally take the lead in the investigation and are supported by their fire brethren.

Investigators have to work with what they do have and the first place to start is by pulling the 911 call. What did the person sound like? Were they excited or excited scared? What are the words they are using? Fire setters often call 911 to start the excitement, so pay special attention to the caller. If possible, locate them and conduct an interview in person.

To warrant an arson investigation, there must be some evidence discovered at the scene. Examples of evidence could be an accelerant residue, an unusual point of origin such as the living room, or an unusual amount of one type of material such as newspapers or wood. Some of the most common types of accelerants used in arson are gasoline, kerosene and turpentine. These accelerants leave a residue behind that can be identified even after the fire.

Arson investigations usually kick off when a body is found at the scene of a fire and an autopsy reveals that the manner of death is homicide. Fire scenes where a body is found should be treated like a crime scene and held until the medical examiner determines the manner of death. Investigators will initially have an "Emergency Exception" for a search warrant so that they can secure evidence of the crime before it is destroyed. However, once the evidence can be located in the fire scene, investigators may need to obtain a warrant for the location. If you are unsure, confer with your supervisor or legal division before doing anything that may jeopardize the case.

Investigating arson is no different than any other crime. The investigator will interview personnel at the scene. One question that may be different than other crimes is asking the first responders if they smelled anything peculiar when they arrived at the scene. This could indicate an accelerant. Unlike other crimes, the investigator should ask the fire officer in charge what his/her professional opinion was and why. Was anyone overly friendly or helpful with the fire personnel? Did they notice any familiar observers at the scene? Did anyone meet them as they arrived? The fire setter may still be at the scene so have someone take photographs or videotape the scene—it may prove to be useful down the road.

Investigators should ask witnesses and neighbors the same question. A carefully conducted canvass for surveillance cameras and additional witnesses asking fire-related questions is important. Did you see anyone walking with a gas can? Investigators should also pay a visit to the local gas stations and home-improvement stores in an attempt to see if anyone was exhibiting unusual behavior or asking fire-related questions.

Arson is a crime of choice by individuals who like to roll the **DICE**:

Destroy evidence of another crime (i.e., murder, rape, etc.)
Insurance Fraud
Competitors in business
Excitement

DESTROY EVIDENCE OF ANOTHER CRIME (I.E., MURDER, RAPE, ETC.)

Perpetrators attempt to destroy evidence with fire. In most cases, it will destroy DNA and trace evidence, but not the body itself in homicide cases. An ordinary fire does not rise to the temperature level needed to "cremate" the body. According to the Cremation Association of America (2000), it takes temperatures of 1,400° to 1,800° to cremate a body and about 1½ to 3 hours of time depending on the size of the individual. Even after that bits and pieces of bone and teeth remain.

The body still can tell the story on how the person met his/her demise. Bullet holes in skulls or chip marks in bones are quite evident to pathologists, even after a fire. This is why it is imperative that patrol officers establish a crime scene to protect whatever evidence remains. This is the key in solving all cases.

If you remembered from the Murder and Death Investigations chapter, one of the first steps in solving a homicide is to identify the victim. The forensic pathologist and investigators will attempt to identify the victim. The charred remains of the human body may be unrecognizable and any identification that they may have had on them was more than likely destroyed. Therefore, pathologists and Investigators must use other factors like jewelry, X-rays and dental records to identify the body. Investigators may have to use Request for Information posters containing specific items that the person had on him/her because photo identification will be impossible.

INSURANCE FRAUD

When individuals can no longer afford a car payment or mortgage payment, they may resort to arson to relieve themselves of the financial burden. Unfortunately for them, evidence of arson is quite obvious. Investigators will search for records of an unexpected increase in insurance on the property as well as complete an extensive financial background investigation on the owner(s). Was furniture moved out of the house or to other parts of the house? Were family photographs present in the house or were they removed? Does the owner have their important documents with them? These are some clues that the fire was set intentionally.

COMPETITORS IN BUSINESS

Local business disputes can get ugly, quickly. Competitors use arson to knock out their competition faster than product pricing. Investigators need to determine who would benefit from the fire and search police reports for any previous threats that were made to the owner.

EXCITEMENT

Arsonists set fires for the pure excitement of watching the fire grow and listening to the sirens. Also, arsonists use setting fires as a form of sexual gratification.

Internet Resources for Investigators

National Fire Protection Association
http://www.nfpa.org/

NIJ Fire and Arson Guide
http://www.nij.gov/pubs-sum/181584.htm

Questions for Discussion and Review

1. Johnny walked up to Mary and stated, "If you don't give me your money, I'm going to burn down your house next week." If arrested, what crime would Johnny be charged with and why?

2. What types of products could be used as an accelerant?

3. Why is the point of origin so important to investigators?

4. What are the four (4) elements of the Fire Tetrahedron?

5. Why should investigators videotape the fire scene?

CHAPTER 17 — MISSING PERSONS INVESTIGATIONS

"Absolutely not. I'm the last person ... I can't find my car keys in the morning. Trying to get out of my house is a nightmare. 'Where's my wallet? Where are my keys? I have to go find a missing person.'"
— Actor Anthony LaPaglia when asked if he could actually find a missing person.

KEY TERMS

NCIC	**Amber Alert**
Special Category	**NamUs**
Custodial Interference	**Anthropologist**
Safe Return Program	

CHAPTER OBJECTIVES

At the end of this chapter the student should be able to:

- Identify who is considered a "Special Category" missing person.
- Identify who should not be considered a missing person.
- Recall investigative steps in solving missing persons cases.
- Discuss the importance of using the National Missing and Unidentified Person System (NamUs)

According to the FBI in 2010, almost 700,000 missing persons cases were entered into the National Crime Information Center (NCIC). Of those cases entered in 2010 by law enforcement, over 85,000 of them remain as active missing persons investigations and almost 45% of them are children under the age of 18 (FBI.gov).

The procedure for missing persons investigations varies from jurisdiction to jurisdiction; however, the goal is the same: find the person! For instance, some police departments preclude the filing of a missing persons report until a certain amount of time has passed, while others take the report immediately upon being called. The filing of a Missing Persons Report is all that is done in many cases and a search may never be conducted unless something can prove that the person is missing involuntarily. In such "Special Category" cases, the police department will launch an immediate search and investigation into the person's whereabouts. Therefore, investigators should assume the person is in danger until the facts prove otherwise.

Missing person cases are very time consuming and eat up a tremendous amount of police resources. Often people leave and just don't want to be found. Could someone have had enough of the daily grind, packed up and left with no forwarding address? Sure they can. Not every missing persons case is one that involves foul play; however, investigators must ensure that it isn't the reason they are missing. Therefore, many police departments have guidelines for what type of case will spark an immediate investigation and which ones will not.

First, let's briefly discuss who is not considered a Missing Person. Police departments will not investigate a missing **COW**:

Committed a crime and is wanted
Over the age of 18 and left home voluntarily
Wanted on a warrant (arrest or bench warrant)

So who do the police look for then? Police departments share a common theme among missing persons cases. Anyone who falls into what is known as a "Special Category" will have an immediate search and investigation.

Special Category searches should always start with the person's home, especially when dealing with the very young or the elderly. An immediate search of the facility or home should be made before anything else is done. The person may need immediate medical attention, so before filing paperwork in these cases, the search is started. Included in this search will be rooftops of residential buildings or nursing homes, elevator shafts, closets, basements, etc.

Investigators should never take the word of a family member, friend or caretaker that a search of the premises was conducted and the person wasn't located. In the case if Jon Benet Ramsey, the father, John Ramsey, told responding investigators that he had searched the house and his daughter could not be located. They initially took the father's word for it, but then later asked a family friend to help John Ramsey search the house for his daughter whose body was eventually found in the basement. Then, upon finding his daughter, John Ramsey wrapped the daughter in a blanket and brought her upstairs, further contaminating the crime scene. Don't let this be you. The case investigator must conduct the search no matter what they are told or who is telling them—there are no shortcuts.

"Special Category" or "High Risk" missings are people who can be classified as **IS GONE**:

Involuntary Disappearance
Suicidal

Gone fishing
Over the age of 65
Not yet 21 years of age
Emotionally, mentally disturbed or in danger for medical reasons

INVOLUNTARY DISAPPEARANCE

This phrase for missing persons is a "catchall" category. If evidence exists that the person did not intentionally disappear on their own accord, then an immediate investigation will be conducted. For example, a twenty-two-year-old woman is out at a bar with friends and decides to stay behind with a guy she just met, but never returns home or, a forty-year-old man leaves his house to make a run to the bank and never returns. Later on that evening his vehicle is found abandoned and on fire in another jurisdiction. Considering the little bit of information in these scenarios, a rational person would come to the conclusion that both disappearances were not voluntary and unfortunately both individuals are the victims of foul play. For example, pocketbooks, wallets, car keys and cell phones are left behind. Many criminals know that cell phones are easily tracked.

SUICIDAL

If the person has ever attempted suicide, talked about suicide, was depressed or left a note stating their intention was to harm themselves, then an immediate investigation will start. Has anything bad happened to the person recently? Lost a job? Breakup? etc. are all questions that investigators must ask family, friends and significant others.

GONE FISHING

Anytime someone has gone fishing, boating or spent a day at the water and hasn't returned, the possibility exists that they may be a victim of a drowning or is seriously hurt somewhere.

OVER THE AGE OF 65

Older people, like children, are more vulnerable to the elements such as the heat or cold. Investigators must act quickly. Investigators may also be looking for patients with Alzheimer's disease, which is a form of dementia that gets worse over time. According to the Alzheimer's Association, one out of every eight individuals over the age of 65 have the disease (ALZ.org). In these cases, the facility or the family may have registered them with the Alzheimer's Association Safe Return Program. Investigators can call the 24-hour hotline at 1-800-625-3780 for help with the search, notifications and other resources. If the person is located, the investigator should call the hotline back and let the Safe Return Program know.

In addition, investigators should ask facility personnel and family members if the person ever did this before and if they did where did they go or where were they found? After the search of the home or facility these are good places to look initially.

NOT YET 21 YEARS OF AGE*

Children and the elderly are the most vulnerable in our society, so extra care must be taken in these cases. Once a teenager turns the age of 18, they are considered emancipated, meaning that they are now capable of making decisions on their own; however, the FBI has included the age up to 21. This is always the most difficult category because unless you can prove some sort of criminality, there is no immediate search for someone

---

*In some jurisdictions, this category is "not yet *18* years of age."

over the age of 18. However, investigators must identify the teenager's best friend, boyfriend, girlfriend, etc., especially when they have disappeared in the past.

EMOTIONALLY, MENTALLY DISTURBED OR IN DANGER FOR MEDICAL REASONS

This category is self-explanatory; however, no matter how old the person is when he/she falls in this category, an immediate search will be conducted. Investigators should look into medicine cabinets and on countertops for any evidence that the person is taking prescribed psychotropic medications. These clues may change the initial procedure of just taking a report into conducting a full-blown search.

Investigative Steps to Consider in Missing Persons Cases

After the initial search of the house and facility, investigators must sit down and conduct an interview with the family member, facility manager or significant other. An important first question is whether the person was reported missing on previous occasions and where they were found. Investigators must always remember that people are victimized by someone they know most of the time, so conducting an immediate interview with the boyfriend may not be the right initial step. However, there is some background information that needs to be obtained, no matter what:

1. Full name of the missing person
2. Race, Gender, Height, Weight
3. Date of birth
4. Eye color/Blood type
5. Social Security Number (if available)
6. Scars, tattoos, birthmarks etc. and the location on the body
7. Address (including apartment number, if applicable)
8. Vehicle information (year, make, model, body type, plate number) if applicable
9. Mental and physical condition of the missing person
10. Where the person was last seen, time the person was last seen, where they stated they were headed or who he/she was with?
11. Last known clothing description
12. A recent photo
13. If they attend school, which one
14. Name, address, phone number of dentist and primary care physician
15. DNA samples, X-rays on file

We have entered a new era of electronic devices used to track the whereabouts of suspects, but we can also use them in missing persons cases. Investigators must conduct a complete victimology on the individual in question to ensure that we ask about social media that the person may have used in the past, i.e., Facebook, Twitter, Xanga, etc., so that the investigator can view recent posts that may provide clues to the disappearance.

Amber Alerts

After obtaining the pedigree information from the complainant, investigators must branch out from the home. The investigator must ensure that the Missing Persons Report is filed with NCIC so that the information is available to law enforcement nationwide, especially in missing children cases for an Amber Alert. In order for an accurate Amber Alert, law enforcement must input the name of the child, the fact that they are 17 years of age or younger, that they have been abducted and in possible danger.

CI Tip Sheet

Amber Alerts require the following four (4) pieces of information:

- ☐ Name of the child
- ☐ His/Her age is 17 or younger
- ☐ That he/she has been abducted
- ☐ That he/she is in possible danger

Each state has its own Amber Alert System and the police agency should already have a procedure in place to use the system. A complete list of Amber Alerts by state can be found in the Internet Resources at the end of this chapter. In addition, the investigator's supervisor should reach out to the department's Public Information Officer (PIO). Investigators must always consult with their supervisor before submitting any information for release to the media. The faster the information reaches the general public, the better chance of developing tips on the whereabouts of the missing person. Newscasts may also grab the attention of the "missing person" who is not missing but has failed to notify someone where they were going.

One aid that may prove useful in planning a search is an aerial map view from one of the many Internet websites. This provides a framework on where investigators can search and may include locations not previously thought of, such as: a park, transit hub, bus depot, taxi stand, abandoned properties, etc., and in addition it provides a point to launch the canvass.

Canvassing, as previously discussed in Chapter 5, is also important in missing person cases. Generally, people are more likely to cooperate with the investigators seeking information on missing persons, especially little children or the elderly. This is where having a recent photo of the person is valuable. Many people do not even know their own neighbors by name, but will recognize them by face. So if only one photo exists of the person, copies should be made and given to all investigators participating in the canvass. Canvassing with a photo of the missing will lead to more information than will the name alone.

When a small child is missing, investigators should also conduct a computer search for possible sex offenders that live in the area before they start knocking on doors.

Vehicles

When an adult goes missing under questionable circumstances, investigators should obtain the person's Department of Motor Vehicle (DMV) records for registered vehicles. In addition, they should ask the family if the individual had an electronic toll reader device. Many of the parkways contain electronic toll trackers, which are currently used for "Rate x Time = Distance" to see how fast traffic is flowing (we all know where this is going).

Investigators can request the electronic toll records to determine where the "pings" were recorded. This may establish date, day and time as well as the direction of travel. Investigators should request reports from all department and county police vehicles, bridges and tunnels that are equipped with License Plate Readers (LPRs). The investigator has the ability with these systems to upload vehicle information so that an alert will be transmitted if the individual's license plate is read.

Investigators should canvass for video surveillance cameras in both residential and commercial areas, including red light traps in and around the time of the incident. There have been a few high-profile abductions that were caught on camera; unfortunately, with sad endings.

Follow-Up Investigation in Missing Persons Cases

After a certain number of days, usually thirty (30), the investigator should retrieve DNA exemplars from family members on a voluntary basis. The department should have a predesigned consent form just for this purpose. It is always best to start with the mother and/or descendants from the mother, i.e., brothers and sisters. Also, the investigator should secure a DNA sample from artifacts left behind by the missing person such as a toothbrush, hair brush and an article of clothing for future identification purposes. Obtaining these samples should be treated like any other evidence. The investigator should wear the proper protective equipment to avoid contamination and should abide by the strict chain of custody procedures. When appropriate, the investigator should also obtain a release of medical records from a family member that is authorized to give such consent.

Custodial Interference Cases

When investigating a missing person (child) that may be a custodial interference case you may have to check passport information. Since September 11, 2001, many of the countries that did not require citizens of the United States to carry a passport, now do. Someday, you may need a passport to travel anywhere within the United States by air. The law enforcement agency can request the U.S. Passport Office to check records of recently filed applications, including photographs with a request made on official department letterhead. This initial fax will begin the investigation; however, the hard signed copy must be forwarded. This request can also be e-mailed to the Passport Office, just make sure you ask the individual for their e-mail address.

     United States Passport Service
     Research and Liaison Branch
     1111 19th Street NW, Suite 510
     Washington D.C. 20522-1705

     Phone: 202-955-0258
     Fax: 202-955-0288

If the investigator determines that the case is a custodial interference case and that the individual that abducted the child maybe fleeing the United States, the investigator should call:

     United States Department of State
     Bureau of Consular Affairs
     Office of Children's Issues

     Phone: 1-888-407-4747
     Fax: 202-736-9132

Unidentified Human Remains

If you are an investigator long enough you will investigate a case where unidentified human remains are discovered either during a cold case dig or they are stumbled upon at a construction site. Investigators must work closely with the Forensic Anthropologist who will ultimately determine if the bone(s) are human or not. There are 206 bones in the human body and each one is identifiable by the well-trained eye. When a cold case dig operation is planned, the medical examiner's office/coroner should be notified so that the anthropologist can be on site. This saves countless hours and prevents wasted efforts.

When human remains are uncovered, the scene will be treated as any other crime scene. The bones will be carefully excavated and photographed as they are uncovered. The area should be searched for articles of clothing or any other items that may aid in the identification. At the very least, a description of clothing recovered can be released to the media and provide some insight on how long the body has been there.

Many departments have a Missing Person liaison in the medical examiner or coroner's office that help facilitate the identification of unidentified human remains by the use of fingerprints. These members of the police department have a difficult task of fingerprinting dead bodies, but when they are successful in retrieving the prints, they are entered in AFIS with the hopes of identifying the decedent.

The National Missing and Unidentified Person System (NamUs)

Policies and procedures have already been set forth in your department's guidelines; however, the National Institute of Justice (NIJ) has a tool that aids investigators called The National Missing and Unidentified Person System or NamUs for short.

NamUs is composed of two (2) databases: The Missing Person Database and the Unidentified Human Decedent database. NamUs accepts information on missing person cases from Law Enforcement, Medical Examiners and the general public. The general public can include victim's family members, victim advocates or concerned citizens; however, they cannot access law enforcement-only information. Currently, there are over 9,600 cases in the system, of which 74% are still active. NamUs was not created to replace the NCIC missing database, but to streamline the system for law enforcement investigators by eliminating the clutter often received from NCIC. In addition, not every agency in the criminal justice system has access to NCIC, i.e., medical examiners, which allows more sharing of information.

The process is simple. An investigator enters the missing persons case into NamUs and the system automatically cross-references entries made by other users. For instance, a medical examiner or family member in another state can enter information on: images of the person, X-rays, tattoos, dental records, clothing description, etc. The family of the missing person also has the option to have a DNA sample put into CODIS to be used for identification purposes.

Unfortunately, according to the Bureau of Statistics, there are over 4,400 unidentified human remains recovered in this country each year and only about one-third of those are cleared through identification. That number may increase as the use of the NamUs database by law enforcement, the public and medical examiners expands.

When to Close a Missing Persons Case

Missing persons cases are never closed unless the person is located. The inability to move forward in the case is not a reason to close it. Cold missing persons cases should be treated like cold homicide cases in the hope that new developments occur. Investigators should stay in contact with the family or reporting party whenever possible and keep them informed of the investigation. This also leaves the door open for information sharing. Missing Persons cases, like homicides, are never closed until we find the person or the body.

Internet Resources

NamUs
http://www.findthemissing.org

Bureau of Consular Affairs—Passports
http://travel.state.gov/passport/passport_1738.html

NCIC: Missing Person File Data Collection Entry Guide
http://cpdmdc.netfirms.com/MP_Data_Packet.pdf

National Center for Missing and Exploited Children
http://www.missingkids.com

U.S. Department of Justice: State Amber Alert Contact List
http://www.amberalert.gov/state_contacts.htm

Questions for Discussion and Review

1. What type of person is not considered missing by police agencies?

2. Where should an investigator search before doing anything when the missing is very young or very old? Why?

3. What does the phrase "Special Category" signify?

4. Why is it a good idea for investigators to have a recent photo of the missing person?

5. List the five (5) categories of "Special Category" or "High Risk" missing persons.

6. What are the four (4) pieces of information that must be entered in to the Amber Alert System?

7. Is it a good idea that some police departments have waiting periods before filing a missing persons report? Why or why not?

8. Why is it a good idea to ask for a DNA exemplar from the mother or a direct descendant of the mother in missing persons cases?

9. What is the name of the program for patients with Alzheimer's?

10. There is only one (1) Amber Alert System in the United States. True/False

CHAPTER 18 — TRIAL PREPARATION

"The trouble with law is lawyers."

— Clarence Darrow

KEY TERMS

ROR	Suppression Hearing
Supreme Court	Culpable Mental States
Grand Jury	Affirmative Defenses
True Bill	Mens Rea

CHAPTER OBJECTIVES

At the end of this chapter the student should be able to:

- Identify the different type of courts the investigator may find themselves in.
- Discuss several pretrial hearings that an investigator might find themselves in.
- Recall the four (4) culpable mental states.
- Discuss defenses that will be brought up in trials.
- Recall what the investigator must do to prepare for a trial.
- Review what the investigator must be prepared to testify on.
- Restate some of the tactics used by defense attorneys.

What Court Am I Going To?

In general, all arrested persons go to a local criminal court where they are booked and arraigned. At arraignment, the judge may dispose of the case, release the individual on their own recognizance (ROR), impose bail or remand the person for trial. In most jurisdictions, investigators may find themselves in Family Court for domestic-related incidents and Juvenile Court for those instances that deal with children usually less than sixteen (16) years of age. Depending on the crime category, misdemeanor or felony, determines what court the individual will go to. Misdemeanors will stay at the criminal court level, but felony cases will be sent over to the local Supreme Court for Grand Jury.

A Grand Jury is composed of 16 to 23 citizens whose function is to listen to the investigator's and the prosecutor's details of the case and decide if there is enough evidence to move forward. Judge input, defense attorneys and witnesses are generally absent from a Grand Jury—generally you, the investigator, is the primary witness. When taking the oath, and every time you give testimony, speak in a loud, clear voice. This is a serious point of the process and it should be done professionally. You are swearing on a Bible that you will tell the truth—the jury is watching your every move.

The Grand Jury is often viewed as an arm of the prosecutor's office and therefore is considered one-sided. The grand jury will convene and vote to pass down a True Bill, also known as an indictment. Because of the way the Grand Jury is set up, this is where the old saying, "You can indict a ham sandwich," came from. Once an indictment has been handed down, a new Supreme Court arraignment will convene to determine if bail will be given and to set the process in motion toward a trial.

Trials are a very rare occurrence. Most cases are plea bargained out to a lesser charge, but that doesn't mean investigators shouldn't be preparing for trial the second they are notified of a major incident. Only in television would you have a crime, an investigation and a trial in 45 minutes with three commercials. Cases may not go to trial for a few years in certain instances, so documentation, record keeping and preparation are the keys to successful prosecutions. The case can be plea bargained at any time prior to start of the trial.

Let the games begin! As the investigator prepares for his first trial, he should be aware of the general process that takes place. The two (2) main actors in the courtroom are the defense attorney and the prosecutor. The investigator prepares for the trial by reviewing the case folder, their notes, lab reports, photos, videos, etc. At some point in time you will sit down with the prosecutor who will "prep" you for the trial by going over evidence procedures, interviews or interrogations that were conducted or any other pertinent material.

During the "trial prep" is the time to go over any problems with the case and get out in front of them. If you or the prosecutor has discovered an issue, then the defense attorney has also. A plan can be developed to get the problem out in the open immediately so it doesn't become the focal point of the investigation. For instance, a problem could be that the investigator failed to document an important interview on an investigative report. A prosecutor will ask you to testify about the interview from your note pad because it was inadvertently left off of an investigative report during all of the commotion that often surrounds live investigations.

The investigator's testimony begins the moment he enters the courtroom, so the investigator has to look and act the part. Think of testifying like you were preparing to walk onto a big stage for a performance. Male investigators are required to wear proper business attire of a suit, shirt and tie. Female investigators are required to wear a business suit or conservative dress. Courtroom testimony for the police is essentially the same for any type of case. Whether it is for a felony drug collar or a petit larceny, the investigator's integrity, appearance, demeanor and credibility are paramount under cross-examination. Don't believe me? The next trial you see on television, just look at the defendant. You wouldn't recognize him. He has been cleaned up; his hair has been cut and he is wearing business attire and sometimes clear glasses to totally change his personal appearance. The defense understands that appearance plays an important role, and so should the investigator.

The investigator's personal appearance plays an integral part of the pretrial preparation. His actions make up the rest. Inappropriate behavior, like fooling around inside or outside the courtroom can sink the officer before he even takes the stand. When he sits in the witness box his feet are planted firmly on the floor, hands on his knees and will sit upright. Leaning back in the chair conveys that the officer is cocky and over-confident. The officer must look at the attorney when he is asked a question and at the jury when he answers it. Remember, actions speak louder than words, so be cognizant of your facial expressions and non-verbal body language.

Testifying in a courtroom is similar to writing a research paper—there is an introduction, a body and a conclusion. Investigative steps need to be broken down into their simplest terms so that they can be followed as a sequence of events. A blow-by-blow description of the circumstances and events that led up to the investigator taking the person into custody should be carefully followed. The investigator, like the student, must put into words all of the things that he felt, found and witnessed. If any jargon is used during his testimony, the investigator should take the time to explain it. Even when it comes to military time, the investigator should also state it in AM and PM terms. Also, because of certain effects of television programs, investigators must explain how certain processes are actually conducted and why. We understand that there is no magic button on our computers that provide us with all of the suspect's information including financial and cell phone information, but the jury doesn't.

Pre-Trial Hearings

Before a trial starts, the investigator may have to testify in what are called suppression hearings. A suppression hearing occurs when the defense attorney files a motion with the judge. It is an important part of the trial and ensures that the defendant will get a fair trial.

There are several suppression hearings and, depending on the juris-diction, they have different names but the same meaning. Each one is designed to test your knowledge of the law and your integrity. When investigators are aware that a case will be going to trial soon, they must contact the prosecutor to confirm their availability to testify; i.e., other court appearances, schedule vacations, illness, pending retirement, etc.

- A Mapp Hearing (*Mapp v. Ohio*, 367 U.S. 643 (1960)) is a hearing that determines the admissibility of evidence *before* the jury is told that it exists. For example, a murder weapon will not be brought into the courtroom until a judge decides before the trial if it will be admissible or not.
  o A Mapp Hearing will:
    - Determine if the search warrant existed at the time the property was seized or if an exception actually existed.
    - Was it executed within the required time frame?
    - Did the officers announce their presence?

- A Wade Hearing (*United States v. Wade* 388 US 218 (1967)), also known as a Gilbert Hearing (*Gilbert v. California* 388 U.S. 263 (1967)), will determine if the police identification procedure (Lineup/Show Up/Photo Array) was too suggestive, which then made it easy to pick the defendant out.
  - o   A Wade/Gilbert Hearing will:
    - Determine if the proper steps were taken during the identification procedure
      - Five (5) fillers? Same gender? Same race? etc.
      - Did witnesses view the lineup separately?
      - Was the defendant asked to speak? Were others required to do the same?
- A Simmons Hearing (*Simmons v. United States* 390 U.S. 377 (1968)) is used to determine the fairness of a photographic identification of the suspect—again to see if the police procedure was too suggestive.
- A Jackson-Denno Hearing (*Jackson v. Denno* 378 U.S. 368 (1964)), also known as a Huntley Hearing (*People v. Huntley* 15 NY 2d 72 (1964), is a hearing that challenges the voluntariness of the statements made by the suspect under custodial interrogation. It will also discuss the correct application of the Miranda Warnings.
  - o   A Jackson-Denno/Huntley Hearing will determine:
    - If Miranda Warnings were given before custodial interrogation
    - If all six (6) warnings were given and how they were given, i.e., word-for-word or other terms to enable understanding
    - If a language barrier existed, did the police use an interpreter?
    - If the rights were waived Voluntarily, Intelligently and Knowingly?
    - If the suspect asked for an attorney
- A Dunaway Hearing (*Dunaway v. New York* 442 U.S. 200, 208 (1979)) is used to determine if evidence should be suppressed because it resulted from an arrest where the police did not have probable cause.

The Culpable Mental States

A perpetrator who commits an offense has criminal liability or mens rea, Latin for "Guilty Mind." He/She can only commit a crime in four (4) ways, known as the culpable mental states or what the person was thinking or not thinking at the time the offense was committed. Culpable mental states play an important role in charging perpetrators with a criminal offense. For instance, intentional murder (premeditation) is a higher charge than criminally negligent homicide. This task falls ultimately on the prosecutor, who will either reduce the charges or raise them.

The culpable mental states can be remembered by using **RICK**:

Recklessly
Intentionally
Criminal Negligence
Knowingly

RECKLESSLY

A person perceives the risk, but disregards it. (A person practicing swinging a baseball bat near a crowd of people.)

INTENTIONALLY

The person meant to do the crime and did it.

CRIMINAL NEGLIGENCE

The person fails to perceive a substantial risk. They are "super reckless." (A person drops a cinder block off of the highway overpass into oncoming traffic.)

KNOWINGLY

The person who committed the crime is aware that their actions are illegal.

Defenses: It Wasn't Me

The number one phrase probably used by the bad guys is, "It wasn't me." A defense must be raised by the defendant and disproved by the *prosecution* (District Attorney's Office) Beyond a Reasonable Doubt. Beyond a Reasonable Doubt means that no questions can be raised about the person's innocence; they did it.

The two defenses that must be raised at the time of trial by the defense are Infancy and Justification.

The Infancy defense can be raised if the person was too young, usually less than (16) years of age. However, if a juvenile less than sixteen commits certain felonies such as: Murder, Manslaughter, Rape, Sodomy, Kidnapping, Robbery, Burglary and Criminal Possession of a Weapon, he/she will be treated as a Juvenile Offender and be tried as an adult in most jurisdictions. Because he/she is being treated as an adult, these cases will be heard in criminal court and not in juvenile court.

The term Justification is what under a normal situation the actions by the defendant would constitute a crime. However, if the defendant was using physical force required and authorized by law or judicial decree then it is justified. Or such action was necessary to prevent, terminate or make an arrest for a crime. This is the defense that protects police officers during the course of their duties and also ordinary citizens. For instance a police officer shoots and kills an individual who was using deadly physical force against another person. This would be classified as a justifiable homicide; however, on the death certificate the Manner of Death will read "Homicide."

Affirmative Defenses are raised by the defendant and must be proved by the *defense* with a Preponderance of the Evidence. Preponderance of the Evidence means the defense has raised more evidence that his client didn't commit the crime or 51% for the defense and 49% for the prosecution.

There are four (4) Affirmative Defenses that can be easily remembered by using the acronym **DR ME**:

Duress
Renunciation

Mental defect
Entrapment

DURESS

The defendant was coerced or forced to do the crime because of imminent use of physical force against him or a third person. A perpetrator grabs your son, puts a knife to his throat and says "If you don't set that building on fire across the street, I'm going to kill your son." You believe that the perpetrator will hurt your soon, so you do it.

RENUNCIATION

The defendant, prior to the commission of a felony, changed his mind and attempted to prevent that felony from occurring. An example of renunciation is as follows: two men walk into a liquor store with the intent of robbing the store. One of the perpetrators notices that an older woman is working alone and decides not to carry out the robbery. He grabs his buddy and attempts to leave. His friend refuses and robs the store anyway.

MENTAL DEFECT

This is the famous insanity defense, which doesn't happen as much as you think. The defendant committed the crime but lacked the responsibility for his actions because of a mental defect or disease.

ENTRAPMENT

The defendant was induced or encouraged to do so by a public servant. The entrapment defense is used a lot in criminal trials involving the buying/selling of illegal narcotics and firearms to a police undercover as well as with prostitution stings.

Cross-Examination

If you treated your investigation from the very beginning as if it was going to court then congratulations, you are 80% of the way there. The other 20% is about your testimony and how well you're prepared. Testifying in court is a lot like being interrogated. The defense attorney asks questions that you have to answer with seldom any room for explanation. The defense attorney crafts questions to make the investigator look bad—real bad. An investigator's testimony is often turned inside out and backwards. Their plan is to have you testify in your defense and not on the case itself. Divert attention to anything but the case and then deny you the chance to explain. It is as simple as that. So, how do you prevent being embarrassed? You prepare and when you think you have done enough preparation, do some more.

At this point in your career you will have to testify in criminal court, especially as an investigator. Do you remember how I spoke about crafting that curve ball question that the suspect is not prepared to answer in Chapter 7 Interview and Interrogation? Well, defense attorneys do it all the time. After the swearing in and the introductions, the defense attorney will quickly turn their attention to you and attack your character. Would you be prepared for this opening question, "Detective, can you explain to the jury what your job function is?" Pause, stutter and stammer and they got you on the ropes already. The twelve people sitting in the courtroom who couldn't figure out how to get out of jury duty are asking themselves, "How can this detective know who did the murder when they can't even explain what they do!"

This was not what you prepared to testify about and that pause and blank look on your face was exactly what they are hoping for. So how should you answer that question? It is easy if you remembered what I discussed in Chapter 1 about the CORE elements of criminal investigation. "Counselor, my job function is to carefully Collect, Organize, Record, Evaluate evidence and information to bring a case to a successful conclusion. In this investigation it led to an arrest." I can almost see the dirty look the defense attorney will be giving you after saying that.

The investigator will be cross-examined by the defense attorney. The defense will attempt to paint the investigator as sloppy and incompetent by "breaking you down." This is an effort to sow the seeds of doubt in the jury and be able to bring up all the "mistakes" in their final summation—or closing argument. For example, you arrested an individual for murder where they allegedly shot and killed the victim during a robbery. The firearm and/or money may never be recovered and the defense attorney will design their questions so that the investigator must testify that the defendant was apprehended without the firearm/money, so the "real" shooter is still out there. This is not the time or the place to argue or show your frustration. You must remain calm and professional. The investigator shouldn't worry about this particular cross-examination tactic, because they will be able to explain to the jury when the prosecutor redirects. This is where the investigator will explain the positive results of the gunshot residue (GSR) testing that was conducted and about the video surveillance evidence that was recovered during the canvass, which captured part of the event on tape.

When the investigator knows how to testify, knows the case and knows what to expect, they are in a better position to cause the defense's case to be **WILTED** like a flower. The investigator must be prepared to testify about the following:

Weather

- On your arrival at the crime scene—testing your observation skills
  - o Especially in outdoor crime scenes
    - Rainy/Sunny
    - Clear/Foggy
    - Sleet/Snow
    - Hot/Cold

Identity of other members of the police department that were at the scene

- Ensure that you have the "Gatekeeper's" list (see Chapter 4)
- Patrol officers
- Supervisors (patrol/investigations)
- Other members of the investigating unit (Homicide Squad, Arson Squad, Crime Scene Unit, etc.)

Layout of the crime scene (indoors/outdoors)

- Have Demonstrative Evidence prepared
  - o Determine which crime scene photos will be enlarged
  - o Determine what other aids will help the jury understand the relationship between the crime scene and evidence recovered
    - Investigative Timeline
    - Criminal Enterprise chart (if applicable)
  - o Smooth Sketch
- Refer to the rough sketch you prepared (see Chapter 4)

Time of the events(s) occurred

- Refer to the investigative timeline you created
  - o How the evidence and the suspect fit into the timeline at the exclusion of all others

Exact location of:

- The address of the crime scene and/or the configuration of the streets
  o Refer to sketch in notepad
- The physical/forensic evidence found at the crime scene
  o Is it necessary to have evidence in the courtroom?
  o If a search warrant was/was not obtained (why not?)
- The body when it was found (homicide cases)

Description if the suspect(s) when they were apprehended

- Clothing worn
  o Corroborate witness/victim statements and video surveillance
- Physical condition
  o A cut, scrapes, scratches, bruises, etc.
    - Hopefully injuries were photographed

The Investigator Testifying in Court

The defense team will have done their homework on you and your history, so be able to explain any wrinkles in your background. For instance, do you have a lot of civilian complaints? The defense will bring them up in an effort to discredit your testimony and paint you as a "hot head." In cases where the defendant has retained his own attorney they also hired their own investigators to examine the crime scene process and the investigation.

The investigator must be flexible and unflappable. Do not get hooked while you are in the courtroom—it will be devastating to the case. When you speak, do not sound like a walking report. The investigator should be very descriptive when they speak. Remember the jury wasn't there so you have to paint them a picture using the senses: Smells, Sounds and Sight.

- Go to the courtroom beforehand so you know exactly where to go
- Always tell the truth—most important
- No case is worth perjuring yourself
- The investigator will be thoroughly prepared before testifying in any court—this is the most important step
  o Review the case folder, notes and physical evidence
- Do not chew gum/mints
- Speak when spoken to
- Avoid using police jargon in your courtroom testimony. I know very few people that use the phrases: "I exited the vehicle," or "I entered the premises."
- If the investigator does not know the answer to the question he/she should respond, "I don't know," not "I don't recall"
- Whenever possible give definite responses—not, "I think," "Maybe," or "You can say that"

- When asked, "Did you discuss the case with anyone?" Of course you did: the district attorney and fellow officers who were at the scene. The answer to this question is *never* no!
- Ask for permission before reading directly from the case folder
- Do not use the word(s): perp, perpetrator and suspect—refer to them as the defendant or by name or as Mr. or Mrs. etc.—as hard as this might be, you have to do it!
- Testify on only things you know—direct them to other members on what they did
- Do not answer questions before they are asked—do not volunteer information
- If either the prosecution or the defense attorney objects to a question, stop talking and wait to answer
- Answer only the questioned that is asked
- If you don't understand the question or you didn't hear it, ask them to repeat it
- Do not nod or use other nonverbal communication
- Do not constantly look at the Prosecutor for help during cross-examination. This gives the impression the investigator is unprepared, unable to answer on his/her own or was coached
- Do not give your opinions unless you are a qualified expert witness
- Watch what you say when court is in recess, you never know who is in earshot
- Be careful of defense lawyer cross-examination traps
  o The start strong and finish strong tactic
    - People remember what was said last, so don't get worn down, stay focused
  o Rapid fire questions
    - Slow them down—it's a trap
    - Pause before answering every question—even the easy ones
  o Asking "Yes" or "No" answers without allowing an explanation
    - Try to explain answers—if you get shut down too many times by the defense it's a positive for the prosecution
      - If not, you will have the opportunity to explain in the direct examination
  o Silent treatment
    - Human nature is to fill the dead space by talking, often too much
    - Speak only when spoken too
    - Again, only answer the question that is asked
  o Baiting the investigator to lose his/her cool—must be unflappable
    - Using the wrong name, rank and/or title constantly
      - Correct them once

Redirect/Recross

When the defense attorney is finished with you, they proclaim, "No further questions." Do not move from the witness stand. The Redirect is limited to what questions or issues were raised during the cross-examination. The prosecutor is now afforded the opportunity to let you explain many of the Yes/No answers that you were forced to answer. You are not out of the woods yet. The defense has the opportunity to conduct a recross of what was said in the redirect.

Internet Resources

Cross Examination Blog
http://wwwcrossx.blogspot.com

Police Magazine Courtroom Testimony Articles
http://www.policemag.com/Articles/List/Tag/Officer-Court-Testimony.
aspx

Questions for Discussion and Review

1.   What is the purpose of the Grand Jury? How many people comprise the Grand Jury?

2.   What is the Grand Jury's function?

3.   List the four (4) Culpable Mental States. What significance do they play in charging crimes?

4.   Why is taking the oath an important stage in an investigator's testimony?

5.   What is a suppression hearing? Who raises the need for a hearing?

6.   Why should investigators be ready to testify about the weather conditions at a crime scene?

7.   What is the difference between the direct examination and a cross-examination?

8.   Why is preparation the most important part of courtroom testimony?

9.   Who raises the Affirmative Defenses? What are they?

10. What is an indictment?

11. What is the main purpose of the Redirect by the prosecutor?

REFERENCES

ABC News Radio. April 22, 2011. "California gang member's tattoo of murder scene leads to crime conviction," Retrieved on December 12, 2011. Retrieved from http://abcnewsradioonline.com/national-news/california-gang-members-tattoo-of-murder-scene-leads-to-crim.html

Adams, S. (1996). Statement analysis. What do suspect's words really reveal? FBI Law Enforcement Bulletin October 1996. Retrieved on January 6, 2011. Retrieved from http://www.crimeandclues.com/index.php/criminal-investigation/statement-analysis/29-statement-analysis-what-do-suspects-words-really-reveal

Alzheimer's Association (2011). Safety Center. Retrieved on September 4, 2011. Retrieved from http://www.alz.org/safetycenter/we_can_help_first_responders.asp

American Foundation for Suicide Prevention (2009). National Statistics. Retrieved on January 26, 2012. Retrieved from http://www.afsp.org/index.cfm?fuseaction=home.viewPage&page_id=050FEA9F-B064-4092-B1135C3A70DE1FDA

Australian Museum. (2003). "Decomposition: what happens to the body after death." Retrieved on October 23, 2009. Retrieved from http://www.deathonline.net/decomposition/body_changes/grave_wax.htm

Bryner, J. (2007). "Mystery deaths plague coroners." Live Science, May 4, 2007. Retrieved on January 27, 2012. Retrieved from http://www.livescience.com/4445-mystery-deaths-plague-coroners.html

Byrd, J. H. (2011). "Insects in Legal Investigations." Retrieved on January 22, 2012. Retrieved from http://www.forensicentomology.com/info.htm

CBS News. October 8, 2011. "Say cheese!" iPhone app catches thief. Retrieved on January 30, 2011. Retrieved from http://www.cbsnews.com/stories/2011/10/08/scitech/main20117622.shtml

Chisum, W. J. & Turvey, B. (2000). "Evidence dynamics: Locard's exchange principle and crime reconstruction." Journal of Behavioral Profiling, January, Retrieved on October 17, 2009, retrieved from: http://www.profiling.org/journal/vol1_no1/jbp_ed_january2000_1-1.html

CJ Foundation for SIDS. (2012). What is SIDS? Retrieved on January 29, 2012. Retrieved from http://www.cjsids.org/resource-center/what-is-sids-suid.html

Clarke, R. (1999). Hot products: anticipating and reducing demand for stolen goods. Police Research Paper 112, London, UK. Retrieved on April 12, 2009, from http://www.homeoffice.gov.uk/rds/prgpdfs/fprs112.pdf

Connors, E., Lundregan, T., Miller, N. & McEwen, T. (1996). Convicted by juries, exonerated by science: case studies in the use of DNA evidence to establish innocence after trial. Retrieved on April 14, 2009, from http://www.ncjrs.gov/pdffiles/dnaevid.pdf

Cremation Association of North America. (2000). The Cremation: Processing the Remains. Retrieved on July 30, 2009, from http://www. funeralplan.com/funeralplan/cremation/cremationprocessing.html

Criminal Profiling. (2001). Autoerotic Death. August 4, 2001. Retrieved on January 26, 2012. Retrieved from http://www.criminalprofiling.com/ AUTOEROTIC-DEATH_s134.html

Cronin, J., Murphy, G., Spahr, L, Toliver, J., & Weger R. (2007). Promoting effective homicide investigations. Police Executive Research Forum, Washington D.C. Retrieved on 10/6/2008. from http://www.cops. usdoj.gov/files/ric/Publications/promoting%20effective%20homicide %20investigations.pdf

DiMaio, V. & DiMaio, D. (2001). *Forensic pathology.* CRC Press, Boca Raton, FL

Domestic Violence Statistics (2012). Domestic Violence Statistics. Retrieved on February 3, 2012. Retrieved from http://domesticviolence statistics.org/domestic-violence-statistics/

DNA.gov (2009). DNA initiative: DNA.gov mitochondrial DNA. Retrieved on April 10, 2009, from http://www.dna.gov/research/mitochondrial_ research/

FBI. (2010). Uniform Crime Report (UCR): Crime in the United States. Retrieved on January 27, 2012, from http://www.fbi.gov/ about-us/cjis/ucr/crime-in-the-u.s/2010/crime-in-the-u.s.-2010

FBI NCIC (2010). National Crime Information Center. Retrieved on September 4, 2011. Retrieved from http://www.fbi.gov/about-us/cjis/ ncic/ncic-missing-person-and-unidentified-person-statistics-for-2010

Fenton, J. (2011). FBI seeks to update definition of rape. Baltimore Sun, September 29, 2011. Retrieved on January 28, 2012. Retrieved from http://www.baltimoresun.com/news/maryland/baltimore-city/bs-m d-ci-fbi-rape-definition-20110929,0,7509980.story

Forensic Dentistry Online. Bitemarks. Retrieved on January 27, 2012. Retrieved from http://www.forensic-dentistry.info/wp/?page_id=9

Gaines, P. (2009). Remember: A Rod has never taken steroids: according to A-Rod. Deadspin.com. Retrieved on April 9, 2009, from http://deadspin.com/5148732/remember-a+rod-has-never-taken-steroids-according-to-a+rod

Giacalone, J. (2006). Writing crime New York style: Miranda. Retrieved on March 31, 2009, from http://www.writing.com/main/view_item/item_id/822133

Giacalone, J. (2009). Five types of canvasses made easy. *Private Investigator Magazine.* March/April

Giacalone, J. (2011). The Social media canvass: a 21st Century law enforcement tool. Retrieved on December 11, 2011, from http://connectedcops.net/?p=5025

Hall, R. (n.d.) "Suicide Risk Assessment: A Review of Risk Factors For Suicide In 100 Patients Who Made Severe Suicide Attempts." Retrieved on October 17, 2009, retrieved from http://www.drrichardhall.com/suicide.htm

Innocence Project. (2011). Fix the system. Retrieved on January 2, 2012. Retrieved from http://www.innocenceproject.org/fix/Eyewitness-Identification.php

Japan Times Online. "Young teen suicides up 22.7% in 2006" June 8, 2007.

Kirk, P. L. (1974). Crime Investigation, 2nd ed., New York: John Wiley & Sons, Inc.

Miller, Greg. (2010). "Scientists explain how familial DNA testing allegedly nabbed serial killer," ScienceMag.com. Retrieved on October 29, 2011. Retrieved from http://news.sciencemag.org/scienceinsider/2010/07/scientists-explain-how-familial.html

National Institute of Justice. (2003). "What every law enforcement officer should know about DNA," Issue 249, July.

New York State Criminal Procedural Law (CPL).

Newsday (2009). Supreme Court limits warrantless vehicle search. April 22, 2009.

Nolte, K., Hanzlick, R., Payne, D., Kroger, A., Oliver, W., Baker, A. et al. (2004). Medical Examiners, coroners and biological terrorism: a guide-book for surveillance and case management. Retrieved on October 23, 2009. Retrieved from http://www.cdc.gov/mmwr/preview/mmwrhtml/rr5308a1.htm

NYC.gov New York City Records. (2009). Photographs 1889 – 1956, Re-trieved on February 24, 2009, from http://www.nyc.gov/html/records/html/collections/collections_photographs.shtml

Office for Victims of Crime. (2008). First response to victims of crime: a guidebook for law enforcement officers. U.S. Department of Justice Office. Retrieved on April 14, 2009, from http://www.ojp.usdoj.gov/ovc/publications/infores/pdftxt/FirstResponseGuidebook.pdf

O'Neill, T. (2002). Look who's talking: most everyone despite Miranda. Chicago Daily Law Bulletin, February 8, 2002. Retrieved on January 6, 2012. Retrieved from http://www.jmls.edu/facultypubs/oneill/Confessions47.pdf

Police Chief. (October 2008). Eyewitness identification: what chiefs need to know now. Retrieved on January 2, 2012. Retrieved from http://www.policechiefmagazine.org/magazine/index.cfm?fuseaction=display_arch&article_id=1636&issue_id=102008

RAINN. (2009). Statistics. Retrieved on January 28, 2012. Retrieved from http://www.rainn.org/statistics

Rabon, D. (2003). *Investigative discourse analysis.* Carolina Academic Press, Durham Carolina

Rosenbloom, S. (2006). In certain circles, two is a crowd. *New York Times*, November 16, 2006. Retrieved on January 6, 2012. Retrieved from http://www.nytimes.com/2006/11/16/fashion/16space.html?pagewanted=all

Smith, A. (2011). DA: Kiss left DNA on rape victim's cheek. *Newsday*, October 20, 2011, page A 19.

Smith, S. (2010). 'Missing' notes emerge in cop killing trial; perjury possible, judge warns. August 30, 2010. Retrieved on February 27, 2012. Retrieved from http://www.wbtv.com/Global/story.asp?S=13065555

STAR Magazine (1994). O.J.'s statement to the LAPD. November 29, 1994. Retrieved on April 11, 2009, from http://www.law.umkc.edu/faculty/projects/ftrials/Simpson/OJSstmnt.html

Turvey, Brent E. (2008). *Criminal Profiling: An introduction to behavioral evidence analysis.* 3rd Edition, Elsevier, Burlington, MA

United States Constitution. (1787).

USDOJ (2006). Criminal victimization in the United States. Retrieved on March 10, 2009, from http://www.ojp.usdoj.gov/bjs/pub/pdf/cvus/current/cv0633.pdf

USlaw.com (2009). Retrieved on October 20, 2009. Retrieved from http://www.uslaw.com/us_law_dictionary/c/Circumstantial+Evidence

United States Fire Administration (2001). Arson in the United States. Retrieved on June 24, 2009, from http://www.usfa.dhs.gov/down loads/pdf/tfrs/v1i8-508.pdf

YouTube (2006). Clinton, I did not have sexual relations with that woman ... Retrieved on April 9, 2009, from http://www.youtube.com/watch?v=KiIP_KDQmXs posted on August 30, 2006.

Wyatt, K. (2008). Anonymous rape tests are going nationwide. Associated Press. Retrieved on April 10, 2009, from http://abcnews.go.com/Health/Story?id=4847901&page=1

Zulawski, D. E., Wicklander, D. (2001). *Practical aspects of interview & interrogation:* 2nd Edition. Boca Raton, Fl: CRC Press.

Court Cases Cited

Aguilar v. Texas 378 US 108 (1964)
Arizona v. Grant 143 p.3d 379 (2006)
Brady v. Maryland 373 U.S. 83 (1963)
California v. Greenwood 486 U.S. 35 (1988)
Carroll v. The United States 267 U.S. 132 (1925)
Chimel v. California 395 U.S. 752 (1969)
Coolidge v. New Hampshire 403 U.S. 443
Daubert v. Merrell Dow Pharmaceuticals, Inc. 507 US 904 (1993)
Davis v. United States, 512 US 452 (1994)
Duckworth v. Eagen 492 U.S. 195 (1989)
Dunaway v. New York 442 U.S. 200, 208 (1979)
Flippo v. West Virginia 528 U.S. 11 (1999)
Frazier v. Cupp 394 U.S. 731 (1969)
Frye v. United States 293 F. 1013 (1923)
Gilbert v. California 388 U.S. 263 (1967)
Grant v. City of Long Beach 315 F. 3d 1081 (2002)
Illinois v. Caballes 543 U.S. 455 (2005)
Illinois v. Gates 462 US 213 (1983)
Jackson v. Denno 378 U.S. 368 (1964)
Kirby v. Illinois 406 US 682 (1972)
Maryland v. Buie 494 U.S. 325 (1990)
Mapp v. Ohio 367 U.S. 643 (1961)
Mincey v. Arizona 437 U.S. 385 (1978)
Miranda v. Arizona 384 U.S. 436 (1966)
Moran v. Burbine 475 U.S. 412 (1986)
New York v. Quarles 467 US 649 (1984)
People v. DeBour 40 NY 2d. 210 (1976)
People v. Huntley 15 NY 2d 72 (1964)
People v. Johnson 81 NY 2d 828 (1993)
People v. LeGrand 8 N.Y.3d 449 (2007)
People v. Jennings 252 Ill. 534 96 N.E. 1077 (1911)
People v. Mitchell 39 NY2d 173 (1976)
People v. Rosario 9 NY2d. 286 (1961)
Rhode Island v. Innis 446 US 291 (1980)
Sheriff v. Bessey 914 P.2d 618 (Nevada 1996)
South Dakota v. Opperman 428 U.S. 364 (1976)
Spinelli v. the United States 393 US 410 (1969)
State v. Cayward 552 S.2d 971 (Florida 1989)
State v. W.B., New Jersey, April 27, 2011
Stovall v. Denno 388 U.S. 293 (1967)
Tennison v. San Francisco, No. 06-15426
Terry v. Ohio 392 U.S. 1 (1968)
Thompson v. Louisiana 469 U.S. 17 (1984)
United States v. Crews 445 U.S. 463 (1980)
United States v. Wade 388 US 218 (1967)
United States v. White 401 U.S. 745 (1971)
Weeks v. The United States 232 U.S. 383 (1914)

INDEX

To see other interesting titles from
Looseleaf Law Publications, Inc.
please visit our website
LooseleafLaw.com
or call for a free catalog
1-800-647-5547